Palgrave Studies in the Enlightenment, Romanticism and Cultures of Print

General Editors: **Professor Anne K. Mellor** and **Professor Clifford Siskin**

Editorial Board: **Isobel Armstrong**, Birkbeck; **John Bender**, Stanford; **Alan Bewell**, Toronto; **Peter de Bolla**, Cambridge; **Robert Miles**, Stirling; **Claudia L. Johnson**, Princeton; **Saree Makdisi**, UCLA; **Felicity Nussbaum**, UCLA; **Mary Poovey**, NYU; **Janet Todd**, Glasgow

Palgrave Studies in the Enlightenment, Romanticism and Cultures of Print will feature work that does not fit comfortably within established boundaries – whether between periods or between disciplines. Uniquely, it will combine efforts to engage the power and materiality of print with explorations of gender, race, and class. By attending as well to intersections of literature with the visual arts, medicine, law, and science, the series will enable a large-scale rethinking of the origins of modernity.

Titles include:

Scott Black
OF ESSAYS AND READING IN EARLY MODERN BRITAIN

Claire Brock
THE FEMINIZATION OF FAME, 1750–1830

Brycchan Carey
BRITISH ABOLITIONISM AND THE RHETORIC OF SENSIBILITY
Writing, Sentiment, and Slavery, 1760–1807

E. J. Clery
THE FEMINIZATION DEBATE IN 18TH-CENTURY ENGLAND
Literature, Commerce and Luxury

Adriana Craciun
BRITISH WOMEN WRITERS AND THE FRENCH REVOLUTION
Citizens of the World

Peter de Bolla, Nigel Leask and David Simpson (*editors*)
LAND, NATION AND CULTURE, 1740–1840
Thinking the Republic of Taste

Ian Haywood
BLOODY ROMANTICISM
Spectacular Violence and the Politics of Representation, 1776–1832

Anthony S. Jarrells
BRITAIN'S BLOODLESS REVOLUTIONS
1688 and the Romantic Reform of Literature

Michelle Levy
FAMILY AUTHORSHIP AND ROMANTIC PRINT CULTURE

Robert Miles
ROMANTIC MISFITS

Tom Mole
BYRON'S ROMANTIC CELEBRITY
Industrial Culture and the Hermeneutic of Intimacy

Erik Simpson
LITERARY MINSTRELSY, 1770–1830
Minstrels and Improvisers in British, Irish, and American Literature

Mary Waters
BRITISH WOMEN WRITERS AND THE PROFESSION OF LITERARY CRITICISM,
1789–1832

David Worrall
THE POLITICS OF ROMANTIC THEATRICALITY, 1787–1832
The Road to the Stage

Palgrave Studies in the Enlightenment, Romanticism and Cultures of Print
Series Standing Order ISBN 1–4039–3408–8 hardback
1–4039–3409–6 paperback
(*outside North America only*)

You can receive future titles in this series as they are published by placing a standing order. Please contact your bookseller or, in case of difficulty, write to us at the address below with your name and address, the title of the series and the ISBN quoted above.

Customer Services Department, Macmillan Distribution Ltd, Houndmills, Basingstoke, Hampshire RG21 6XS, England

Literary Minstrelsy, 1770–1830

Minstrels and Improvisers in British, Irish, and American Literature

Erik Simpson

First published 2008 by
PALGRAVE MACMILLAN

Palgrave Macmillan in the UK is an imprint of Macmillan Publishers Limited, registered in England, company number 785998, of Houndmills, Basingstoke, Hampshire RG21 6XS.

Palgrave Macmillan in the US is a division of St Martin's Press LLC, 175 Fifth Avenue, New York, NY 10010.

Palgrave Macmillan is the global academic imprint of the above companies and has companies and representatives throughout the world.

Palgrave® and Macmillan® are registered trademarks in the United States, the United Kingdom, Europe and other countries.

ISBN-13: 978–0–230–20051–7 hardback
ISBN-10: 0–230–20051–6 hardback

This book is printed on paper suitable for recycling and made from fully managed and sustained forest sources. Logging, pulping and manufacturing processes are expected to conform to the environmental regulations of the country of origin.

A catalogue record for this book is available from the British Library.

Library of Congress Cataloging-in-Publication Data
Simpson, Erik, 1972–
    Literary minstrelsy, 1770–1830: minstrels and improvisers in British, Irish, and American literature / Erik Simpson.
        p.   cm. — (Palgrave studies in Enlightenment, romanticism, and cultures of print) Includes index.
    ISBN-13: 978–0–230–20051–7 (alk paper)
    ISBN-10: 0–230–20051–6 (alk paper)
    1. English literature—19th century—History and criticism.
    2. Minstrels in literature.   3. English literature—18th century—History and criticism.   4. English literature—Irish authors—History and criticism.   5. American literature—19th century—History and criticism.   6. Authorship in literature.   7. Romanticism.   I. Title.
    PR468.M55S56 2008
    820.9′008—dc22   2008016325

10   9   8   7   6   5   4   3   2   1
17   16   15   14   13   12   11   10   09   08

Printed and bound in Great Britain by
CPI Antony Rowe, Chippenham and Eastbourne

For my parents,
Richard and Deborah Simpson

Contents

Acknowledgements

This book has grown out of a dissertation written at the University of Pennsylvania with the careful and generous guidance of Stuart Curran, Michael Gamer, Penny Fielding, and the late David DeLaura. I am deeply grateful to the first three for their continuing support of the project as it became this book, and wish only that I could have continued to draw on David's learning and wisdom. James English and Madelyn Gutwirth read chapters of the dissertation and offered valuable comments, and the project has long benefited from the hot intellects and warm characters of the Penn eighteenth-century studies reading group, in whose meetings Jack Lynch, Brett Wilson, Dan White, Julie Schutzman, Allen Grove, Susan Essman, and Lynn Festa showed me how scholarly communities work at their best. In our dissertation writing group and subsequently, Jim Kearney and Emily Zinn have been great readers and better friends. At Grinnell, my colleagues have provided in abundance the encouragement and advice I needed as a new member of the faculty. Among them I especially thank Roger Vetter, who shared his time and photographic eye with me as I considered cover art for the book. Grinnell's magnificent students and alumni have helped me keep the joys of intellectual inquiry always in view.

The project has received institutional support from a Mellon dissertation fellowship and a number of grants from Grinnell College, including a Harris Fellowship funded by the late Jack and Lucile Hanson Harris. I also thank the library staffs of the British Library, the National Library of Ireland, the National Library of Scotland, the Van Pelt Library of the University of Pennsylvania, the Beinecke Library of Yale University, the Harry Ransom Research Center at the University of Texas at Austin, the Library Company of Philadelphia, the University of Iowa, and Burling Library of Grinnell College, as well as the readers of my work for *ELH* and *European Romantic Review*, in which versions of two chapters have previously appeared, and Palgrave Macmillan. The book has also benefited from the keen editorial eye of Eileen Bartos and the support of Paula Kennedy at Palgrave Macmillan and that of the series editors, Anne K. Mellor and Clifford Siskin.

To my grandparents Ruth and Wendell Milz and the late Venice Simpson, to my mother and father Deborah and Richard Simpson, and to my brother Tom, I owe boundless thanks for their interest in my life and livelihood, for creating the family of which I am so fortunate to be a part. My parents inspired me to teach by their examples, and they have brought their skill to bear on this work, reading every chapter of this book, usually more than once, often on short notice.

In this accounting of blessings the greatest come last: I am fortunate indeed to have shared the time of this book's composition with Carolyn Jacobson and, more recently, our son Peter. Nothing delights me more than the prospect of many more years of reading and writing with them.

1
The Minstrel Mode

Writing about minstrels: the heard overheard

This study explores a literary convention: the representation of a poet, harp, or lyre in hand, performing for an audience. Before 1750, minstrels and bards had traditionally played only a peripheral role in British literature, appearing as fleeting decorations in numerous works but rarely, if ever, taking center stage. After 1750, the situation changed. Some authors began to pay sustained attention to minstrels, bards, and their continental cousins (such as troubadours, *improvvisatori*, and *improvvisatrici*). At the same time, other British authors, most notably William Wordsworth and Samuel Taylor Coleridge, largely rejected the minstrel mode and began to develop the conventions of what later came to be called Romantic authorship. One goal of this study is to introduce minstrel writing – the phrase I will use to describe representations of poetic composition through minstrels and similar figures – as a model of writing that developed in dialogic opposition to that of Romantic lyricism.

Minstrelsy does appear in Romantic poetry, generally to signify social activity from which the action of a poem is separate. Coleridge's ancient mariner, for instance, prevents the wedding-guest he encounters from entering a wedding celebration featuring 'merry Minstralsy' (l.40). Wordsworth in *The White Doe of Rylstone* (1815) sends characters into the 'din of arms and minstrelsy' (II.417), but the poem does not follow them. Instead, the narrative lingers to explore the thoughts of those left behind. We see here a split between writers who wanted to explore minstrelsy as a metaphor for their own authorship and those, such as Wordsworth and Coleridge, who sought to represent the best poetry as composed from a contemplative position outside of the economic and political exchanges that form the basis of the minstrel's professional existence. Wordsworth himself acknowledged such a divergence of aims in the faint praise he offered to Walter Scott's *Marmion* (1808). Wordsworth wrote to Scott,

> Thank you for Marmion . . . I think your end has been attained; that it is not in every respect the end which I should wish you to propose to yourself you will be well aware, from what you know of my notions of composition, both as to matter and manner. (*Letters* [*Middle*] I.264)

Scott's poetry, whose 'matter' is explicitly concerned with the poet's place in 'the din of arms and minstrelsy', could win only grudging approval from Wordsworth.

William Hazlitt also saw the work of Scott and Wordsworth as tending to different ends, each with its own 'defects and excellences':

> [Wordsworth] is the most original poet now living [in 1818]. He is the reverse of Walter Scott in his defects and excellences. He has nearly all that the other wants; and wants all that the other possesses. His poetry is not external, but internal; it does not depend on tradition or story, or old song; he furnishes it from his own mind, and is his own subject. (V.156)

Hazlitt oversimplifies both poets' work in many ways; Wordsworth routinely addressed subjects beyond 'his own mind', and Scott's writing sometimes describes the mental state of the composing poet. In fact, Wordsworth and Coleridge tend to separate themselves most carefully from minstrelsy precisely in works that come closest to minstrel writing's fantasy of poetic composition as performative storytelling, such as Coleridge's 'Rime' or Wordsworth's *The Excursion*. In all their excess, however, Hazlitt's blunt dichotomies do draw on differences in Wordsworth's and Scott's self-representations, especially Scott's embrace of the minstrel as his poetic persona (fueling Hazlitt's perception of an 'external' poetry that 'depend[s] on tradition or story') and Wordsworth's persistent rejection of minstrelsy as a foundational metaphor for his writing.

Hazlitt's dichotomies become still more extreme in the criticism of writers such as John Stuart Mill, whose brand of Victorian Wordsworthianism leads him to say that 'internal' poetry, in Hazlitt's phrase, is by definition the only writing that constitutes poetry at all. Mill's famous antithesis that '[e]loquence is *heard*, poetry is *over*heard' (348) constitutes part of a theory that specifically excludes minstrel writing's characteristic fantasy of a poet in front of an immediate audience: 'the peculiarity of poetry appears to us to lie in the utter unconsciousness of a listener' (348), Mill writes, and 'no consciousness that any eyes are upon us must be visible in the work itself' (349). To emphasize the interiority of the poet's compositional process as the source and proper subject of good poetry is to push minstrel writing aside. Whether in prose or verse, minstrel writing presents the poet observed, interacting with a live audience at a moment of simultaneous inspiration, performance and reception.[1] Minstrel writing stages the 'heard' mode of poetry within the text: the minstrel's audience is not primarily the reader but rather one or more fellow characters. The author who represents a minstrel performing for an audience not only imagines poetry as 'heard' through that fantasy of a live audience but also allows authorship to become a two-faced or three-faced or four-faced enterprise, in which the minstrel character, and often a narrator and an editor, make different kinds of claims to representing the author's sincere voice.[2] Minstrel writing involves the paradoxical multiplication of Romantic sincerity.

The minstrel's role is often to be fundamentally responsive, sometimes also to be rhetorically persuasive (to partake of Mill's 'eloquence'). To readers accustomed to the values of Romantic individualism, the sociability of the minstrel's compositional process appears corrupt, dependent, subservient – to produce poetry in immediate response to a listener's needs is inherently to be a flawed poet.[3] Some Romantic-era writers used portrayals of minstrelsy to express frustration with their inability to achieve a position of artistic disinterest because they relied on their own patrons or the literary market for support. Other writers, however, proudly aligned themselves with the minstrel's social process of composition as a sign of the poet's sympathy with an audience or even, as part of a world-view supporting landed aristocracy over the incursions of republican democracy, as a celebration of the proper interdependence of poets and the great families who administer the state. The figure of the minstrel could represent many sides of poetry's social existence.

The harp and the pen

As they advocated their own theories of writing, Wordsworth and Coleridge shed the textual and figurative apparatuses of minstrelsy by exchanging metaphors of musical performance for those of writing. They both characterized their support of common written language as opposition to the writer's use of the minstrel's instruments – harps, lutes, and lyres. Writing to Coleridge in 1798, Wordsworth establishes a hierarchy of 'pencil' over 'lute', writing of Bürger, 'I love his *"Tra ra la"* dearly; but less of the horn and more of the lute – and far, far more of the pencil' (*Letters* [*Early*] I.235). Later, in the opening pages of his *Biographia Literaria* (1817), Coleridge draws a clearer distinction by tracing a similar metaphor back to the 1790s. After stating his ambition 'to effect, as far as possible, a settlement of the long continued controversy concerning the true nature of poetic diction' (5), Coleridge recalls the influence of his childhood schoolmaster, James Boyer. Coleridge writes that Boyer

> showed no mercy to phrase, metaphor, or image, unsupported by a sound sense, or where the same sense might have been conveyed with equal force and dignity in plainer words. Lute, harp, and lyre, muse, muses, and inspirations, Pegasus, Parnassus, and Hippocrene, were all an abomination to him. In fancy I can almost hear him now, exclaiming *"Harp? Harp? Lyre? Pen and ink, boy, you mean!"* (9–10)

Boyer's enforcement of 'manly simplicity' (8), to use Coleridge's phrase, performs at least two functions here.[4] Coleridge signals to the reader, perhaps defensively, that he admired the 'language of men' before he met Wordsworth or went to Germany. More important for my purposes, the passage also locates poetic merit away from harps and lyres, the conventional accoutrements of minstrels, bards, and improvisers.[5]

Like Wordsworth and others, Coleridge presents the opposition between the harp and the pen as one between childish flights of fancy on the one hand, and realism, restraint, and 'manly simplicity' on the other. Yet Coleridge no more reached the bulk of his audience by means of '[p]en and ink' than Scott reached his own audience by singing. Both writers communicated through the mechanisms of a burgeoning print culture, whose editors, presses, advertisements, and consumers are as obscured by Coleridge's nostalgic fantasy of the pen as by Scott's of the minstrel. Coleridge's fantasy won out; writers still 'pen' their works, but they have dropped their metaphorical harps. When the *Biographia* was published in 1817, however, the pages of British and Irish writing teemed with harps, lyres, and their players, from Scott's many minstrels to Byron's Turkish tale-tellers and *improvvisatori*. In that year, Thomas Moore's *Lalla Rookh* (1817), a minstrel tale for which Moore had received an advance of 3,000 guineas (an amount unprecedented for a poem), began its sensational run. Surrounding Coleridge was a profusion of

poets pretending to be literal lyricists. The minstrel, bard, and improviser were celebrated denizens of British poetry not only in Coleridge's
youth but also at the time of the *Biographia's* publication. Trying to stem
the tide of minstrel writing in 1817, Coleridge may well have felt as
beleaguered as a hapless English soldier facing Bonnie Dundee and the
Highlanders at Killiecrankie – a metaphor that Scott's vast readership
had been trained to understand.

Thus, deep as Wordsworth's connection to the ballad revival was,
his method of adopting that material differed dramatically from that
of the minstrel writers. Wordsworth characterized the Poet as a lone
man with the time, physical ability, and economic wherewithal to wan-
der the countryside. Minstrelsy, in contrast, provided conventions of
authorial fantasy for writers who could not (or had reason not to)
enact the Wordsworthian model using a straightforward lyrical voice –
among them women, United Irish sympathizers, working-class poets,
and the lame (Scott and Byron). Every major writer of minstrel, bard,
or *improvvisatrice* narratives in the period had cause to understand the
Wordsworthian Poet as a persona he or she could not inhabit. For minstrel writers, such a mode of authorship was not only an unlivable fairy
tale, but also one that lacked the political flexibility and wide audience
that the minstrel mode provided.

By the end of the nineteenth century, Wordsworth's notions of poetic
propriety had carried the day. Blackface or 'Negro' minstrelsy transformed popular conceptions of the minstrel on both sides of the Atlantic.
At the end of the century, thanks in part to stricter copyright laws, the
volumes of writers such as Moore, Scott, and Hemans that filled the
bookshelves of readers in the nineteenth century began their migra-
tion to the second-hand bookstores of the twentieth, not for decades to
be reproduced in modern editions. And literary history largely revised
away the paraphernalia of minstrelsy, the implements that deflected
the modern author's pen and ink on to the harp and lyre of historical
imagination.

Roots: minstrel writing in the eighteenth century

Though most of this study analyzes nineteenth-century texts, it refers
frequently to eighteenth-century works that established the practice of
imagining authorship through the portrayal of bards and minstrels. A
series of foundational pieces of minstrel writing emerged between 1757
and 1774. First came Thomas Gray's 'The Bard: A Pindaric Ode' (1757)
and James Macpherson's Ossianic poems (1760 and following). Then,

Thomas Percy's 'An Essay on the Ancient English Minstrels' (1765) provided the source material for two more works: Percy's own *The Hermit of Warkworth: A Northumberland Ballad* (1771), and James Beattie's *The Minstrel: Or, the Progress of Genius* (1771–4). In works published before that time, minstrels did occasionally contribute more to a text than singing at the culminating marriage of a comedy, but the few who garner more than a passing mention are generally not minstrels at all, but other characters who play that part to gain access to courtly or aristocratic functions (as do, for example, Viola/Cesario in *Twelfth Night* or Rafe, Dicke, and Robin in John Lyly's *Gallathea*). When Gray, Macpherson, Percy, and Beattie made the minstrel's or bard's character central to their imaginative works, however, they created the minstrel mode of the following generations.

An early encounter between two of these writers is instructive. As he composed what would become *The Minstrel*, Beattie sent the unfinished work and a sketch of the whole to Gray. Gray replied in a letter dated 2 July 1770:

> The design is simple, and pregnant with poetical ideas of various kinds, yet seems somehow imperfect at the end. Why may not young Edwin, when necessity has driven him to take up the harp, and assume the profession of a Minstrel, do some great and singular service to his country? (what service I must leave to your invention) such as no General, no Statesman, no Moralist could do without the aid of music, inspiration, and poetry. (Gray, *Poems* I.383–4)

One of Beattie's leading modern champions, Everard King, has submitted that '[o]ne is surprised . . . that Gray does not view the poem as an attempt to show the development of the poet's own mind and imagination' (54). Gray's reaction is indeed surprising if one considers Gray only as the author of his 'Elegy Written in a Country Churchyard', as that pre-Romantic poet of introspection.

We see here a tension between two genealogies of Romantic-era poetry. King's response presupposes the centrality of a poet's autobiographical psychology; hence his surprise that the Gray of the famous elegy does not find in Beattie a prefiguring of Wordsworth, as King himself does. On the contrary, Gray perceives in *The Minstrel* a missed opportunity to take up the public function of the poet through the figure of the minstrel. In other words, Gray, speaking as the author of 'The Bard' rather than of the 'Elegy', sees the possibility that would come into being, though more through Percy and Macpherson than through Beattie: minstrelsy would become a mechanism by which many writers explored the poet's ability to provide 'great and singular service to his country' by direct action.

In fact, when Beattie planned his poem, and even as he published the first book, he did imagine a public career for his hero in line with Gray's and Percy's writings on minstrelsy.[6] The title of *The Minstrel* marked the poem as a kind of sequel to Gray's then-famous 'Bard', and the opening sentence of Beattie's Advertisement acknowledged a debt to Percy: 'The first hint of this performance was suggested by Mr. Percy's ingenious *Essay on the English Minstrels*, prefixed to his first volume of Reliques of Ancient English Poetry, published by Mr. Dodsley in the year 1765' (iv).[7] Like many other antiquarian narratives of bards and minstrels, Percy's essay emphasizes the high regard in which the nobility held ancient poets. Percy explains ways in which military and political figures took on the role of the minstrel to infiltrate enemy camps – King Alfred spied on the Danes as a minstrel, according to Percy, and then a later Danish king returned the favor by spying on King Athelstan – thus adding a soldierly aspect to minstrelsy. Beattie's plan for his poem, as expressed in a 1767 letter to Thomas Blacklock and probably also to Gray, did indeed follow the martial model of Percy's essay. Beattie imagined for his minstrel a 'genius for poetry and adventures', and though a hermit discourages the minstrel from adventuring, 'on a sudden, the country is invaded by the Danes or English borderers (I know not which), and he is stript of all his little fortune, and obliged by necessity to commence minstrel' (Forbes I.103).[8] Following Percy's example, that is, Beattie imagined minstrelsy as a mode of public service necessitated by a military invasion.

After the publication of *The Minstrel*'s first book, which describes the childhood experiences of its title character Edwin, Beattie turned from his plans to portray the military service of his minstrel to an acceptance of the introspection of his 'lone enthusiast' (I.lvi) as an end in itself. Beattie revised the Preface, omitting the opening acknowledgement of Percy's inspiration. Then, minimizing the importance of the Preface's claim that Edwin lived in a 'rude age', the second book rejects the utility of historical detail in favor of present-day introspection:

> But sure to foreign climes we need not range,
> Nor search the ancient records of our race,
> To learn the effects of time and change,
> Which in ourselves, alas! We daily trace. (II.ii)

The poem ends with the narrator, now explicitly contemporary and autobiographical, mourning the death of John Gregory. Nothing like the planned invasion ever materializes. In the 1774 edition, the move from examining historical minstrelsy to exploring the present-day Beattie's mind is complete, and Beattie *qua* proto-Wordsworthian is born.

Beattie's revisions enabled *The Minstrel* to assist in the creation of both traditions of Romantic-era writing that I have described. The first edition demonstrated that Percy's antiquarian work could provide the raw material for successful modern adaptations that, unlike James Macpherson's Ossianic poetry, wore their modernity proudly. At the same time, oddly, Beattie's minstrel never becomes a minstrel, even according to Beattie's own plan. To the retrospective eyes of Scott, in fact, Beattie had described a character who could never have become a minstrel like Scott's own characters. Scott guessed that Beattie came to have 'a suspicion that he had given his hero an education and a tone of feeling inconsistent with the plan he had laid down for his subsequent exploits' (quoted in King 161).[9] With no invasion and no minstrelsy, Beattie's poem anticipates not the minstrelsy of Scott but the authorial theory of Wordsworth: what began in the minstrel tradition of public, martial narratives became by omission an account of introspective sincerity for its own moral purposes. In other words, leaving the poem unfinished made it more like Gray's 'Elegy' – that is, a contemplative poem about the poet's mind, composition, and mourning – and less like Gray's 'Bard'.[10]

As a result, from the perspective of later representations of minstrelsy proper, Beattie's *Minstrel* was not even the most influential adaptation of Percy's *Reliques* published in 1771.[11] That distinction belongs to Percy's own *The Hermit of Warkworth*, which became the direct inspiration, in content and method, of Scott's metrical romances. *The Hermit* is a border tale, as Scott's tales would be; Scott would use Warkworth and the Percy family to set the scenes of *The Lay of the Last Minstrel* (1805) and *Marmion* (1808), his first two full-length metrical romances, and would copy Percy's plot of accidental murder closely in *Rokeby* (1813). Percy's widely read poem comes with antiquarian paratexts, including the descriptions of modern landscape that became characteristic of Scott's editorial persona.[12] By placing an avowedly original poem in an antiquarian apparatus, *The Hermit* introduced the split authorial voice that, as I will argue, would separate minstrel writing's annotations from those of its eighteenth-century predecessors.

Percy also modeled for Scott the practice of flattering a more prosperous branch of his own family, dedicating *The Hermit* 'To Her Grace

Elizabeth, Duchess and Countess of Northumberland, In Her Own Right Baroness Percy, &c. &c. &c.' The verse dedication reports that 'the Muse' has inspired a tribute to Percys old and new:

> Surely the cares and woes of human kind,
> Tho' simply told, will gain each gentle ear:
> But all for you the Muse her lay design'd,
> And bade your noble Ancestors appear … (v)

In the poem itself, the eponymous hermit tells a story of the past prosperity of the Percys, when the grandfather of the story's young hero held parties at which minstrels sang the achievements of the family (20). The connection between that minstrelsy and the latter-day Percy's dedication of *The Hermit* can hardly be missed. We also see here the trope of the minstrel disguise, adapted from the *Reliques*, as Bertram (a friend of grandfather Percy who turns out to be the mysterious hermit himself) uses disguises to search for his captured lover. He dresses as a poor Palmer, for instance, and

> Sometimes a Minstrel's garb he wears,
>   With pipes so sweet and shrill;
> And wends to every tower and town;
>   O'er every dale and hill. (30)

Thus Percy establishes not only the most important textual form of later minstrel writing, the imaginative work surrounded by the author's own notes, but also a key point of minstrel writing's content, the use of 'a Minstrel's garb' to imagine the poet's literal and metaphorical access to the public life of politics and war.

If Percy's work had merely provided a model upon which Scott based his metrical romances, *The Hermit of Warkworth* would still merit more attention than it presently receives. But it did more than that: its hermit became the melancholic, secret-carrying hero that Scott adapted in *Marmion* and that later became 'Byronic'. It also inspired Hannah More's first full-length published poem, *Sir Eldred of the Bower* (1776), which is a patent imitation of *The Hermit* in form and content, and then her tragedy *Percy* (1777), another keystone in the Percy–Douglas tradition following Percy's poem and John Home's *Douglas* (1757). Percy later extended his influence by moving to Ireland, where he 'tended his Dromore diocese though the volatile period that erupted in the Irish Rebellion of 1798' (B. Davis ix) and befriended Charlotte Brooke, who wrote *Reliques of Irish*

Poetry (1789). Brooke's *Reliques* included an original tale that, like *The Hermit*, created a new story from antiquarian sources. Brooke's was the first important work of that kind in Ireland, and that tale's Preface constituted the first widely read imagination of female minstrelsy in Britain or Ireland. In other words, Thomas Percy was not only a respected antiquarian who provided source material for other writers during the ballad revival. He was also arguably the most important writer of original verse among eighteenth-century minstrel writers. He created a model that directly influenced key figures, male and female, in England, Scotland, Wales, and Ireland.

An equivocal minstrel: the case of Macpherson

Though Gray, Percy, and Beattie created many conventions of later minstrel writing, none established the crucial figure of the minstrel engaging a live audience. Macpherson's Ossianic writings did that, but they also complicated the issue of authorship. Because of Macpherson's protestations against his authorship of Ossianic poetry, discussing his importance for minstrel writing requires conditional assertions. If authors took Macpherson at his word and regarded his poems of Ossian as translations of ancient originals, then Macpherson's Ossianic texts provided a northern source of ancient poetry whose descriptions of bards could become source material for modern writers. On the other hand, for those who regarded Macpherson's Ossian as essentially a hoax – a series of modern prose poems based loosely on oral tradition – Macpherson's writing became one of the first self-annotated imaginative works about bards and minstrels. That is, the more one regards Macpherson as a fraud, the more he becomes the first eighteenth-century minstrel writer, and one of the most influential.

Seen retrospectively, Macpherson's pronouncements about authorship and literary value come loaded with irony. In 1762, Macpherson – known today, when known at all, as an author of spectacular but fleeting influence – dismissed the value of immediate success in literature, citing the questionable taste of the crowd in his Preface to *Fingal*:

> The poets, whose business it is to please, if they want to preserve the fame they have once acquired, must very often forfeit their own judgments to this variable temper of the bulk of their readers, and accommodate their writings to this unsettled state. A fame so fluctuating deserves not much to be valued. (n.p.)

Only time can sort the merits of literature from the personalities of authors, Macpherson argues, so 'Poetry, like virtue, receives its reward after death' (n.p.). As Macpherson acknowledged defensively, such an argument could work to help a disingenuous forger achieve immediate success by fabricating the endurance of a work. That strategy produces a strange mirroring of Macpherson's and Wordsworth's arguments about reception: both poets serve their different purposes by arguing for the authority of the generations who live after an author dies. Whereas Wordsworth would use that logic to explain his own lack of commercial success, among other things, Macpherson deploys it to a different end by framing his immediate audience in 1762 as itself the voice of a later generation that can judge the work of Ossian.

'The eternal question, concerning the authenticity or spuriousness of Ossian', as the *Annual Register* for 1807 termed it (998), ate at the foundations of Macpherson's rhetoric, creating endless possibilities for unwitting or intentional double entendre. Macpherson's editorial persona, for instance, creates unintentional humor in moments of ostensible speculation about what may well have been his own intentions: 'Perhaps the poet alludes to the Roman eagle' (93). The humor stems from what would become a standard component of minstrel writing: two authorial personae existing in tension with each other. In spite of Macpherson's claims to the contrary, we see in his Ossianic texts an early example of Percy and Scott's method of annotating one's own work. Macpherson's editorial voice, sounding at times like Scott's, contains ancient superstition in a rationalist Enlightenment framework, as in this note:

> It was the opinion then, as indeed it is today, of some of the highlanders, that the souls of the deceased hovered round their living friends; and sometimes appeared to them when they were about to enter on any great undertaking. (10)

When Malcolm Laing used further annotations to attack Macpherson in Laing's 1805 edition of the poems, Scott himself noted the irony of Laing's method: Laing's notes, Scott writes, 'are intended, contrary to general usage, to destroy the authority of the text' (Review 433). But in destroying Ossian's authority, Laing's notes helped create Macpherson's status as an author annotating his own creative work in the minstrel mode.

Scott's comment arises in his review of Laing's edition and Henry Mackenzie's Highland Committee report on the poems' authenticity.

Those works and Scott's review all appeared in 1805, the same year Scott published his first full-length metrical romance, *The Lay of the Last Minstrel*. Scott's own writing would have given him an unusual sense of the way Macpherson's writing could be important even if falsely advertised. Even as he declares Laing the victor of the authenticity debate, Scott presents his verdict as a reclamation of Macpherson as an influential modern author in the same vein as John Home, whose play *Douglas* (1757) was based on traditional materials. Scott says that Laing's argument 'compels us to allow, that the poems of Ossian, as translated by Macpherson, bear the same relation to the original legends, that the Tragedy of Douglas does to the Ballad of Gil Morris' (462). Scott's final maneuver is to reclaim Macpherson as a modern 'bard' from 'almost as barbarous a corner of Scotland' as Ossian, a poet 'capable not only of making an enthusiastic impression on every mind susceptible of poetical beauty, but of giving a new tone to poetry throughout all Europe' (462).[13]

After 1805, other writers followed Scott in recasting Macpherson as a modern poet. For example, Byron's 'The Death of Calmar and Orla, An Imitation of Macpherson's "Ossian" ' appeared in *Hours of Idleness* in 1807. It includes an explanatory footnote saying that 'Laing's late Edition has completely overthrown every hope that Macpherson's Ossian, might prove the Translation of a series of Poems complete in themselves' (*CPW* I.375). Byron could accept the fact of Macpherson's imposture and then write an imitation of Ossian taking Macpherson's work at least in part as original prose poetry rather than as translations of earlier verse. To write a prose imitation of Macpherson was to treat Macpherson as an original author, writing in prose by choice – to treat him as he had pleaded not to be treated.

Two epigraphs further illustrate the new Ossianic possibilities available to writers after 1805. Sydney Owenson's *Lay of an Irish Harp* (1807) and Jane Porter's *The Scottish Chiefs* (1810) use epigraphs from Macpherson that speak of awakening and of ancient voices. Owenson's reads, 'Voice of the days of old, let me hear you – Awake the soul of song' (front matter), and Porter's, 'There comes a voice that awakens my soul. It is the voice of years that are gone; they roll before me with all their deeds' (front matter). By attaching the metaphor of awakening to 'national' subject matter (both Macpherson's and their own), Owenson and Porter echo what Ernest Gellner calls 'the nationalist ideologue's most misguided claim: namely, that the "nations" are there, in the very nature of things, only waiting to be "awakened" (a favourite nationalist expression and image) from their regrettable slumber, by the nationalist "awakener" ' (47–8).

For Owenson and Porter, however, it is stories of the past, not a nation, that awaken. In both of their novels, Ossian becomes a displaced muse, a figure for a misty bardic past whose spirit can be separated from the time and place of Macpherson's Ossian. Rather than a poet uniquely grounded in his natural and temporal environment – a figure appropriate to earnest political nationalism – the debunked Ossian became a sign of national poetic spirit adaptable to the more moderate and ambiguous political purposes of writers such as Owenson and Porter.

'Ossian' Macpherson thus became an oddly paradigmatic case of minstrel authorship, displaying the flexibility of minstrel writing's conventions and the extreme ends to which they could be employed. Paradoxically, Macpherson reached this status by proclaiming that he was not a minstrel writer at all, but rather a collector, a passive medium for the creations of an inspired original bard. That is to say, Macpherson helped shape minstrel writing by claiming not to be part of it. For many other writers of the time, his fall from bardic inspiration into the self-conscious derivativeness of modern minstrelsy was a literary *felix culpa*.

The author and the minstrel

The case of Macpherson, which involves a set of contested texts transformed into the stuff of the following generation's literary and political contestations, illustrates some of the variety and adaptability that characterized the minstrel writing of the early nineteenth century, from Scott's publication of *The Lay of the Last Minstrel* in 1805 to the emergence of blackface minstrelsy in the 1830s. This minstrel writing includes representations of ancient and contemporary minstrelsy, and of male and female minstrels. It cuts across established categories of literary genre, including metrical romances, historical novels, and national tales. Its writers use minstrels for a wide range of literary and political purposes; indeed, the widespread use of the conventions of minstrel writing made it especially susceptible to revision and allusion. What the diverse texts of minstrel writing do share, however, is the semi-autobiographical representation of a performing poet. Minstrel writing uses the minstrel to portray the author's role and often some of the author's characteristics, but that portrayal maintains a separation between minstrel and author. Generally, the minstrel is only one of multiple authorial personae in a piece of minstrel writing, as the minstrel develops by contrast to more modern, scholarly narrators and editors that claim to represent other timbres of the authorial voice – or, to alter the metaphor, these personae are recognizably different voices that all seem to speak as the author.

Before returning to address further the authorial personae of minstrel writing, I pause to explain my choice of *minstrel* as the blanket term for minstrels, bards, *improvvisatori*, *improvvisatrici*, and occasionally troubadours. I will make finer distinctions when necessary, but in general, I follow the example of early nineteenth-century writers, who treated 'minstrel' as a broad category and routinely called improvisers, bards, and troubadours by that name. Differences between minstrels and bards carry most weight in the eighteenth-century writings of nationalist antiquarians. There, as a rule, *bard* connotes Celtic foreignness, whereas *minstrel* refers to a later figure of the English and Scottish Border country.[14] Choosing selectively from early examples allows one to construct a distinction: within eighteenth-century antiquarian writing, bards are foreign, ancient figures – as Anne Janowitz puts it, 'until the seventeenth century ["bard"] had been used only as a foreign word, associated with the vernacular of Scotland, Ireland, and Wales' (66) – whereas minstrels came later and tend to be Border figures, often invoked to support cordial relations between Scotland or Ireland and England. As Maureen McLane has noted, 'It is telling … that Katie Trumpener called her recent book *Bardic*, and not *Minstrel*, *Nationalism*; for the cultural nationalism she tracks is one of heroic resistance from the periphery, its bardic mouthpieces prophetic, albeit doomed, protestors of the seemingly inevitable march of progress' ('Figure' 433).

It is also worth noting the many exceptions to these rules of usage in the Romantic period. By the early eighteenth century, *bard* had long been a generic term for a poet, especially but not always a poet of the past. The term *minstrel* carried more specific associations with vagabond entertainers, but its metaphorical associations allowed birds, for instance, to be called minstrels but seldom bards. By the nineteenth century, common usage complicated matters further, blurring especially the line between Celtic bards and English or Border minstrels: *bard* continued to refer to poets in general, notably the consummately English Shakespeare, and minstrels came rhetorically to populate the Highlands and Ireland, with Thomas Moore, for example, becoming Ireland's 'Minstrel Boy'. Even Carolan, one of the most prominent bards in Irish writing, goes by 'minstrel' as well as 'bard' in one of Sydney Owenson's explanatory footnotes to *The Wild Irish Girl* (90). The demands of meter confused the situation still more: poets gained flexibility by selectively calling a minstrel a bard or vice versa. The culmination of this terminological confusion is evident in the title of 'The Minstrel Bard' (1808), an early poem by Felicia Hemans. To the extent that a distinction between the terms persisted, however, most minstrel writing did portray a 'minstrel' or minstrel-like figure secondarily called a 'minstrel'. The minstrel's status as following the bard chronologically provided a useful metaphor for the author of minstrel writing, who also came belatedly relative to minstrels depicted as thriving in earlier times; hence the motif of the last bard or minstrel, the final surivivor from a culture preceding the author's own.

This sense of the minstrel's secondariness was reinforced by representations of minstrels as collecting poetry in addition to composing it. The split between performing and editorial personae in the texts of minstrel writing mirrors the split between composition and collection in the minstrel. The spectacle of performing persona is almost universally the best-remembered feature of a minstrel text, and the one that attracts the most commentary. The fantasy of such performance impressed itself on the readers of the time to the extent that they tended to call authors metonymically by the names of the minstrel performers they created: Macpherson became known as 'Ossian', Beattie as Edwin, Moore as the Minstrel Boy, Owenson as Glorvina, Germaine de Staël as Corinne, Walter Scott (the poet) as a more generic Border Minstrel, James Hogg as the Ettrick Shepherd or the Mountain Bard, Byron as Harold.

The equation of writer and minstrel is always too simple. The performing minstrels of minstrel writing are both recognizably autobiographical and also *not* autobiographical in any literal way. Often, this contradiction is evident in a split between orality and textuality. The creative processes of writer and character, though obviously analogous, can never be identical, and the reader must recognize that the performing minstrel is a fantasy whose significance stems from the separation between fantasy and reality. Critics then and now have tended to erase the discontinuities between writer and character in favor of simple identification, even when the discontinuities provide important information. Neglecting the differences between Owenson and her heroine Glorvina, for instance, has tended to minimize the difference between *The Wild Irish Girl*'s pre-Union setting and post-Union production, a displacement crucial to reading the book's political positions.

It is no wonder that Owenson and Staël, the writers most responsible for creating a tradition of female minstrelsy, both resented being conflated with their fictional heroines. Appropriately, Byron – himself, of course, constantly conflated with his characters over his protestations – figures in telling anecdotes about both Staël's and Owenson's personae. At the party where she first met Byron, Owenson was furious at being forced to play Glorvina. (Owenson's first biography states that Glorvina was based on Elizabeth Malby [Fitzpatrick 108–9], though later critics have taken for granted that the character is a thinly veiled self-portrait.) Later, 'Byron insisted on calling [Staël] "Corinne" knowing full well that [she] always vehemently resisted all attempts to connect her autobiographically to her heroine' (Frank 325). But resist these identifications as they might – and they did not always resist – writers in the minstrel mode created such confusions by choosing the minstrel mask.

These confusions stem from the fact that, as constructed in minstrel writing, minstrels seldom display the ironic self-awareness required of the authors who create them. The minstrel's process of composition involves the articulation of a sincere emotional response to the minstrel's immediate circumstances; this requires an emotional transparency – a staged version of deep Romantic sincerity – that makes deception impossible, and minstrel writing includes much praise of the emotional transparency of, among others, Highlanders, the Irish, and good women. Minstrel writing thus creates its minstrels as contradictory figures from the start: their attractiveness lies in the deep feeling occasioned by their presence before audiences, but their actual audiences are readers. In minstrel writing, that is, the conventions of oral immediacy are constantly belied by the form of their presentation. The minstrels are thus like characters in sentimental drama who proclaim the signs of sensibility to be beyond acting even as they were being acted.[15] Like the actor, the minstrel writer speaks in character, putting on a self-conscious rhetorical act even as his or her text proclaims the virtues of having that within which passeth show.

Minstrel writing, in other words, balances on an edge between lyric and dramatic monologue: the author speaks in character but tempts the reader to consider the character as a mouthpiece of the sincere authorial self. To illustrate the point further by contrast, we can look to Wordsworth's approach. Wordsworthian authorship, though it does allow for speaking in character, relies on the clarity of bounded speakers' selves. In the Advertisement to the 1798 *Lyrical Ballads*, Wordsworth ensures that such boundaries remain intact, saying that '[t]he poem of the Thorn, as the reader will soon discover, is not supposed to be spoken in the author's own person: the character of the loquacious narrator will sufficiently shew itself in the course of the story' (*Prose* I.117). The latter part of the sentence wears its anxiety prominently. If the 'character of the loquacious narrator will sufficiently shew itself', it should not require supplemental clarification. Wordsworth's insistence reflects the work the claim does in another direction, however: by calling attention to the difference between Wordsworth and one of his speakers, it authorizes the reader to read *other* poems as indeed 'spoken in the author's own person'. The Wordsworthian model accommodates a transparent lyrical voice and the impersonation of other subjects' sincerity, but Wordsworth draws a thick line between them.[16]

This passage in the 1798 Advertisement might seem to contradict the later Preface's fantasy of sympathetic identification, in which Wordsworth expresses a literary version of Adam Smith's sense of sympathy's process. Smith writes that '[b]y the imagination we place ourselves in [our brother's] situation, we conceive ourselves enduring all the same torments, we enter as it were into his body, and become in some measure the same person with him' (9). Wordsworth, terming sympathetic identification a desirable 'delusion', makes it the starting point of composition in the 1802 Preface to *Lyrical Ballads*:

> it will be the wish of the Poet to bring his feelings near to those of the persons whose feelings he describes, nay, for short spaces of time perhaps, to let himself slip into an entire delusion, and even confound and identify his own feelings with theirs; modifying only the language which is thus suggested to him, by a consideration that he describes for a particular purpose, that of giving pleasure. (*LB* 256)

In presenting sympathetic identification as the source of poetry, Wordsworth comes very close to a model of sentimental authorship, in which strong feeling produces an immediate, sincere effusion of text.[17]

Wordsworthian authorship comes not from that feeling, however, but from the period of contemplation and filtering that follows. 'Here, then', Wordsworth continues, 'he [the poet] will apply the principle on which I have so much insisted, namely, that of selection' (256), which takes place through simulating the original emotion in the state of 'tranquillity' described in this famous passage:[18]

> I have said that Poetry is the spontaneous overflow of powerful feelings: it takes its origin from emotion recollected in tranquillity: the emotion is contemplated till by a species of reaction the tranquillity gradually disappears, and an emotion, kindred to that which was before the subject of contemplation, is gradually produced, and does itself actually exist in the mind. In this mood successful composition generally begins, and in a mood similar to this it is carried on... (266)

However inspired by common speech, Wordsworth's poet composes in writing and privately, separated from the source of the inspiring words or feelings. In contrast, Gray's bard, Scott's last minstrel, Staël's Corinne, and Owenson's Glorvina, for all their differences, all explore the fantasy of poetry being produced under the immediate influence of strong emotion and directed to an identifiable audience. To this Wordsworth adds an intervening stage of spatial and emotional retreat.[19]

One cannot say that Wordsworth's theory rejects emotionalism or sentimentality per se; 'an emotion, kindred to that which was before the subject of contemplation', which 'does itself actually exist in the mind' is central to the mood in which 'successful composition generally begins' (266). Wordsworth makes no distinction of degree or kind between the two 'kindred' emotions; this is not an anti-sentimental theory. Context separates the initial emotion and the second, and the second becomes the producer of 'successful composition' precisely by removing the object of sympathy from the scene. In 1798, at the height of reactionary fear of ill-considered crowd behavior, Wordsworth puts a literal distance between the poet and the polity. In that space – the space of distance, of solitude, of reflection – grows Wordsworthian authorship.[20]

Minstrel writing, on the other hand, opposes this model with a mode representing poetry as an enterprise with immediate social inspiration and public consequences, as a process of engaging an audience in the inspired production of a text. As Staël's Corinne observes, improvised discourse is 'language full of life that solitary thought could not have brought into being' (45).[21] In Corinne's case and many others, that audience is the body politic. Minstrel writers, in short, represent minstrels as in some sense the *acknowledged* legislators of the world, or at least as political actors – though their world is generally displaced chronologically or geographically from present-day Britain.

The semi-autobiographical speaker described above therefore embodies a fantasy of authorship as an immediate response to an imminent stimulus, generally consisting of a live audience. Much minstrel writing, however, does address the process of writing, publishing, and distributing a material text through its framing apparatuses. Here the fantasy of oral performance dissipates, and we see other voices that compete for identification with what Wordsworth calls 'the author's own person': minstrel writing's antiquarian editors and novelistic narrators, along with the voices of its appendices and advertisements, prefaces and epigraphs. Minstrel writers allow their variously projected and ironized personae to operate simultaneously, with the minstrel and the collector lying on a continuous arc of ventriloquism. The resulting effect is the simultaneous creation and demolition of the fantasy of oral performance. On the one hand, the minstrels in these works preserve the romance of an intimate connection between poet and listener; even when surrounded by crowds like Corinne at the Capitol, they tend to speak or sing especially to one person, as Corinne does to the man who will become her lover. In minstrel writing, however, such moments come packaged in texts of many layers of commentary that call attention to the techniques of print authorship and thereby acknowledge the loss of that fantasy. The exploration of this simultaneous creation and loss often takes place in the paratextual apparatus of the minstrel text.

The paratextual personae of minstrel writing

> What has made Lord Kaims's 'Elements of Criticism' so popular in England is his numerous illustrations and quotations from Shakespeare. If his book had wanted these illustrations, or if they had been taken from ancient or foreign authors, it would not have been so generally read in England. This is a good political hint to you, in your capacity of an author...
> Dr John Gregory to James Beattie, 1 January 1768
> (quoted in Forbes I.110–11)

Minstrel writing is peculiarly rich in paratexts: prefaces, footnotes, supplementary authenticating materials, and the like. In 1808, a few years after *The Lay of the Last Minstrel* began the heyday of minstrel writing, the growing tendency of writers to annotate poetry inspired Thomas Moore to offer this piece of wit in his Preface to *Corruption and Intolerance*:

> The practice, which has lately been introduced into literature, of writing very long notes upon very indifferent verses, appears to me a rather happy invention; for it supplies us with a mode of turning stupid poetry to account; and, as horses too dull for the saddle may serve to draw lumber, so Poems of this kind make excellent beasts of burden, and will bear notes, though they may not bear reading. Besides, the comments in such cases are so little under the necessity of paying any servile deference to the text, that they may even adopt that socratic dogma, 'Quod supra nos nihil ad nos' ['what is above us is nothing to us']. (v–vi)

Moore's satire here is good-natured; he was an avid annotator himself, and not just satirically so. The more serious function of his joke is to point out a disruption of literary hierarchy: notes had begun to rise above their former station, doing much more than dryly explaining their texts.

This way of using annotation was largely new. Before the middle of the eighteenth century, hundreds of British works had advertised themselves as coming 'with notes'. The notes, however, were attached to works that could not, in the modern sense, be said to be 'authored' by the annotator: translations (mostly from Greek and Latin), bibles and other religious documents, collections of laws, or literary works by writers other than the annotator.[22] In the early eighteenth century, these annotations of later writers explicating the texts of earlier ones figured prominently in the Augustan 'Battle of the Books' debate, with those claiming the side of the Ancients crying out against the editorial zeal of the Moderns, most famously in the satirical exaggeration of editorial apparatuses in Swift's *Tale of a Tub*.[23]

Then, starting in 1759 and 1760, came the nearly simultaneous success of Laurence Sterne's *Tristram Shandy* and Macpherson's Ossianic poetry. Sterne's novel stands as the culmination of Scriblerian satire of excessive annotation.[24] Macpherson's Ossian introduced a largely new mode: that of an author annotating his or her own creative work.[25] Of course, Ossianic poetry was a highly ambiguous model in this way, since it claimed *not* to be original but rather to be another in a recognized line of annotated literary inheritances. Macpherson's work – or, more accurately, the accusations of his critics – raised the possibility that he had created a prominent self-annotated imaginative work. Percy's *The Hermit of Warkworth* then did explicitly what the Ossianic poems had done scandalously: Percy surrounds an original work, though one in the style of older work, with scholarly annotations by the avowed author.[26]

Some writers followed the examples of Macpherson and Percy in the late eighteenth century, but when Moore writes in 1808 of a recent profusion of notes, I believe he refers specifically to a more recent development, the sharp increase in annotation occasioned by the success of Robert Southey and especially Scott. Works characterized by authorial self-annotation had slowly begun to accumulate at the end of the century, and then the Bristol circle upped the annotative ante: Joseph Cottle's *Alfred, An Epic Poem* (1800) and Southey's Cottle-published *Thalaba the Destroyer* (1801) both feature many scholarly footnotes. In 1805, Southey's *Madoc* and Scott's *Lay of the Last Minstrel* replaced footnotes with extensive endnotes, in the format now familiar to readers of Scott's poetry in most of its published settings. The extent and complexity of the notes in such commercially successful books immediately popularized the convention of footnoting one's own imaginative works. Jane Porter and Sydney Owenson provide cases in point: Porter's *The Scottish Chiefs* (1810) is much more heavily footnoted than her earlier *Thaddeus of Warsaw* (1801); and Owenson's novels and poems both follow the same pattern, with works written after 1805 carrying many more annotations than her first novels. When Moore refers to heavy annotation as a 'practice, which has lately been introduced into literature', then, he speaks of a sudden, widespread shift in literary conventions driven in large part by minstrel writing.

This shift is usually invisible in modern accounts of the note. The most prominent such study, Anthony Grafton's *The Footnote*, details the rapidly increasing prominence of historians' documentation at this time. (It opens, 'In the eighteenth century, the historical footnote was a high form of literary art' [1].) However, Grafton's genealogy of the note, because it neglects historical fiction (broadly conceived), omits many of the most important writers of historical notes during the eighteenth and early nineteenth centuries. Grafton invokes Scott only in passing and does not mention Scott's notes. Grafton is an historian himself, and one can hardly fault him for constructing his genealogy in his own field. To understand minstrel writing, however, we need a different approach, one alive to the uses of specifically literary practices of annotation.

Martha Woodmansee has argued that the modern author, as 'an individual who is solely responsible...for the production of a unique, original work' (35), emerged as a rhetorical construction of the Romantic era. Following Foucault's suggestion that we place our own notions of authorship in the context of their eighteenth-century development, Woodmansee documents the development of the Romantic author as a phenomenon driven by economic as well as aesthetic interests in Germany and Britain. To examine minstrel writing is to jump to a parallel track of literary history. Minstrel writing developed, accompanied by popular and critical acclaim, alongside Romantic authorship in the late eighteenth and early nineteenth centuries. While also partaking of contemporary notions of artistic genius, minstrel writing calls attention to the historical and contextual functions of the literary artist. The minstrel's social art, like that of a modern jazz musician, relies fundamentally on interactions with fellow creators, on an ideological commitment to live performance, and on the preservation of a repertoire of 'standards' that may or may not be supplemented by original compositions. Minstrel writing is a body of work by authors who chose to combine myths of original, spontaneous composition with those of authorial collection. This study examines the consequences of that choice.

Chapter structure: points of contention

Competition and contestation infuse minstrel writing for a number of reasons, including the real and imagined military functions of ancient minstrels, the commercial success of minstrel writing, and the explicit ties of minstrel writing to political patronage. Each chapter of this book will address a series of texts to explore points of contention within minstrel writing: how Irish writers responded to British constructions of Border minstrelsy; how women writers reacted against the pervasive masculinity of minstrel writing to create a modern, female minstrelsy through the figure of the *improvvisatrice*; how Byron and Wordsworth engaged and separated themselves from minstrel writing and from each other's interpretations of minstrelsy; how later minstrel writing made contestation its content by staging prize competitions; how early American blackface minstrelsy grew out of and against the conventions of British and Irish minstrel writing.

This book strives to break new ground in part by letting the figure of the minstrel itself determine the genealogies of the analysis. Where most recent scholarship on minstrel writing addresses it through the lenses of gender, genre, nationality, or a given author's corpus, this book examines the intersections of those categories without taking any of them to be overridingly central: it asks what happens to gender, genre, and nation when the character of the minstrel defines a literary genealogy.[27] It is the only study to date whose methodology allows (and requires) close examination, for instance, of relationships among *The Lay of the Last Minstrel* (1805), *The Wild Irish Girl* (1806), and *Corinne* (1807), all of which appeared in the space of two years, enjoyed remarkable popular success, and deploy many of the same conventions, including the portrayal of oral performance of Scottish or Irish traditional verse.

This is, of course, an exercise in genealogy; the content, method, and criticism of minstrel writing all partake of genealogy. The popularity of minstrel writing, especially after 1805, allowed writers to assume a wide audience familiar with its conventions and thereby to press the characters and motifs of earlier texts into the service of new literary purposes. Wide circulation enabled minstrel texts to create meaning through allusion and revision as well as through explicit statement. Minstrel writing's emphasis on textual genealogy – both in the portrayed minstrels' function as keepers of a repertoire of songs and in the authors' unusually explicit acknowledgement of the modern texts on which they draw – made it remarkably well suited to writers who had political reasons to be indirect. The same property made it equally *ill* suited to excite the admiration of critics who excluded context from literary judgement.

The ability to imagine political participation through poetry made minstrel writing a compelling option for writers, especially women, who were discouraged from more direct political action. In 1806 and 1807, the character of minstrel writing was transformed by the emergence of women minstrel writers and representations of female minstrels. Those years saw minstrel writing's transition from its eighteenth-century manifestations as a mode, almost always, of men writing about men, to a means by which the gender of authorship was contested. Eighteenth-century minstrelsy wore its masculinity on its sleeve: when Percy calls the English minstrels 'an order of men' (*Reliques* ix), he means *men*. Joseph Cooper Walker in *Historical Memoirs of the Irish Bards* (1786) writes that in spite of his extensive research, he 'cannot find that the Irish had female Bards, or BARDESSES, properly so called' (19).[28] Similarly, Percy remarks in his 'Essay', 'I do not find that any of the real Minstrels were of the female sex' (xviii).[29]

The minstrel's masculinity was more than incidental to the construction of his historical character. For Hugh Blair, Ossian's greatness depends both on his ability to work with a tradition of bards preceding him and his coming before 'the two dispiriting vices' of 'covetousness and effeminacy' infected poetry (352). While 'effeminacy' only sometimes carried the gendered connotations it does today, other writers used more explicit language: in Beattie's *The Minstrel*, for instance, Edwin's young adulthood is marked by the 'dignity' given by 'the downy cheek and deepen'd voice' (II.vi). Because ancient minstrelsy had overwhelmingly been men's work, men writing in the Romantic era could play with minstrel personae, with the idea that they were and were not minstrels themselves. That play became a significant feature of the minstrel mode. That eighteenth-century minstrels and bards were male and masculine meant, however, that women writers could not identify so easily with the minstrel characters. Some women did work around the problem by addressing the historical content of minstrel works while removing or minimizing the role of minstrels themselves.[30] Nonetheless, before 1806, women rarely wrote works that addressed minstrelsy and bardic composition as a central concern.[31]

From 1806 onward, however, women entered the field of minstrel writing without apology or qualification. Owenson's *The Wild Irish Girl*

(1806) and Staël's *Corinne, or Italy* (1807) move the ancient British minstrel to environments where women as well as men could imagine themselves as minstrels. They do so by first modernizing the setting, so their female characters can leave the antiquarian ground where men would provide nearly all the models. Owenson's Glorvina (the heroine of *The Wild Irish Girl*) closes that distance: her environment is that of the end of the eighteenth century. Glorvina also sings in her house, moving away from the myth of the solitary wanderer (or 'lone enthusiast' (I.lvi) in Beattie's then-famous phrase) that restricted minstrelsy to men.[32] Chapter 2 of this book examines Owenson's work as part of minstrelsy's complicated relationship to 'national' writing by paying close attention to Owenson's poetic and editorial personae in *The Wild Irish Girl* and *The Lay of an Irish Harp* (1807).

Owenson's Glorvina becomes a female minstrel at the expense of the minstrel's customary public function; although Owenson participated in public discourse by writing *The Wild Irish Girl*, Glorvina performs only for private gatherings. In *Corinne* Staël gave British women an imagination of Italy as a place where one could imagine publicly sanctioned female performance. Moving minstrelsy away from Britain and Ireland lent female minstrelsy enough exoticism to allow representations of unapologetic public performance. Only a year after Glorvina's debut, *Corinne* features a strikingly similar heroine: like Glorvina, Corinne is an artistically talented antiquarian guiding a stubbornly prejudiced visitor through her country. Unlike the housebound Glorvina, however, Corinne unashamedly sings in public, explicitly enabled to do so because she has left England. In Italy, she says, 'It is common practice . . . to do as you please in society; there are no set standards, nothing to take into consideration' (95). Corinne also improvises, employing a method of composition that, unlike Glorvina's recitation, allows or even requires an audience. And Corinne gets no happy ending: she loses out and withers away, left with neither her lover nor the career she sacrificed for him.

Corinne thus represents an intersection of a distinctively modern female minstrelsy with the long-established conventions of Sapphic suffering. *Corinne* gave women a way to talk about the difficulties of being a woman writer, creating the phenomenon Ellen Moers analyzes as 'The Myth of Corinne' in *Literary Women*. *Corinne* also made the problems of the woman writer emblematic of the problems of Italy's sufferings under colonial rule and connected both of those to a theory of improvisational development, and it detached the portrayal of minstrel figures from the ground on which their authors lived, making improvisation the artistic mode of exile. Whereas Scott's minstrels and Glorvina sing to the countries to which they were born, the half-English Corinne chooses Italy over England, and Italian exile becomes a major theme of the book. Staël's new myth provided an alternative formulation linking authorship, history, gender relations, and modern politics as seamlessly as Scott had, with most of the political polarities reversed. Chapter 3 explores the development of the *improvvisatrice* through Staël and her successors.

Moving from minstrel writing itself to its effect on Romantic poetry, Chapter 4 addresses the degree to which Beattie's *Minstrel* and minstrel writing more generally formed the ground on which Wordsworth and Byron engaged each other during the Regency. In his poems and prose of that period, Wordsworth characterized his poetry as a project that echoed but superseded the practice of ancient minstrelsy. At the same time, as he narrated his own development as a poet, Wordsworth borrowed extensively and pointedly from Beattie's myth of the minstrel's 'progress of genius' to create parallel tracks of developing personal morality and poetic genius.

Byron, on the other hand, treated modern minstrel writing more sympathetically, arguably becoming its most brilliant practitioner and at times its most devastating satirist. No other writer engaged as many strands of minstrel writing as thoroughly as Byron, from the Ossianic imitations of *Hours of Idleness* (1807) to the wholesale satirical revision of Beattie and Scott in *Childe Harold's Pilgrimage* I (1812), the Turkish tale-teller narrating *The Giaour* (1813), and the *improvvisatore*-narrator of *Don Juan* (1819–24).[33] Though neither Wordsworth nor Byron was a minstrel writer in the same way as Scott, Owenson, or Moore, they both shaped their Regency-era work in large part by defining their approaches in relation to ancient and modern minstrelsy.

Also during the Regency and continuing into the 1820s, a group of writers began to consider the competitive dynamics of the literary market through the vehicles of contests and prizes. Imagining the burgeoning and competitive book trade as a minstrel contest, writers could address their own situation in the marketplace through established conventions of contest poems and the newly emergent category of the prize poem. I argue in Chapter 5 that minstrel prize and contest poems constitute a collective reflection on what had become solidly established practices of minstrel writing. Contest poems set conventionally nationalized minstrels and bards in competition with each other, as in James Hogg's *The Queen's Wake* (1813) and Letitia Elizabeth Landon's *The Troubadour* (1825) and *The Golden Violet* (1827). Concentrating on the idea of the literary prize rather than the contest itself, Felicia Hemans's *Wallace's*

Invocation to Bruce (1819, published as 'Mrs. Hemans's Prize Poem') dissects the tensions created between economic and patriotic interests in minstrel writing. Such works constitute a last generation of minstrel writing in its British Romantic-era form. They display a movement from political to economic concerns after the fading of the Napoleonic threat.

The internationalism of minstrel contest poems prefigures the developments analyzed in the sixth and final chapter, which addresses a transitional period that enabled the development of 'Negro minstrelsy', especially in the United States. This chapter addresses the underexamined period between the emergence of Scott's minstrelsy and the time when blackface performance came to be called *minstrelsy* in the 1830s and 1840s. During this period, all the varieties of British minstrel writing I have described still enjoyed a wide transatlantic readership, and blackface performance had not yet taken its place as the primary cultural referent of the term *minstrelsy*. Using James Fenimore Cooper's *The Last of the Mohicans* and its parallel minstrelsies of Native Americans and white colonists as a touchstone, this chapter explores multiple aspects of minstrelsy in this transitional period, including a new internationalization of the minstrel mode and a corresponding development of 'minstrels' as books rather than people – as collections of international songs. The chapter analyzes Cooper's use of the comic minstrel David Gamut to build on Scott's last minstrel myth by describing postcolonial America arising from the parallel (and equally mythical) expirations of the Mohicans and minstrels.

The book closes with a consideration of the consequences of this internationalization of minstrelsy for the beginnings of blackface 'minstrelsy' under that name. When blackface performance took over as the dominant cultural association of the term *minstrelsy* – that is, when the minstrel character collapsed onto the body of the performer and the audience was literalized – minstrelsy lost the dynamic of the 'heard overheard', described above, that defines this study. Blackface performance created a fundamentally different kind of ventriloquism that has been widely analyzed and that lies outside the purview of this book; therefore, this study leaves off as the age of blackface minstrelsy's wide popularity begins in the middle years of the nineteenth century.

2
The Minstrel in the World: Sydney Owenson and Irish Internationalism

The conscious, consistent foundation of minstrel writing is the deployment of personae that are crucially autobiographical, in ways that encourage fantasies of transparent identifications of author and character, and just as importantly *not* autobiographical, in ways that emphasize breaks between authors and their historical environments. Such breaks constitute the explicit rationale for creating minstrel writing: authors take up the subject of minstrelsy in writing precisely because minstrelsy has disappeared or is disappearing. By creating a model of the collector-author who speaks of a chronological environment other than his or her own, this trope of the disappearing minstrel justifies imaginative travel to geographical settings other than the author's. In Sydney Owenson's 1805 novel *The Novice of Saint Dominick* – whose working title was *The Minstrel* – the narrator remarks that 'a minstrel's garb is a passport every where' (I.275). Owenson was in her mid-twenties when *The Novice* was published; this chapter will use the early part of her career as its central example to study how Owenson exploits minstrel writing's capacity to act as a passport to places, times, and public participation that the author, *in propria persona*, could not attain. The minstrel's garb enabled authors to explore literary worlds that break ties to a local context – the ties underlying both Wordsworthian localism and what Katie Trumpener describes as bardic nationalism.

Minstrel writing's general preoccupation with autobiographical fiction is uncommonly important in Owenson's case. Deeply informed by the conventions of sensibility employed by James Macpherson, Goethe, and the Della Cruscan poets, Owenson's writing develops generic tensions between sensibility and minstrel writing. Like her predecessors in the literature of sensibility, Owenson creates speakers who claim deeply sincere self-expression, the ability to transmit feeling without deception or irony from speaker to reader. Indeed, much of what critics have written about Owenson assumes a transparent sincerity that allows many of her characters to speak as Owenson herself.

However, as Julie Ellison writes, '[s]ensibility is sophisticated. Its genres can reflect on their own conventionality' (447). Owenson uses the conventions of minstrel writing to undermine sensibility's claims to emotional transparency. Like other authors of minstrel writing, Owenson creates characters who invite autobiographical comparisons but also display clear breaks with the author. For one simple example, Glorvina, the domesticated minstrel-heroine of *The Wild Irish Girl* (1806), is like Owenson in certain ways, and Owenson toyed with playing the role of Glorvina; Owenson wore a 'Glorvina cloak' at times and allowed herself to be nicknamed Glorvina among friends. Far from justifying the common practice of equating Owenson's thoughts with her character's, however, Owenson's playful impersonation of her character displays her sense of the fantasy involved in becoming Glorvina.

The differences between author and character are clear enough: Owenson's youth as the daughter of a Dublin actor hardly mirrored Glorvina's life as old Irish royalty, and the novel's chronology limits Glorvina's historical knowledge by placing her story before the turn of the nineteenth century. That is to say, Sydney Owenson knew much more than Glorvina about the Ireland of 1806. When Glorvina uses the language of sensibility to claim transparent sincerity, therefore, Owenson invites the reader to sympathize with Glorvina's feeling but also to contextualize it, to consider the tensions, ironies, and moments of playful self-awareness that arise from the differences among Owenson and her personae – that is, from Owenson's command of the minstrel mode.

Post-Union Irish internationalism

Considering Sydney Owenson's early writing requires attending to a period often overlooked in narratives of Irish history. The years between the Union of Ireland with Great Britain (1800–1) and Waterloo (1815) – the years of Walter Scott's rise to prominence, of the climax of the Ossianic controversy, and of deepening war between Britain and France – fall between conventional Irish historical touchstones of the Union and the later rise of Catholic nationalism led by Daniel O'Connell.[1] In Roy Foster's *Modern Ireland*, for instance, the period in question falls at a section break, and even Foster's minutely researched volume says almost nothing about the time between Emmet's death in 1803 and the late

Regency. However, Foster does emphasize the international character of the United Irish movement in the early 1790s:

> 'Nationalism' as such had not been part of the original United Irish package. They were internationalist liberals, anti-government rather than anti-English. Even when anti-Englishness took over, they had little time for 'ethnic' considerations; recent fashions for traditional music and poetry, and archaeological divinations of a 'Celtic' past, seemed to middle-class radicals at best silly and at worst savage. (269)

As Foster presents the matter, identification with Continental concerns characterized the early United Irish movement but faded during the 1790s, and leaders such as Theobald Wolfe Tone became increasingly opposed to England in particular rather than to tyranny in general.

Foster's account does not explain a burst of high-profile internationalism *after* the Union, instead locating such sentiment in the 1790s and again in the early 1900s, with very little of the kind in between. A retrospective attention to materials that anticipate narrower kinds of Irish nationalism has helped much of Owenson's and Thomas Moore's writing to fall out of view. Though Owenson's *The Wild Irish Girl* and Moore's *Irish Melodies* focus intently on the Irish situation, they are far from representative samples of their authors' work before 1820.[2] Owenson's first novel, *St. Clair* (1803), takes place in Ireland but only incidentally so,[3] and *The Novice of Saint Dominick* (1805) unfolds in France and Italy. After *The Wild Irish Girl* of 1806, Owenson published a conspicuously internationalist volume of poetry, *The Lay of an Irish Harp* (1807), and the rest of her career blended Irish materials with those of other nations in works such as *Woman; or, Ida of Athens*, *The Missionary* (about an Indian princess), and the controversially frank travel books *France* and *Italy*. Moore's case is perhaps even more extreme. As much as he cared about the *Irish Melodies*, his other projects seldom touched on Ireland more than peripherally before 1820. He made his reputation as the translator of Anacreon's odes, and much of his other work was Byronically scandalous – erotic, irreverently skeptical, scathingly satirical, and wildly popular – before scandal had become Byronic.

But why should that internationalist writing, so highly visible at the time, have receded into the margins of both literary and historical accounts? One reason, perhaps, is that Irish literary history tracks a sequence of events whose primary impact was felt in Ireland: the formation of the United Irishmen, the Belfast Harper's Festival, the rebellions, the Union, the emergence of O'Connell. Such a narrative is easy to build in retrospect, but at the time, all thinking about Ireland had to be influenced by the fact that the Union might quickly become a footnote to the story of France taking over the British Isles; suppression of the 1798 rebellion hardly ended the threat of French victory in Ireland and Britain. Wellington's victory at Waterloo gave Ireland a reason to place a memorial at his birthplace, but it also meant that Ireland was no longer a key link in the development of a worldwide empire built – ostensibly, at least – on the universalist spirit that had informed Moore's and Owenson's conceptions of a new Ireland. That possibility died only with Napoleon's defeat, not with Wolfe Tone's.[4]

In this environment, Moore and Owenson turned to representations of minstrels and bards. Both gathered and created Irish songs, represented minstrels in their works, and came to be regarded as performing their minstrel characters themselves at social gatherings, Moore as the minstrel boy and Owenson as Glorvina. Minstrelsy offered them the ability to connect with a well-established mode of Scottish writing in ways that could call attention to the trauma of Ireland's failed rebellions through a literary mode popularized by Unionist Scots. Whereas the Scots portrayed historical traumas that had receded into a more or less distant past, however, Irish writers changed the inflection of historical minstrelsy by discussing events closer to their own time.

A common nationalist narrative about Owenson's place in her times builds on her own comments about the milieu of *The Wild Irish Girl*. Owenson's stated concerns about 1806 involved government surveillance by Dublin Castle. In retrospect, Owenson wrote that

At the moment the 'Wild Irish Girl' appeared, it was dangerous to write on Ireland, hazardous to praise her, and difficult to find a publisher for an Irish tale which had a political tendency. For even ballads sung in the streets of Dublin, had been denounced by government spies, and hushed by Castle sbirri; because the old Irish *refrain* of Eiren go Bragh, awakened the cheer of the ragged, starving audience, who had much better have raised the chorus of 'Eiren go Bread.' Graves were then still green, where the victims of laws, uselessly violated, were still wept over by broken hearts; and the bitter disappointment of a nation's hopes, by the recent and sudden desertion of Pitt, the most powerful champion of Catholic Emancipation, which gave the ascendancy new power, and sunk Catholicism in deeper despondency, was only slowly yielding to the benign influence of a new and liberal administration of Irish affairs, during the temporary return to power of the Whigs, under the vice-royalty of the Duke of Bedford. (quoted in Fitzpatrick 110–11)[5]

Owenson's publisher, Richard Phillips, who had offered her a good price for *The Wild Irish Girl*, shared her sense of the delicate situation:

> Phi[l]lips, however, had no sooner examined the work, than a panic filled his usually impassive temperament. 'The sentiments enunciated', he said, 'are too strongly opposed to the English interest in Ireland, and I must withdraw my original offer.' (Fitzpatrick 111)

Having been imprisoned for publishing Paine's *Rights of Man* in Leicester (Stevenson 62), Phillips knew of what he wrote. He did nonetheless finally publish the book. While public and critical reactions were largely positive, some reviews viciously attacked the novel and its author.

Such moments illustrate Owenson's nationalist side. However, the moderateness of that nationalism and the vehemence of her attackers also made her useful in a new British government policy of conciliation, and her next work, a drama whose name has not come down to us, debuted with the express endorsement of the Viceroy.[6] During the run of that comic opera in 1807, Owenson published *The Lay of an Irish Harp*, her second volume of poetry, which had been composed over the previous years. *The Lay* is therefore the only one of Owenson's published works written in arguably the most politically delicate stage of her life, the brief time after the publication of *The Wild Irish Girl* but before she had gained the protection of the Viceroy (and, in 1812, that of a title). As Lady Morgan, Owenson would later address contemporary politics directly, even arguing for some benefits of the French Revolution long after most of its supporters had fallen away. In *Italy* (1821), for instance, she adopts a voice Byron would call 'fearless': she writes, 'it is notable that there are no legitimate beginnings of empires; and that all monarchical governments, owing their origin to the wants or the crimes of man, are founded in conquest, or are consolidated by usurpation' (I.2–3).[7] This voice was unavailable to Owenson in 1806 and 1807.

By making relatively few references to the Irish situation, *The Lay of an Irish Harp* in one way avoided some of the controversial flashpoints of *The Wild Irish Girl*. In another way, however, the volume of poetry made connections more potentially inflammatory than those of its predecessor by linking the situations of Ireland and Continental countries, primarily France and Italy – countries with Catholic histories forming an axis of Napoleon's empire. By examining *The Wild Irish Girl* and *The Lay of an Irish Harp* together, this chapter will consider Owenson's literary responses to Ireland's circumstances after the rebellions and the Union as a way to reconsider the relationship between nationalism and writing about bards and minstrels in Romantic-era writing.

Nationalism and internal evidence: dating the action of *The Wild Irish Girl*

Near the beginning of *The Wild Irish Girl*, the novel's main epistolary narrator, Horatio, hears a rustic Irishman named Murtoch sing 'the *Cualin*' (29). The song, Horatio learns, is the 'lamentation of the poor Irish for the loss of their *glibbs*, or long tresses, of which they were deprived by the arbitrary will of Henry VIII' (28). Horatio, the prejudiced Englishman who will learn to love Ireland and the novel's eponymous heroine, reacts to the song thus:

> Almost every word of Murtoch's lamentation was accompanied by the sighs and mournful lamentations of his auditors, who seemed to sympathize as tenderly in the sufferings of their progenitors, as though they had themselves been victims to the tyranny which had caused them. The arch-policy of the 'ruthless king,' who destroyed at once the records of a nation's woes, by extirpating the 'tuneful race,' whose art would have perpetuated them to posterity, never appeared to me in greater force than at that moment. (29)

Horatio places 'ruthless king' in quotation marks because he borrows the phrase from the opening line of Thomas Gray's 'The Bard: A Pindaric Ode' (1757): 'Ruin seize thee, ruthless king!' (53). By quoting Gray, Horatio invokes a chain of metonymies: Horatio connects the English prohibition of long hair to the English suppression of Irish bards, which he links via Gray to the legendary suppression of the Welsh bards by Edward I, Gray's 'ruthless king'. That is, the reference works along the lines of what Katie Trumpener describes as 'bardic nationalism': Horatio and Owenson use the sign of the bard to link Irish and Welsh resistance to English tyranny.

Trumpener argues that for Celtic writers, 'Bardic nationalism insists on the rich fullness of national knowledge, on the anchoring of discursive traditions in landscape, in a way of life, in custom. The English, in comparison, have only borrowed words' (34). Trumpener describes a model of literary circulation in which Celtic antiquarians supplied source materials for English poets, who 'tried to impersonate the bardic voice and to imitate bardic materials, without grasping their historical and cultural significance' (6). This model relies on the contention that the 'English appropriation of bardic poetry' (7) characterizes 'the bard (and the minstrel after him) as an inspired, isolated, and peripatetic figure' (6). When Horatio describes Irish bardic performance through Gray, however, we see something more complicated than a pale English imitation of genuine bardic materials – something, in fact, that illustrates fundamental differences between bardic nationalism and the minstrel writing of the early nineteenth century. Note the complications of this moment in *The Wild Irish Girl*: an Anglo-Irish writer presents a newly thoughtful Englishman quoting a Welsh bard created by an English poet for explicit Unionist purposes to address an Irish bardic past and a modern Irish performance. In a novel driven by the interplay of economic, literary, and cultural debts, layers of borrowing and quotation prevent neat divisions of national or literary creators and borrowers.

Gray's poem itself illustrates some of the complications that will recur in the novel. Before it made its way into *The Wild Irish Girl*, 'The Bard' was perhaps the first widely read imaginative work based on eighteenth-century antiquarian research into bards and minstrels. Gray was no Welsh nationalist, as his poem makes clear. Rather, Gray contains the nationalist resistance Horatio quotes from the poem's first line ('Ruin seize thee, ruthless king!') in a progressivist history that ultimately glorifies the ascension of the Tudor line: 'ye genuine Kings, Britannia's Issue, hail!' (l.110). The poem portrays the crimes of Edward I as a temporary perversion of legitimate English power rather than a manifestation of its inherent problems. Gray's approach provided a model for many Romantic-era writers throughout Great Britain and Ireland who concentrated on moments of national resistance to England precisely in order to explain how they led to present-day solidarity.[8] In such cases, writers emphasizing the imperative for cooperation in resistance to external threats did not adapt bardic conventions 'without grasping their historical and cultural significance', in Trumpener's phrase. Rather, that significance, with its links to nationalist resistance, was what made those conventions such useful material for Unionist myth-making.

In *The Wild Irish Girl*, Horatio's letter supports a similar reading of Henry VIII's tyrannical treatment of the Irish: even as Horatio admires the power of Murtoch's song to excite the sympathy of his audience, Horatio notes that modern Irish women do wear their hair long, contrary to the English prohibition that had inspired the song. Their hair 'sometimes flows over their shoulders', he says, 'sometimes is fastened up in tresses, with a pin or bodkin' (29). Horatio hints, at least, that the sorrow occasioned by English tyranny has drifted into the past, preparing modern Ireland for the kind of resolution that Wales has enjoyed in Gray's portrayal. As effectively as Trumpener's model of English–Celtic literary relations works to explain the work of nationalist antiquarians and some of their literary followers, its underpinning dichotomies cannot account for the complications of many other important texts about bards and minstrels. In the case of *The Wild Irish Girl*, those complications result in ambiguities Owenson creates with prominent silences, from the lack of commentary on recent Irish history to the conspicuous absence of Glorvina's voice during the events surrounding her climactic marriage.

The man Glorvina weds, Horatio, late in the novel uses a mathematical metaphor to describe their relationship: 'like the *assymtotes* of an hyperbola', he writes, 'without absolutely rushing into contact, we are, by a sweet impulsion, gradually approximating closer and closer towards each other' (165). (An asymptote, in this usage, is a straight line whose distance to a curving line approaches but never reaches zero; that is, the asymptote and the curve move ever closer to each other but never touch.) The metaphor seems to work well to describe the courtship: Horatio fills his letters with attempts to find words for the increasing intimacy of his relationship to Glorvina, and the novel leads the readers through hundreds of pages of slowly increasing romantic tension, only to leave off just before the relationship's sexual consummation. Horatio's asymptotic metaphor leads us to see the novel as tending inevitably towards the marriage at the end, and to see the novel's politics as resting on the crux of that marriage – the transformation of the asymptotic relationship into a true meeting – as a metaphor for political union between England and Ireland. As Kathryn Kirkpatrick's edition of *The Wild Irish Girl* points out, however, Horatio's metaphor is seriously flawed. Kirkpatrick's note says that an asymptote is not a hyperbola,[9] which is technically true but misleading: Horatio is correct that hyperbolas have asymptotes, but incorrect to say that they approach without touching. In fact, the asymptotes of a hyperbola approach the hyperbola itself without touching it, and the two asymptotes cross each other. In short, the asymptotes approach each other, meet, and then move inexorably apart.

Whether or not Owenson intended Horatio's mistake, the mathematical flaw leaves us with a different metaphor through which to view the novel: that of *false* asymptotes, lines that someone, especially an English man, imagines coming slowly together 'by a sweet impulsion' but actually approach, depart from, or cross each other depending on the place one observes them. For example, Horatio's father, whom the novel reveals to be Horatio's secret rival, would presumably imagine himself to be approaching Glorvina just as Horatio does. In his case, however, the lines break off from their seemingly unwavering approach – or, like the real asymptotes of a hyperbola, they cross for an instant and then begin to separate as rapidly as they had come together. More difficult to assess is perhaps the most important asymptotic movement of the book: the convergence of the plot and the notes as they approach the 1798 rebellion and the Union with England. The temporal worlds of the novel never touch those years, and the resulting gap in historical explanation creates the difficulty of locating the politics of *The Wild Irish Girl*.

The temporal split between the editorial perspective and the novel's plot aligns *The Wild Irish Girl* with other minstrel writing that uses similarly split structures. Thanks to Scott and others, readers in 1806 understood that minstrel texts frequently separated editorial voices from their fictions in order to call attention to the ways that the portrayed characters differ from their contemporary authors and readers. As Penny Fielding has argued, in Scott's self-consciously British project of *Minstrelsy of the Scottish Border*, 'it is not the ballads themselves that are to contribute to Scotland's national history, but the editor's notes and dissertations'; Scott 'displays a marked reluctance to let [the ballads] speak for themselves' (51). The distance between text and paratext that Scott put to the use of editorial control also creates a potential for tension and irony that Owenson fully exploits.

The tensions of *The Wild Irish Girl* often become apparent in chronology. Critics of the novel, while they sometimes remark in passing that it takes place in the eighteenth century, tend nonetheless to treat it as a picture of its author's 'contemporary' times.[10] But the time of the novel's setting and publication are only almost contemporary: the editorial voice knows about the time of the rebellions and the Union, but the characters do not. That time, roughly 1798–1803, is the asymptote that the two sides of the narrative seem to approach but not touch: the plot starts in the eighteenth century and moves forward, while the notes place themselves in 1806 and gradually come nearer to addressing the rebellions.

This structure places *The Wild Irish Girl* in a subgenre of Romantic-era fiction that we might call the slightly historical novel. Whereas *Waverley*, for example, calls attention to the difference between the plot's time and that of the novel's publication, these novels set their action slightly in the past with little or no direct commentary on the displacement. Whereas Scott generally portrays events that he and most of his readers had not witnessed, slightly historical novels portray events within the recent, living memories of adult readers. Often, the time difference places national events of major importance between the consciousnesses of the novel's characters and readers. Some specimens of this subgenre include Charlotte Smith's novels addressing the recent progress of the French Revolution, *Desmond* (1792) and *The Banished Man* (1794); Maria Edgeworth's *Castle Rackrent* (1800), in which the gap between characters and readers includes the Irish rebellion of 1798; Jane Porter's *Thaddeus of Warsaw* (1803), whose action begins with the Russian invasion of Poland in 1792; Germaine de Staël's *Corinne* (1807), whose gap most notably includes the French takeover of Italy during the Napoleonic wars; Mary Shelley's *Frankenstein* (1818), whose pan-European scope and later date creates a larger gap that includes most of the Napoleonic wars; and, in the midst of these, *The Wild Irish Girl*.

These latter three novels – *The Wild Irish Girl*, *Corinne*, and *Frankenstein*, chronologically – are related still more closely. All three take place near the author's own time, and all three have inspired readers to take the novels as pictures of the authors' contemporary worlds and more or less veiled autobiographical selves. All three disrupt that contemporaneousness with the same device: an epistolary structure with letters dated '17—'. Omitting Edgeworth's and Scott's characteristic historical specificity and meditations on the changes between historical action and the author's present time, these slightly historical novels use the dates of their letters to leave readers, if they wish, to construct for themselves the shifts in context between their own time and '17—'.

The Wild Irish Girl plays with the reader's perception of this historical gap through an editorial persona (lacking in *Corinne* and *Frankenstein*) that does have access to the reader's own time. When the editor's notes threaten to touch the rebellions directly – a late note does mention the 'atrocities' (176, emphasis original) of Wexford[11] – the notes disappear. They abandon their documentary function just as they begin to trouble the novel's silence regarding the Irish complaints about English actions during and after the fighting. A newly bloodied and resentful Ireland is precisely what Horatio's philosophy has not dreamt of.

After the note about Wexford, the last long note of the novel re-emphasizes the silence about Ireland's recent historical crisis through an account of a man known as a two-headed bard. That note ends with one of the oddest moments in a book crammed with oddities:

In February 1806 the author, being then but eighteen miles distant from the residence of the Bard, received a message from him, intimating that as he had heard she wished to purchase his harp, he would dispose of it on very moderate terms. He was then in good health and spirits, though in his hundredth and ninth year. (202)

The transaction begs for a sentimental explanation. Why must the bard sell his harp? What has changed in Ireland that makes the sale necessary? How did he react to parting with his beloved instrument? How did 'the author' feel upon seeing the bard reduced to something like beggary? In the novel proper, Horatio has already explained the delicacy necessary when offering money to a bard: 'So great was my veneration for this "bard of other times,"' he says, 'that I felt as though it would have been an indelicacy to have offered him any pecuniary reward for the exertions of his tuneful talent' (202).[12] No explanation of the apparent contradiction is forthcoming, however: once again, Owenson allows the novel to approach an analysis of historical crisis and its consequences, but she allows questions and silences to substitute for that analysis.[13] She is herself a bard of two heads, or more than two, offering the reader many faces and mouths of authorship, none of which speaks to the driving historical crises of Ireland's and the novel's recent past.

In the action of the novel proper, the problems introduced by the near-erasure of Ireland's recent past begin with the related issue of determining the novel's chronology. To venture a dreadful but useful pun: as Horatio discovers, dating the wild Irish girl (or, for a reader, *The Wild Irish Girl*) is more difficult than it first appears. The reader knows immediately that the novel takes place in the eighteenth century; as already noted, the novel's letters carry the date '17—', placing the action before Ireland's 1800 vote for unification and the 1801 Union. Owenson's editorial persona, on the other hand, speaks from a time very close to the first readers' own: the notes refer to events taking place as late as 1806 (202). At the outset, therefore, we know that Owenson situated her editorial voice as looking back at least six years to the action of the novel.

The few critics who have attended to the novel's chronology have emphasized the late revelation that Horatio's father seems to have disguised himself as one of the rebels of 1798. I will return to that revelation, but I will first note the muddle of chronological information that precedes it. The reader receives the novel's clearest signal of the plot's placement in the past when Father John describes to Horatio the character of the *'poor scholar'* (127, emphasis original). Owenson's note to that passage informs us that Horatio sees something no longer extant in Ireland: 'The French Revolution, and the foundation of a Catholic college at Maynooth, in Leinster, has put a stop to these pious emigrations' (128). The college in Maynooth was founded by the Irish Parliament and funded by the British government, to avoid the training of priests in revolutionary France, in a well-known process in 1795. On its own, the sighting of the *'poor scholar'* therefore seems to place the action of the novel before 1795 and perhaps also, given the note's explanation, before the French Revolution itself, or at least before the war between England and France limited travel to the Continent in 1793. Other evidence for dating the novel's action comes primarily from the characters' debate about Macpherson's Ossian, in which they refer to sources from the 1780s and in which Horatio addresses the 'spirit' of Macpherson (116), who died in 1796. That is to say, before Horatio's father brings the 1798 rebellion into view, Owenson gives the reader scanty and contradictory evidence of the novel's temporal setting, with no indication that the characters, generally so talkative about matters of Irish history, know of the rebellion.

The reader gains crucial additional information when Horatio, with the help of Glorvina's nurse, begins to piece together the story of his rival, the man who will turn out to be his father. Horatio discovers that a man claiming to be 'some unfortunate gentleman who had attached himself to the rebellious faction of the day' (214) came to the castle seeking shelter '[o]n a stormy night, in the spring of 17—, during that fatal period when the scarcely cicatrised wounds of this unhappy country bled afresh beneath the uplifted sword of civil contention' (213–14). Few critics noticed this passage before Mary Jean Corbett made it central to her ingenious reading of the novel; all, including Corbett, assume it to say that Lord M— arrived at the castle during the 1798 rebellion. Indeed, that time fits the description better than any other: the reader already understands the novel to take place in the 1780s or 1790s, and the 1798 rebellion did begin 'in the spring' (in May). Mention of 'the rebellious faction' seems to seal the association and thereby neatly to place the action of the novel in 1799, the only year fitting the pattern '17—' during which characters could refer to 1798 as a year in the past. This is an odd and tenuous solution to the problem of dating the novel's action, but when the reader accepts it (as this reader does), it only raises further and more troubling questions.

These questions begin to arise at the start of the passage about Horatio's father. The reference to the previous year as 'the spring of 17—' is forced. Why is this not a more natural suggestion of the rebellion's recentness such as 'the spring of last year'? Also, why would the 1798 rebellion be said to open 'scarcely cicatrised' wounds – a description perhaps more closely fitting Robert Emmet's summer 1803 uprising, looking back on the 'wounds' of 1798? More significantly, why would the Irish nationalist family's nurse, describing the arrival of an English-man involved in the fighting, describe an overtly nationalist rebellion as 'civil contention'? And most broadly, why is the reader left to piece this information together late in the novel? If the action takes place in 1799, how have these characters, in their extensive debates about Anglo-Irish politics, avoided a detailed discussion of the rebellion?

When the novel suddenly solidifies its setting, shifting from a gener-alized past before the Union to the specific circumstances of 1799, the new clarity of setting recontextualizes the rest of the characters' con-versations about Anglo-Irish relations as obscuring the rebellion – the most obvious and traumatic topic they could address. Only the family nurse, a woman on the fringes of the political and familial negotiations of the characters, can bring up the rebellion in these direct and emo-tional terms of blood and wounds. Her reference to 'civil contention' recalls the novel's earlier, incongruous attention to the founding of the Catholic college at Maynooth, an institution founded to blunt the forces of rebellion by maintaining some Catholic allegiance to Dublin Castle.[14] The *'poor scholar'* – the French-educated Catholic priest – in retrospect seems to have wandered into the novel out of his own time to repre-sent the old Catholic allegiances that made Ireland a threat to England during the Napoleonic wars, only to be countered by new institutional alliances including the Union itself.

The ambiguities arising from the novel's silences have created a split among modern critics attempting to interpret the politics of Glorvina's marriage and of Lord M—'s letter that closes the novel. Robert Tracy's much repeated notion of 'the Glorvina solution' (10) has largely held sway among the novel's critics: Tracy contends that the marriage legit-imizes Anglo-Irish landholding by merging the interests and progeny of the royalty of Inishmore with those of Lord M— and Horatio (8).[15] On the other hand, Joseph Lew emphasizes the moments in which Owenson likens England's presence in Ireland to other Imperial occupations, and Julia Anne Miller draws out the disruptive potential of Glorvina's accu-sation of murder – 'Which of you murdered my father?' (24) – uttered in a convenient and oddly fleeting moment of delirium, just before she marries into the 'murder[ing]' family.[16] Ina Ferris's recent study is one of the few to address the logic of both sides of the split; after noting many readers' suspicion of the implied British audience of Owenson's and other national tales, Ferris notes that 'this is imperial romance with a distinctly abrasive edge' (*Romantic* 48).[17]

Like 'The Bard', in other words, *The Wild Irish Girl* mobilizes nation-alist and Unionist sentiment; unlike Gray's poem, however, it does not subsume one into the other in a clear developmental narrative. This complexity arises from the characteristics of minstrel writing: Owenson deploys multiple semi-autobiographical personae, most importantly the domestic minstrel Glorvina, who voices some of Owenson's sentiments and who resides in a pre-rebellion past. By dividing Owenson's authority (in both senses) among these personae, the novel can produce the logic of economic Unionism and nationalist resistance simultaneously.

More specifically, the novel presents an argument for reform and reconciliation, but it does so in the subjunctive mood. The ending constructs a model of reform that could have resulted in happier relations between England and Ireland, but it does so in a fictional world separate from that of Owenson and her readers. To imagine something like an equal marriage of England and Ireland is to imagine a time before the historical Union and the violence and corruption that made it possible; to think that better landlords can cure Ireland's ailments is a fantasy of that earlier time. Where Miller sees a silencing of Glorvina, we might also see as a silencing of the editor, a character in *The Wild Irish Girl* who understands the traumas of Ireland's recent past, or even as the pervasive, voluntary silencing of nearly all the characters on the subject of the Union. Only women on the fringes of power – Glorvina's nurse and Glorvina herself in a moment of delirium – suggest the violence beneath the polite negotiations of the novel's ending.

When the asymptotes of past and present fail to come together at the Union, Owenson leaves a gap in *The Wild Irish Girl*'s historical narrative that destabilizes any reading of the novel as narrowly propagandistic. Rather, the novel invites precisely what we see in its modern critical reception: multiple and directly contradictory readings of its political import, depending on the selection of evidence each critic chooses to deploy. These multiple readings arise from questions of proof and interpretation that the novel stages explicitly as problems of 'internal evidences' (106) or 'evidence of internal feeling' (118). This motif allows the novel to stage thwarted readings of people and texts that mirror the reader's own difficulties: the Prince applies 'internal evidences' to the poems of Macpherson's Ossian, which is the 'beautiful but unfaithful' (112) text analogous to the beautiful but unfaithful Englishwoman with whom Horatio had once fallen in love. For all of his celebrations of the silent language of sensibility in the novel, in fact, Horatio proves an inept reader of that language, whether it is embodied in people or texts.[18] For nearly the whole novel, Horatio confidently misreads Glorvina and arguably the Prince as well, with troubling and nearly tragic consequences. The absence of a political account of the Union makes *The*

Wild Irish Girl analogous to its heroine: the novel invites its readers to consider the pleasures of its artlessness, while through the conventions of minstrel writing, it artfully produces tensions that belie its apparent simplicity.

Scottish minstrelsy, editorial sentimentality, and *The Lay of an Irish Harp*

Because of the conventional assumption of personal sincerity in lyric poetry, the critical tendency to seek the transparent voice of Sydney Owenson in *The Wild Irish Girl* is even more pronounced in the little existing commentary on *The Lay of an Irish Harp; or, Metrical Fragments* (1807), the volume Owenson published in the wake of *The Wild Irish Girl*'s success. That commentary consistently portrays *The Lay of an Irish Harp* as a collection of thinly veiled autobiographical effusions. This approach follows the lead of William John Fitzpatrick's 1860 biography of Owenson, which barely touches on the volume, only quoting a brief passage to 'furnish some insights into the idiosyncrasies of the fair writer' (152). Likewise attentive to personal 'idiosyncrasies', Lionel Stevenson's 1936 biography opens its commentary on the volume with a critical evaluation, seeing, among other faults, 'a pedantic display of French and Italian' and what he rightly calls the 'mock-modesty' of the conventionally self-deprecatory Preface, which Stevenson finds 'annoying' (90). Stevenson then devotes his analytical energy solely to speculation about the biographical contexts of the volume's love poems. More recently, critics have focused on Owenson's novels and political writings rather than her poetry, thus passing over the *Lay* entirely, and Mary Campbell's 1988 biography reinscribes Stevenson's reading.[19]

From its title onward, however, *The Lay of an Irish Harp* calls the reader's attention to ways in which it addresses larger issues than Owenson's 'idiosyncrasies'. The impersonal metonymy of the title works against reading the book as a volume of poetry representing Owenson's unique psychological experience of her environment. It claims rather to be the production of a generic 'Irish Harp', the voice of the nation itself as figured through the conventional symbol of the bardic harp, and the volume's lyrics seem to come from an entity combining elements of Owenson, Glorvina, and a more generalized Irish speaker. That national voice arises not from insular nationalism, however, but from connections to other countries and other writers. Even the confessional sincerity of the volume's lyrics comes packaged as part of a broader, pan-European literature of sensibility. A product of her moderate, internationalist stance in 1807, *The Lay of an Irish Harp* embodies Owenson's attempt to create an Irish and Continental counterpoint to the masculine, Francophobic productions of British minstrel writers.

Owenson's departure from *The Wild Irish Girl* in the *Lay* is perhaps most evident in the epigraphs and footnotes of the *Lay*. Unlike those of *The Wild Irish Girl*, the paratexts of *The Lay of an Irish Harp* have little to say about Ireland. The poems' annotations include none of the Irish antiquarianism that the novel's notes feature so prominently. Rather, the *Lay*'s paratexts position the volume in the context of two international traditions: that of Scottish and Border minstrelsy on the one hand, and that of Continental sentimentalism on the other. There is also a more subtle difference between the two books. Coming from the voice of an editor more sober and learned than the narrator, the novel's annotations had participated in the tradition of those of James Macpherson, Edward Gibbon, Thomas Percy, and the newly celebrated Walter Scott. The annotations in *The Lay of an Irish Harp*, on the other hand, move away from the tradition of scholarly notes by injecting the conventions of sentimental prose into the volume's editorial voice.

Owenson thus creates what would seem an oxymoronic kind of annotation that merges the performing and editorial personae of *The Wild Irish Girl*: the sentimental scholarly note. Earlier volumes of the poetry of sensibility (such as *The Florence Miscellany* and later Della Cruscan collections, or Moore's Thomas Little poems) did not include extensive footnotes explaining their sources.[20] Though occasionally including a note to explain a literary reference or foreign term, they glorified immediacy, sincerity, and the physical effects of sensibility, often with a pointed rejection of the literary learning that characterized the modern collector-minstrel. Learned notes such as Owenson's own in *The Wild Irish Girl*, on the other hand, emphasized the weight of tradition. Scholarly annotation developed in the backward-looking and conventionally masculine territories of biblical commentary, Classical translation, and antiquarian history. Owenson's notes to *The Lay of an Irish Harp*, in contrast, invoke a community defined by shared feelings. The volume emphasizes internationalism rather than nationalism, Continental connections rather than British introspection, Ossianic sensibility rather than antiquarian self-control.

In her literary works, her letters, and her memoirs, Owenson mentions as her primary influences writers who took sentimentality seriously and applied it to the political questions of the day: the Della Cruscans, Helen Maria Williams, Macpherson/Ossian, Goethe, Rousseau, and (later)

Germaine de Staël. Functioning largely on the level of allusion, *The Lay of an Irish Harp* moves between the effusive poems and the notes' references to other sentimental texts, linking the highly personal emotions of the poems to the volume's contexts. This movement ultimately connects the volume to Continental political and literary thought in opposition to British minstrel writing, especially James Macpherson's Ossianic poetry and Walter Scott's *Lay of the Last Minstrel* (1805).

In the parallel between the Scottish and Irish post-Union situations lies the interest of Owenson's reaction to Scott in *The Lay of an Irish Harp*.[21] This work represents an early utterance in a long literary conversation between Owenson and Scott, a conversation usually discussed now as a matter of Owenson's later influence on the method of the Waverley novels. Owenson never mentions Scott in *The Lay of an Irish Harp*, but the contours of the omission point to Scott in many ways. By 1807, both Owenson and Scott were well-established creators of minstrels and bards. They had each published a full-length minstrel text in 1805: Scott's *Lay of the Last Minstrel* and Owenson's *The Novice of Saint Dominick*, whose main male character is a fifteenth-century French troubadour whom the novel routinely calls a minstrel. The title of Owenson's *Lay of an Irish Harp* in 1807 certainly would have called Scott's title to many readers' minds, and the opening poem of Owenson's *Lay* features her own last minstrel – 'the *last* of the inspired throng' (3), with 'last' in italics lest the allusion be missed. But this minstrel is not of Scott's world.

In his *Lay*, Scott had placed the 'last minstrel' in the time of the Glorious Revolution; that minstrel is the lone representative of a band made extinct by Elizabethan edicts that 'called his harmless art a crime' (*PW* 3).[22] As was often the case, Scott used materials that could easily constitute the seed of rebellious Scottish nationalism. As in the later novels, however, Scott controlled that potential with an apparatus of antiquarian notes, his mechanism for containing nationalist resistance as had Gray's historical narrative in 'The Bard'.[23] As a result, *The Lay of the Last Minstrel* characterizes resistance to the English as compelling but ultimately obsolete, as a romantic remnant of a past before Tory Unionism became the more reasonable position for a patriotic Scot. For example, in Canto V, Stanza VI, the 'hostile armies', 'by habit, and by nation, foes', meet and have a moment of identification when they raise their visors, with 'many a friend, to friend made known'. The armies even play dice and football together, though the truce can change to war at any instant.[24] Scott makes the difference between peace and war, like the separation of England and Scotland, a matter of habit and circumstance, not a difference of essential national character.

While Owenson follows Scott in portraying her minstrel as a political outcast – 'Tis said *Oppression* taught the lay / To him' (3), she says – she reverses the connotations of that oppression. Scott's minstrel is alienated by the Anglo-Scottish conflict of a distant past, conflict that must, in Scott's view, be overcome by a united Britain in resistance to a threatening France. Owenson, on the other hand, invokes Anglo-*Irish* conflict and then leaves it pointedly uninterpreted. In an explanatory note to the title of the volume, she tells of her visit to the 'province of Caonnaught' (the location of the short-lived 'Republic of Connaught' [1] in 1798 and earlier the place of Irish refuge from Cromwell's army), during which she wanted to hear 'the Irish Harp'. 'But', she says,

> the hope I had long cherished of hearing the *Irish Harp* played in perfection was not only far from realized, but infinitely disappointed. That encouragement so nutritive to genius, so indispensably necessary to perseverance, no longer stimulates the Irish bard to excellence, nor rewards him when it is attained; and the decline of that tender and impressive instrument, once so dear to Irish enthusiasm, is as visibly rapid, as it is obviously unimpeded by any effort of national pride or national affection. (2)

We can interpret the minstrel's abstract '*Oppression*' by relating this fall from 'national pride' that has killed off native music to the Wolfe Tone rebellion, the Union, and/or Emmet's rebellion, all of which had taken place within the decade that preceded the trip Owenson describes. As in *The Wild Irish Girl*, however, Owenson leaves her readers to fill in the details of the political reality underlying a recent silencing of bards and minstrels.

This moment of conventional nostalgia for Ireland's bardic past has little explicitly to do with the rest of the volume, but it allows an implicit transition to Macpherson's Ossian, a common source of such nostalgia and a prominent source of Scottish–Irish controversy. Macpherson provides the epigraph of Owenson's volume: 'Voice of the days of old, let me hear you – Awake the soul of song' (1).[25] Though Macpherson's poetry had circulated for more than four decades at this point, that very circulation and the attendant controversies made the poetry a usefully ambiguous touchstone. 'Ossian' could signify the Scottish creation of Macpherson and his supporters, or it could invoke the many Irish reclamations of the old bard, including Charlotte Brooke's Ossianic translations in *Reliques of Irish Poetry* and the poem that nearly got Thomas Moore expelled from Trinity College, an 'imitation of Ossian' that he later called 'seasoned with plenty of the then favorite condiment – treason' (quoted in Waller x).[26] Malcolm Laing's debunking edition and Henry Mackenzie's report on the authenticity question, both published in 1805, strengthened the Irish case by concluding against the straightforward authenticity of Macpherson's work. More than ever, Irish writers could make Ossian into a ready symbol of deceptive and improper British attempts to incorporate an Irishness that remained unalterably alien.[27]

Like Moore before her, however, Owenson revived Ossian in a context where Ossianic nationalism could not be so easily displaced into the distant past or a field of merely literary imagination. Instead, after making Ossian a kind of presiding spirit of the volume's opening, Owenson connects the Irish and Ossianic sentiments of the opening with Continental writing throughout the rest of the book. While Owenson concentrates on conventionally feminine subject matter in the poems proper, the prose apparatus around the poems, while also not explicitly political, calls forth a remarkable set of associations. The second fragment has an epigraph from Rousseau, for example, and that starts a string of epigraphs and notes from French and Italian writers (this coming after not only the French conquest of Italy but also the English bureaucratic annexation of Ireland): Rousseau, Voltaire, Corneille, Montesquieu, Tasso (in French and then Italian), de la Faire, Guarini, De Mouslier, Petrarch, and more. The community of sources is largely Continental and modern, almost entirely not British (save one quotation from Cowper and the ambiguous Ossianic epigraph), and even – in stark contrast to *The Wild Irish Girl*'s sources – not Irish.[28]

The note to Fragment II of *The Lay*, 'La Rose Fletrie', provides perhaps the most complete example of Owenson's process, set under an epigraph from Rousseau: 'Que l'amour est doux si l'on aimer toujours! / Mais helas! il n'y a point d'eternel amour' ['How love is sweet if one loves forever! But alas! There is no eternal love'] (8). With a flowing, anapestic feel anticipating that of Moore's *Melodies*, the poem opens with a conventional analogy between lost love and a withered rose:

> Oh! return me the rose which I gather'd for thee
> When thy love like the rose was in bloom,
> For neglected it withers, though given by me,
> And shares with thy love the same doom. (8)

The remainder of the poem examines the rose metaphor in detail. In the eighth stanza, attached to a pun on 'wilt' (11), comes a detailed note, something between a personal anecdote and a documentary footnote.

This note begins with an epigraph from the English Cowper on the ability of song to invoke a scene, relates that to Owenson's own attachment to the Irish 'air of Erin go bragh', then quotes Voltaire on the odor of roses. This passage follows:

> And the effect produced by the recurrence of a sweet strain, or a delicious odour, heard and inhaled under the influence of circumstances dear to the heart or interesting to the fancy, may be deemed *twin* sensations: for my own part (and perhaps I am drawing conclusions from an individual rather than a general feeling) I have never listened to the air of *Erin go brach*, or breathed the perfume of the *rose geranium*, without a thrill of emotion which was sweet, though mournful, to the soul, and which drew its birth from a feeling memory … inseparably connected with the melody of the one and the perfume of the other. (11–12)

What Owenson seems to brush aside as merely personal conjoins two symbols with widely understood connotations: the sentimental cliché of the symbolic rose and 'the old Irish *refrain* of Eiren go Bragh', as Owenson put it in the passage describing 1806 quoted above, which emphasizes the air's power over the 'ragged, starving audience' of post-Rebellion Ireland.

The remainder of the note further undermines the opening gesture of self-absorption by first declaring the association of odors and melodies 'just and natural', then, with crafted spontaneity, conjuring a broadly international community of like-minded writers.[29] Owenson writes,

> It is indeed but just and natural that the safest and purest of all the senses should claim the closest kindred with the memory and the *soul*. 'L'oreille est le chemin du ceur', ['the ear is the way to the heart'] said Voltaire. And the rose had never witnessed its frequent apotheosis, had its bloom been its *only* or its sweetest boast.
>
> My memory at this moment supplies me with innumerable poems addressed to the Rose. Among the most beautiful are, I think, one by *Anacreon*, so elegantly translated by Moore; one by *Sappho*, one by *Ausonius*, one by *Francisco de Biojo* (Parnasso Espagnol), one by *Camoens*, one by *Bernard le Jeune*, one by *Cowper*, two by *Metastasio*,

one from the *Persian*, and one by a German poet (whose name has escaped recollection) beginning,
'*Der Fruhling* [sic] *wird nunbald entweichen.*'
['Spring will soon escape/be gone.'] (11–12)

The possibility of excessive self-examination is raised only so it may be forcefully dismissed as the paragraph moves on. The process of the note serves both to establish Owenson's erudition – the pose is far from that of the self-effacing Preface of the volume – and to make a case for humanity's shared emotions. It invokes conventions of Continental republicanism, however, in a self-protective manner, for Owenson never breathes a word of her sources' opinions of less flowery matters.

That note is the longest and most intricate of the volume, but other notes exhibit similar strategies. A note to Fragment VI describes through Locke and Rousseau 'the delicious feelings that accompany those moments vibrating between *waking consciousness* and the senseless torpidity of sleep' (29), leaving us to think what we will of the philosophers' ideas about governments, social contracts, patriarchies, and the like. Throughout the volume, the poem's speakers concentrate on their own feelings and longings in a way that Campbell calls 'frankly autobiographical' (76). It may be so, but if it is, the material certainly selects elements of highly conventional sentimental autobiography, and the notes reinforce the sense that no reader should see the feelings of any speaker as hers alone. Instead, we are told, they are the feelings of a wide community of writers joined across chronological and geographical lines.[30]

Owenson's example points to broader issues raised by the uses of minstrelsy at this time. *The Wild Irish Girl* and *The Lay of an Irish Harp* both deploy the conventions of minstrel writing, especially the tension between autobiographical and non-autobiographical components of literary personae. This allows Owenson to play with the tension between sincerity and conventionality in sentimental writing more generally. The content of Owenson's work that has struck many readers as 'unmistakably Sydney Owenson' (46), in Stevenson's phrase, is ironically the most self-consciously conventional Della Cruscan material Owenson writes. Owenson had steeped herself in Della Cruscan work and consciously imitated Anna Matilda (the female lead character of Della Cruscan poetry, a pseudonymous creation of Hannah Cowley). Owenson wrote of Bracklin Castle, where she stayed with the Featherstone family before she started publishing, that 'the *fadasies* of Della Crusca [were] her *ne plus ultra* of literary acquirement', and she also said that Anna Matilda's '*Farewell to*

Della Crusca' was her 'constant study' (Stevenson 42, italics in original). Even after *The Wild Irish Girl* was published, she reacted to the surprise visit of a Dr. Kirwan thus: 'I flew first to the harp to get up an attitude (like poor Maturin), and then back to the table to seize my pen like "Anna Matilda"' (Stevenson 95).

The Lay of an Irish Harp connects itself to Della Cruscan verse with a witty note to the title of Fragment VI: 'she who writes FROM THE HEART, may insensibly forget that she is writing for the WORLD' (30). In that gratuitously capitalized 'WORLD', the internationalism and the publication history of the Della Cruscan poets intersect. They literally wrote for *The World* magazine; Anna Matilda makes a the same pun on the title in one of her poems 'To Della Crusca':

> But when at length Remembrance bids
> The filmy slumber quit my lids,
> Saying 'the WORLD its Wit hath brought,
> 'Its various point, its well turn'd thought,
> 'But DELLA CRUSCA lends no ray' –
> Oh *what* is Morning – *what* is May? (*Poetry of the World* I.108)

The Della Cruscan poets also wrote for 'the world' in another sense. The dramatized flirtation of the poems routinely connected lovelorn sensibility to the woes of contemporary politics.[31]

To misperceive Owenson's self-consciously Della Cruscan verse solely as the production of transparent sincerity is to re-enact the problems of reading that Owenson stages in *The Wild Irish Girl*. In that novel, according to Horatio, Glorvina's virtue rests on her inability to deceive. When Horatio thinks Glorvina has misled him, his moral universe begins to crumble:

> But it is the silence of Glorvina in the subject of this generous friend, that distracts me; if after all – oh! It is impossible – it is sacrilege to doubt her – she practiced in deception! she, whose every look, every motion, betrays a soul that is all truth, innocence, and virtue! (169)

In fact, Glorvina is indeed 'practiced in deception'. She has deceived Horatio and his father, in both cases with her customary passivity. As Lord M— puts it in retrospect, 'She was silent – she was obedient – and I was – deceived' (249). By the end of the novel, however, any hint of past deception is overwhelmed by the reinscription of the transparently sincere Glorvina that Lord M— and Horatio have wished into existence, the minstrel of literary fantasy who sings spontaneous, artless songs that reflect her emotions and those of her patrons.

To this day, many of Sydney Owenson's readers see her as Horatio did Glorvina: as a producer of transparently readable texts who is 'incapable of deception' – or at least not capable of being as playful, ironic, and allusive as I have argued her early texts to be. Owenson's biographers relentlessly identify her with the heroines of her novels and the speakers of her poems, even when contrary evidence warns us against doing so. 'It need scarcely be said that Glorvina is drawn from the same model [Owenson herself] who had already sat for Olivia and Imogen' (73), writes Stevenson, and Campbell tells us that 'Glorvina is, of course, an idealized Sydney' (68). Even some of the most persuasive recent readings of the novel work to locate an unequivocal voice of 'Owenson' among its many competing perspectives.[32]

Owenson's supposed transparency is part of a larger critical problem in dealing with any literature that glorifies improvisation, effusion, genuineness, and, conversely, the lack of ability to dissemble. *The Wild Irish Girl*'s moral order rests on Glorvina's transparency, however much a closer inspection might reveal flaws in the glass. Similar fantasies of spontaneous, sincere communication between a poet or musician and an audience lie at the heart of many other narratives with minstrel and improvisatrice characters. But this construction of spontaneous, inspired sincerity is still a construction. Neither oral nor improvised, and eminently capable of including misdirection or code, such narratives exploit transparent sensibility, but they do not embody it. The very points at which Owenson's poetry has struck its readers as most self-absorbed are those at which, in another view, her engagement with 'the WORLD' becomes most complex and cosmopolitan.[33]

In a larger sense, sensibility's claim to access feelings that are at once individual and universal allowed writers useful overlaps among personal, national, and universal feeling; hence Owenson's ability to write at once as herself, as Glorvina, as 'an Irish harp', and as addressing 'the WORLD'. Combined with the genealogical and historical conventions of minstrel writing, this flexibility of the literature of sensibility allowed it to become the vehicle of a kind of national internationalism, from Gray's domestication of Welsh resistance to Owenson's imagination of a new, cosmopolitan Ireland through French and Italian sources. If, in Benedict Anderson's famous words, a nation is 'an imagined political community – and imagined as both inherently limited and sovereign' (6) – the practice of minstrel writing complicated nationalism in Britain and Ireland by imaginatively unsettling the borders and sovereignty of

England, Ireland, Scotland, and Wales. We see in the writing of Owenson and many others the practice of staging voices from two or more periods with different national parameters (as in the case of pre- and post-Union Ireland), creating a sense of historical rupture alongside sentimental claims to feelings that transcend national and historical divisions. In the early work of Sydney Owenson, characters are and are not personae of the author; Ireland is and is not a sovereign nation. One cannot explain the particular without reference to the collective, the conventional, the generic – and the contradictory impulses of Owenson's texts are those of minstrel writing itself.

3
'The Minstrels of Modern Italy': Germaine de Staël, Improvisation, and Myths of Corinne

When Germaine de Staël's *Corinne, or Italy* made its sensational debut in 1807, it presented to British readers a familiar image: a poet performing verses to the accompaniment of a harp or lyre. Such images had become a commonplace of British and Irish writing in the preceding decades, in texts ranging from Ossianic poetry to Sydney Owenson's novels. The plot of *Corinne* relies on British representations of bards and minstrels and their familiarity to a pan-European audience; the eponymous Corinne knows Ossian and old Scottish songs, which she performs to win Oswald, Lord Nelvil's reluctant heart. However, Staël also departs dramatically from the conventions of British minstrel writing. Her novel's characters and its critics both notice the oddity, to British eyes, of a performing woman. That innovation has attracted much modern critical attention to what Ellen Moers calls 'the myth of Corinne' and 'the fantasy of the performing heroine' (174). But Corinne also differs from her British counterparts in her compositional method: she improvises, while they recite pre-existing works. As Caroline Gonda has noted, *Corinne* 'did more than any other work to popularize the idea of the improvisatore or improvisatrice' (198), and it did so in a way that gave Britain its first major theory of improvisation.[1] The novel imagines improvisation not only as a compositional method but also as a means of conceiving the histories of people and nations, in a way that constitutes a sweeping response to then-dominant representations of British minstrelsy. As important as Staël's work was for women writers, it also initiated a related but broader 'myth of Corinne' in English-language writing, that of improvisation itself.

Today we use the term broadly: one can 'improvise' anything from a jazz solo to a quiche. Literary critics have written of medieval improvisation, of Iago's improvisation in *Othello*, of the improvisatory styles of Defoe and Sterne.[2] Illuminating as those studies are, all of them use 'improvisation' anachronistically, as the term did not exist as an English word until the end of the eighteenth century. Even when a language of improvisation did emerge, it described a specific practice in Italy, one routinely characterized as an impossibility in Britain. This chapter will detail the development of an English-language rhetoric of improvisation before *Corinne*; analyze Staël's transforming impact on that development; and then trace later writers' reactions to Staëlian improvisation, including those of a series of women writers arguing against improvisatory performance as a model for female conduct.

Isaac D'Israeli set his 1803 poem *The Carder and the Carrier* in 'amorous Florence, that propitious clime / Where Love is constant tho' he talks in rhyme' (1–2). A footnote describes those lines as '[a]lluding to the numerous Improvisatori, the Minstrels of modern Italy' (1). In 1803, when D'Israeli needed to explain 'improvisatori' for an English-speaking audience, he chose the ready means of equating *improvvisatori* with the already-famous figure of the minstrel.[3] The footnote qualifies the analogy in two ways: as modern and Italian minstrels, *improvvisatori* stand in opposition to the self-consciously archaic Britishness of their counterparts in, for instance, Walter Scott's *Minstrelsy of the Scottish Border* (1802–3). D'Israeli's rhetoric epitomizes the development of literary representations of *improvvisatori* and *improvvisatrici* that would flourish in the first decades of the nineteenth century, as an increasing number of writers used the modern Italian figures to rewrite and revise the conventions of British minstrelsy.

As D'Israeli's effort to explain the nature of 'improvisatori' implies, 'improvisation' had a much shorter history in English than did 'minstrelsy'. Although the musical term *ex improviso* (or, later, *ex improvviso*) had appeared occasionally, improvisation as such had no discernible English-language existence before the middle of the eighteenth century. As Gonda has seen, the *Oxford English Dictionary* places the first use of any English variant in 1765 with Smollett writing of an 'improvisatore' as 'one of the greatest curiosities you meet with in Italy'.[4] Smollett's line captures the flavor of the great majority of eighteenth-century uses. They locate *improvvisatori* in Italy and present them as 'curiosities', as things that must be explained to an English audience. And the performers were generally represented as men: the *OED* citation of pre-1800 variants of 'improvisation', in fact, links improvisation with male or ungendered poets in Italy. The *improv(v)isatrice* does not appear until 1804, and then only parenthetically as a synonym for 'poetess'.[5]

Improvisation, as it would come to be called, was more than simply a new way of talking about spontaneous composition or effusion, and its incompatibility with England was more than a trick of vocabulary. British and Irish writers who wanted their readers to take improvisation seriously had to overcome longstanding aesthetic biases against Italian musical art. As pleasing as Italian compositions might be from a strictly aesthetic standpoint, the argument went, they have only aesthetic attraction, as opposed to the emotional and moral merits of bardic performances. Variations of this idea attracted numerous advocates, among them Joseph Cooper Walker in Ireland, who sympathetically quotes 'Anderson's' sentiment that '[m]ost of the modern Italian compositions only trifle with the ear; the Welch [sic], the Scotch, and the Irish music reaches the heart' (n.66); and James Hogg in Scotland, in whose *Queen's Wake* (1813) Queen Mary has acquired a flawed, Italianate taste in the French court.

In the *Edinburgh Review*'s predominantly laudatory notice of *Corinne*, Francis Jeffrey reminded his readers of the larger significance of such theories of national music. Overstating the half-Italian Corinne's Italianness, Jeffrey states, 'it is Great Britain and Italy, the extremes of civilised Europe, that are personified and contrasted in the hero and heroine of this romantic tale' (183). Jeffrey then clarifies the hierarchy of 'the extremes of civilised Europe':

> We are persuaded we shall not, even by Mad. de Staël, be accused of any immoderate partiality in favour of our countrymen, when we say that an Englishman bears a much greater resemblance to a Roman, than an Italian of the present day. Here, therefore, the possession of liberty and laws, and, above all, the superiority which a man derives from having a share in the government of his country, has, in opposition to climate and situation, produced a greater resemblance of character, than the latter was able to do, when counteracted by the former. (194)

Jeffrey here and throughout his review willfully ignores Corinne's complicating arguments on these very points.

The terms of Jeffrey's argument point to the reasons why Corinne provided such a powerful model for other writers. A certain kind of British patriotism depended on precisely the distinction Jeffrey draws, the contention that the Britain fighting Napoleon was analogous to ancient

Rome but not to modern Italy, the Italy of the *Florence Miscellany* and the Della Cruscan poets, the Italy ruled in 1807 by Napoleon himself.[6] By constructing English strength in opposition to Italian weakness, Jeffrey's argument points to the potential for other writers to invert his hierarchy by reclaiming Italy as possessing something positive that England lacked.[7] This is not to say that Staël, herself a vocal proponent of the English government's theory and practice, would have disputed Jeffrey's broad conclusions. ('England', she wrote, 'is the only great European empire that has achieved the final state of perfection of the social order known to us' [*Considérations* 92].) However, Corinne does contest facile claims to the superiority that Jeffrey takes for granted, and her case rests on the novel's presentation of artistic and political improvisation.

Improvising history in Britain and *Corinne*

Corinne's debut in England illustrates how new the idea of improvisation remained to British readers in 1807. Writing in French and comfortable with the Italian terms for improvisation, Staël deployed terminology that seems to have baffled her 1807 translators. In the novel's French, Corinne is an 'improvisatrice' (I.50), she possesses the 'talent d'improviser' (I.65), and her poem at the Capitol is an 'Improvisation' (I.73). These words and phrases, seemingly simple to translate into their English equivalents, instead reveal the lack of a modern vocabulary of improvisation. D. Lawler's translation describes 'Corinna' (as both 1807 English versions call her) as an 'improvisatrix' (I.54), with a note promising to explain the term later. The sole vaguely relevant note, however, suggests only further frustration: Lawler later translates Corinne's 'talent d'improviser' as 'her talent for extempore poetry' (I.69) with a footnote that reads, '[f]or that particular species of poetry here alluded to, called, in Italian, *Improvisatore*, the translator can find no English denomination' (I.69).

The other 1807 translation, an anonymous one, lacks Lawler's boldness of coinage. There, Corinne is not an improvisatrix but simply a 'composer of extempore rhymes' (I.51–2). The translators explain the problem in a note, using an odd variant of '*improvvisatore*': 'The *improvvisitore*, or art of composing extempore verses, is an accomplishment peculiar to the Italians' (I.52).[8] Even a generation later, the 1833 Isabel Hill translation[9] adopts a more modern vocabulary for improvisation but only in some cases: Corinne's improvisation at the Capitol is a 'chant' (25), and although her gift is called one of 'improvisation' (43), it also takes other names more typical in older works, such as 'faculty of extemporising' (43). *Corinne*'s wide circulation in both French and English thus created a paradoxical effect. Its French text gave British readers a new theory of improvisation, with its modern vocabulary largely visible in direct cognates. At the same time, its English translations, especially those of 1807, reveal how little that same British audience had previously understood of improvisation.

The lack of significant precedent in English allowed *Corinne* to establish the popular connotations of Italian improvisation, which it presented as a practice with artistic and political implications. Corinne's improvisation at the Capitol, much cited as an inspirational presentation of public female genius, also demonstrated the ideological work improvisation could do. Asked to improvise on the glory of Italy, Corinne slowly builds a triumphant historical narrative, to the delight of her Italian audience. Then Corinne sees Oswald and responds to his emotions: '[d]ivining the thoughts going through his mind, she was impelled to meet his need by talking of happiness with less certainty' (30). Here the teleology of the poem breaks down, and Corinne improvises, changing the direction of her narrative to accommodate Oswald's reaction, introducing a note of northern melancholy and earning his applause.

By altering a narrative of Italy's past, Corinne suggestively connects her content and her process: as an improviser, she can rhetorically change the course of history if necessary. At a time when revolution, reform, and reaction dominated European thought, a new theory of historical flexibility could reverberate far beyond the steps of the Capitol. (Staël herself had earlier asked, 'who can live, who can write at the present moment, without feeling and reflecting upon the revolution of France?' [*Treatise* 31].) *Corinne* presents improvisation as a political path between stasis and revolution, as an artistic theory of post-Terror moderate liberalism. As a model of innovation bounded by context, Staël's improvisation carved out space between a reactionary emphasis on the authority of previous generations, on the one hand, and Painite optimism that any generation could break free from that legacy on the other.[10] Minstrel writers such as Percy and Scott emphasized the weight of British tradition, creating a retrospective national culture through the collection and repetition of carefully shaped cultural materials. Staël's presentation of improvisation, on the contrary, emphasized the contingencies of poetic creation, the way that the plan of a work – or a nation – could change as it was created. But this freedom has limits. The improviser's skill consists of responding continuously to new events, maintaining flexibility within the boundaries established by a developing performance. Napoleonic autocracy lacks conversational interchange, an aspect of improvisation

Corinne emphasizes in describing rural improvisers as using 'language full of life that solitary thought could not have brought into being' (45).[11]

The improviser cannot break cleanly with her own history, as revolutionary nations strive to do. *Corinne*'s narrator emphasizes repeatedly the constraints of personal and political history: '*We are surrounded by the remains of history,* said Cicero. If he said so then, what do we say now!' (85). Italy's immediate past as the object of imperial ambitions, culminating in Napoleon's 1805 coronation as King of Italy, provided an apt example of a nation's inability to control its destiny.[12] At the microcosmic level, the novel enacts a similar tension, vacillating between constructions of irresistible fate and other hints that undermine that inevitability. Corinne, for instance, experiences her doomed relationship with Oswald as foreshadowed by the heavens: 'I have always known the sky to look paternal or angry, and I tell you, Oswald, tonight it condemned our love' (196). If we need a further suggestion that these are star-crossed lovers, Corinne provides it later by acting the part of Juliet while Oswald watches. But the narrator also assumes paradoxically that 'destiny' is not destined at all but contingent: 'Had she acted upon this impulse, what a different destiny she and Oswald would have known!' (355). A destiny Corinne can change is no destiny at all, but the tension between fate and choice fits well into the model of improvisation Staël establishes here. The project of improvisation is to acknowledge the constraints of history, constraints so strong they can feel like inexorable fate, and to produce from that context a new direction.

In constructing her theory through the figure of the *improvvisatrice*, Staël created a new kind of minstrel, presenting a cultural system through which women could imagine a minstrelsy of their own. In Britain, writers had for nearly half a century presented minstrelsy as an overwhelmingly male mode of performance, with heavy doses of insular British conservatism and Francophobia.[13] Scott's work brought minstrelsy to the center of British letters, and women were largely excluded from one of the popular and lucrative literary modes of the day. Corinne understands the ways of British bardic and minstrel mythologies, and she can sing according to British conventions. She improvises for her Italian audience, but alone with Oswald, she talks of Ossian and wins his heart by singing old Scottish songs.

Even as she demonstrates her mastery of minstrel-style singing, however, Corinne's improvisations turn minstrelsy's conventions upside-down. A critic says of James Beattie's *The Minstrel* that 'the ancient minstrel is invoked as a kind of patriarchal muse who will lend reverential awe and authority to the poet's quest' (King 249). *Corinne* offered women a corresponding *matriarchal* muse of minstrelsy, a means by which to connect the Sapphic tradition of women's performance to a modern, realistic heroine.[14] And the contrast runs even deeper: for instance, writing about minstrelsy commonly romanticized the past, imagining the community of the British nation by having minstrels create its history. Corinne, on the other hand, argues for an improvisational nationalism, a way of constructing national pride without a progressive teleology. Again, the debate turns on fate: Oswald says, 'I judge nations strictly … I always think they deserve their fate, whatever it may be' (54). Oswald wants to imagine Britain through a kind of cultural nationalism that constructs his nation's present eminence as the happy, necessary result of its past.

Corinne counters him from an Italian perspective, constructing Italy's less happy history by emphasizing contingency and internal diversity:

> Perhaps I am mistaken, but the faults of the Italians inspire me with nothing but pity for their fate. Throughout the ages, making this beautiful country a prey for their endless ambition, foreigners have conquered her and torn her to shreds, only to reproach her bitterly for the faults of nations vanquished and torn to shreds. The Italians gave Europe the arts and sciences and now she turns her gifts against them … It is so true that governments form the character of nations that remarkable differences in manners are to be seen in the different states that make up this same Italy. (101)

Corinne opposes Oswald's teleological nationalism with improvisatory history.

The novel does not, however, let Britain stand as a stable imagined community opposed to Corinne's Italy. Instead, it slowly undermines Oswald's assumptions about his own country. Most fundamentally, the narrative cannot settle on whether Oswald comes from Scotland or England; though he is introduced as a 'Scottish peer' and does indeed return to Scotland at the end, he frequently refers to his native 'English' customs in a way that can seem bizarrely careless in a novel that relies so heavily on notions of national difference. Whether resulting from carelessness or strategy, the confusion destabilizes a novel built so carefully on national sentiment in general and British patriotism in particular.[15] English and not English, Scottish and not Scottish, and never easily *British*, Oswald embodies the instabilities of British national identities.

At some points, however, the novel's apparent confusion between England and Scotland disappears, and Staël reveals her familiarity with

Scotland's special resonance in sentimental and patriotic discourse about bards. Scottish poetry makes another appearance as Corinne takes Oswald on a tour of her private gallery, finishing with a landscape featuring a 'bard' and the spirit of that bard's father. Oswald, trying to maintain his reserve, begins to show emotion, and Corinne takes advantage of his vulnerability: 'Corinne took up her harp, and in front of this painting began to sing Scottish ballads whose simple notes seem to keep pace with the sound of the wind moaning in the valleys...and both of them freely gave way to their tears' (157). Corinne understands the power of Scottish conventions to reach Oswald, and she later stresses the connection between Scottish and Italian minstrelsy by comparing Dalmatian improvisers to Ossian in particular and to 'the Scottish bards' in general (301).

At such moments, the presentation of Scotland plays into the novel's general emphasis on the inability of an imperial power to assimilate another land effectively. This emphasis arises in part through the protagonists, whose love cannot overcome their attachments to their respective countries. The novel presents Oswald's father as prophetic in seeing that Corinne

> would inevitably lead my son away from England, for such a woman can never be happy here, and Italy alone is right for her...in countries whose political institutions give men honourable occasions to act and prove themselves, women should remain in the background. How could a person such as [Corinne] be satisfied with such a lot? (329)

Whereas a Unionist plot might present a final marriage that overcomes the strife of a battle-scarred romance, the plot of *Corinne* stages irreconcilable cultural difference, strongly implying a critique of the competing expansionisms of Britain and France.

France had recently taken control of most of Italy when Staël wrote *Corinne*; mention of the French victory is pointedly omitted from the novel, but readers could hardly fail to consider the novel's commentary on Italy's history in light of the Napoleonic takeover. For Italy as for Corinne, improvisation allows a measure of freedom and flexibility. *Corinne* fully acknowledges that flexibility in the heroine's ability to alter her history of Italy to suit the needs of her audience. At the same time, the novel moves beyond its predecessors, as well as many of its successors, by recognizing the constraints of improvisation, the way that it constantly creates new contexts that demand attention and limit the artist's options. Italy can alter itself but must still be Italy; Oswald can change but must remain English; Corinne can love an Englishman but cannot finally leave Italy; Napoleon (as Staël believed but left unstated in the novel) can conquer and reform, but his empire cannot integrate the people he controls.

Improvising a persona: Landon's *The Improvisatrice*

In *Literary Women*, Moers connects Letitia Landon's *The Improvisatrice* (1824) to *Corinne*, describing Landon as 'one of Corinne's disciples, known as "L.E.L." and as the author of a poem called "The Improvisatrice"' (181). Indeed, similarities between the two works in plot and sentiment abound: they share dark-haired heroines identified with Sappho, heroes who sacrifice passion for duty, and a sense that female genius is fated to suffer. As Angela Leighton puts it, '*The Improvisatrice*...is unmistakably modeled on *Corinne*' (58). There are, however, important differences between the texts: Landon writes in verse, with inset tales of gothic exoticism; she uses the first person rather than Staël's third; and her heroine has none of Corinne's detailed characterization. Even more strikingly, Landon's initial first-person narrator, presumably the title character, never mentions improvisation or even improvises, strictly speaking, according to Corinne's definition or a modern one. Nor does the poem include any other improvisers. Instead, the term *The Improvisatrice* uses for its poets – among them the narrator, Petrarch, and Sappho – is *minstrel.* Improvisation enters Landon's work not as the activity of a character but as the governing principle of an unstable narrative presence. The poem's plot, form, and rhetoric come largely from the British minstrel tradition, especially as adapted by Byron, Thomas Moore, and then Landon's more immediate predecessor, Thomas Lovell Beddoes.

Beddoes's *The Improvisatore, In Three Fyttes* (1821) anticipates, and perhaps explains, Landon's strange disjunction between title and content. In the poem itself, Beddoes never uses the word 'improvisatore' or any of its variants, nor does he invoke any of the conventions that had traditionally set *improvvisatori* apart from minstrels and other oral poets. In short, Beddoes's 'improvisatore' is most distinctive, according to the conventions current at the time, for not being an *improvvisatore* at all. Beddoes presents his Italian title only to abandon its implications immediately, as the poem returns to the British antiquarian ground of an older minstrel tradition. As would be true in Landon's *The Improvisatrice*, the figure to which we must suppose the title to refer is called a 'minstrel'. Beddoes strives for something like Beattie's rude minstrelsy; the title page's epigraph, credited to 'Webster's Appius and Virginia', reads, 'I have sung / With an unskilful, but a willing voice.' The poem's first couplet leaves no doubt that the verse takes its lack of skill seriously: 'Dank is the air and dusk the sky, / the snow is falling featherily' (1), says the narrator. The strained diction and gloomy, non-specific landscape announce a world of intentionally artless locodescription, far in every sense from Corinne's cosmopolitan historicizing.

Though not explicitly set in Britain, *The Improvisatore* takes place in the conventionalized past-tense landscape of British romance. The poem embodies 'the desire' in Romantic ruin poetry 'to experience the heterogeneity of the past as a homogeneous featureless past' (Janowitz 63). We know that *The Improvisatore* takes place in a time of English knights and wars but not *which* time. Anything like Corinne's concern with the details of Continental history has no place here. The contrast grows still greater when we see that the minstrel does not improvise, at least according to his audience. In the induction to the second fytte, Agnes commands the minstrel to play 'a tale of fairy lore', saying, 'thou knowest / Full many a tale of shrieking ghost' (39). A collector rather than a generator of poems, the minstrel takes his stories from a store of popular tales instead of improvising new ones.

Even stranger, perhaps, is the role of women in *The Improvisatore*. Beddoes dedicates the poem to his mother, and the third fytte's eleventh stanza is a tribute to 'woman', though it finds reasons for praising her that relate only to serving or pleasing men. For example, the stanza opens,

> Oh woman! flower among this wilderness
> Of wickedness and woe, whose soul of love
> Lies scent-like inmost, steaming out above
> Its incense of soft words; how sweet to sip
> Entranced the voice of rapture from thy lip,
> And taste thy soul in kisses. Thou dost bless
> Our early life with looks . . . (98–9)

As distasteful as these raptures might already seem to a modern reader, their placement makes them odd in the poem itself as well. In the following two stanzas, '[a] beauteous daughter of mankind' appears in one of the many terrifying (and patently symbolic) caves of the poem (101). This woman is killed, magically but directly, by an admiring male gaze: one Rodolph's 'look, his breath, had choaked her soul, death's hand / Had stiffened her tresses' (102). As the reader of the poem has come to expect, Rodolph ends up crying out horribly and moving off to face an unspeakable fate. Voicing conventional praise for womanhood while demonizing its active female characters, *The Improvisatore* blends misogyny and morbidity, without a trace of Corinne or Italy. It fairly demands a response from a sympathetic reader of *Corinne*, and Landon provides one.

Landon's initial narrator – again, the only candidate for the title role of 'improvisatrice' – explicitly describes her method of inspired repertory performance:

> . . . mingled with these thoughts there came
> A tale, just one that Memory keeps –
> Forgotten music, till some chance
> Vibrate the chord whereon it sleeps! (15)

This passage describes minstrel performance well, but it displays none of improvisation's defining characteristics: subjects given by an audience, spontaneous composition, or the ability to change direction during composition.[16] The narrator's songs repeatedly invoke the conventions of Scott, Byron, and Moore but set them in the *Corinne*-like plot, using those conventions to overturn the gendered assumptions of minstrel writing while using its familiar form.[17]

With the change in the protagonist's gender comes a wholesale change in point of view, as stories of lost love, routine in Beddoes, are retold from women's perspectives. Though the landscape of the tales often features the same markings that the Beddoes poem did – a tree under which a love affair ends, for a simple example – the anguish of separation is caused not by sublime natural force (lightning, in the first fytte of *The Improvisatore*) but by a man's betrayal. By embedding and nesting an array of complementary women's stories, Landon creates an internal mechanism linking women's positions across times and across cultures, through their stories' structural similarities and descriptive details. The heroines all have black hair, for instance, a connection to which the poem pays a good deal of seemingly needless attention.

The poem repeatedly connects the narrator's black hair to Sappho's, and the plot echoes the dark-haired Corinne's rivalry with her blonde half-sister. Unlike the meticulously developed Corinne, however, Landon's narrator has virtually nothing else to distinguish her: no name (while Corinne has two), parents, history, or bodily appearance. She *is* her hair, her costume, her genius, her nationality, and her love for

Lorenzo. (That love almost becomes her name, at least rhetorically: 'LORENZO! – how I sighed that name', she says, 'As breathing it, made it mine own!' [46].) But she is nothing else: she is not a character but a vanishing act, not a text but a set of allusions. Even the portrait Lorenzo keeps to remember the narrator pictures not her – 'his Minstrel Love', as this memorial names her – but Sappho.

An experienced reader of minstrel writing might look for grounding in an editorial apparatus, but Landon offers only a brief Advertisement. From beginning – a prefatory remark objecting to prefatory remarks – to end, the Advertisement provides not a grounding but a complicated set of diversions. It reads in full,

> Poetry needs no Preface: if it do not speak for itself, no comment can render it explicit. I have only, therefore, to state that *The Improvisatrice* is an attempt to illustrate that species of inspiration common in Italy, where the mind is warmed from earliest childhood by all that is beautiful in Nature and glorious in Art. The character depicted is entirely Italian, – a young female with all the loveliness, vivid feeling, and genius of her own impassioned land. She is supposed to relate her own history; with which are intermixed the tales and episodes which various circumstances call forth.
>
> Some of the minor poems have appeared in *The Literary Gazette*. (n.p.)

This Advertisement implies that the poem will 'speak for itself', but many of its important aspects are not 'explicit'. First, as we have noticed, it does not depict improvisation, 'that species of inspiration common in Italy', in any straightforward way. Moreover, the 'entirely Italian character' spends much of the poem in costumes and voices of other places, unlike Corinne, who sings only of Italy and Britain, her two native lands. Furthermore, we learn very little of the pointedly anonymous main character's 'own history' – far less than we learn about many other characters in the poem. And, finally, we learn that 'Some of the minor poems have appeared in *The Literary Gazette*', a fact that undermines the illusion of a distinctly Italian compositional 'genius' even before the poem begins.

The Advertisement, like much of Landon's poetry, sketches the broad outlines of a conventional imagined world – in this case, that of an *improvvisatrice* roughly like Corinne – and then points to the precise details that remind us that the conventions are only conventions, and Landon retains control over their deployment. Landon's Advertisement is an anti-Preface, a witty inversion of the explanatory apparatuses that accompany the poems of her predecessors and even those of Corinne. Corinne is a compulsive annotator, a character who can hardly take a step without 'rendering ... explicit' everything she sees around her. True to the Advertisement's word, on the other hand, Landon's Corinne-like *improvvisatrice* explains virtually nothing.

What the poem's narrator withholds in traditional characterization she could supply with a stylistic signature, a voice distinct from those of her recited songs and of Lorenzo's story. In *The Improvisatore*, Beddoes had used a variety of meters and rhyme schemes, in large part to separate the various layers of the storytelling from one another. Such metrical separation was a common device in minstrel poems with inset songs. Landon, too, employs a variety of meters and rhyme schemes, most of them based on tetrameter couplets and quatrains of varying feet.[18] Landon uses that variety, however, to blur and destabilize characters rather than to delineate them. The narrator's voice sometimes matches that of an inset song, sometimes differs very little (as in the first shift from the narrator to Sappho, which changes the rhyme scheme slightly but not the meter), and sometimes differs a great deal. Rather than remaining a stable base against which the other voices are set, the narrator's voice shifts as if in sympathy with the inset poems, floating among Scott's iambic tetrameters, Moore's anapestic lines, and other variations, frequently shifting form within a character's speech (as other writers had done) and *not* shifting when new voices enter the poem.

The effects of this unstable characterization are clearest at the poem's end. Where improvisation is absent in the content of the poem, it is present in form, as the speaking voice shifts in context, finally – in the poem's last remarkable turn – extending beyond the narrator's own life. Taking over in the same meter, a new narrator materializes without warning to describe the previous narrator's posthumous legacy in these lines:

> Lorenzo! be this kiss a spell!
> My first! – my last! Farewell! – Farewell!

> ———————

> There is a lone and stately hall,
> Its master dwells apart from all. (102)

The horizontal line following the narrator's death is the same line the poem used earlier to denote the end of that narrator's songs. Death in *The Improvisatrice* is but another change of character; improvisation, the poem's organizing principle rather than only a way to sing; the *improvvisatrice*, the material of further improvisation. Improvisation in *Corinne* had been a consummately oral and immediate art, utterly dependent on a speaker's spontaneous eloquence. *The Improvisatrice*, by contrast, takes improvisation metaphorically, transforming the precedents of Staël and Beddoes into a text that acts out improvisation in a way that challenges even the most basic conventions of narrative sincerity.

Neither Corinne nor Italy: a female countertradition

If 'Hannah More was the most influential woman living in England in the Romantic era' (13), as Anne Mellor has recently argued in *Mothers of the Nation*, Staël was arguably the most influential woman living on the Continent. Mellor's study illuminates the importance of More's work as well as Staël's by highlighting the limits of *Corinne*-based genealogies of women's writing: Mellor 'suggest[s] . . . that to consign all women's poetry published in England between 1780 and 1830 to this tradition of the poetess seriously misrepresents a great deal of it' (70). I will here argue a different but related point. I contend that some of the public-minded women Mellor describes defined themselves in direct opposition to *Corinne*. They did so by accepting Staël's identification of Corinne with Italy and then dismissing the positive value of that identification, instead constructing Corinne-like performance as a dangerous manifestation of foreign contamination.[19]

Corinne's gender theory insists on the importance of contingency and local convention. *What* the proper lady is, according to the novel, depends crucially on *where* she is. For many women, this cultural relativism provided an invaluable outlet for a creative imagination. As Moers and others have explained, *Corinne* gave such women a way to take new artistic liberties simply by imagining themselves to be in Italy. But other women, more invested in absolute political and social norms, insisted on the danger of Corinne's approach. The makings of opposition to *Corinne* surface in an unlikely place: Sydney Owenson's second novel, *The Novice of Saint Dominick* (1805). Owenson's novel anticipates a line of anti-improvisatory writing that asserts universal rules of conduct against *Corinne's* liberating relativism. *The Novice* details the development of Imogen, a virtuous heroine who takes up minstrelsy to ease her suffering as a female genius. As Owenson's *The Wild Irish Girl* (1806) would do later, *The Novice* anticipates *Corinne* in striking ways.[20] But Imogen must fall before she rises. She gives into temptations of self-display, and the depth of her corruption becomes clear when she engages not just in public performance but also in *Italian* public performance: improvisation.

In volume three of *The Novice's* four, the historical romance of the first two volumes becomes a moral tale about fashionable corruption.[21] Imogen sustains her modest virtue, at least in part, for over a thousand pages, until improvisation marks its final dissolution:

> It was then emulation chased the last lingering shadow of diffidence; and genius, flinging aside the veil which modesty and reserve had thrown over it, appeared in all its cloudless lustre, bright, splendid, and luminous. The variety of those talents which education had so highly cultivated; that elegant store of information which an early thirst for study had accumulated; that original *naïveté* of manner which naturally united the polish of a court to the piquant wildness of simple rusticity; with the youth, the beauty, and rank of their singular possessor, rendered the lady de St. Dorval the cynosure of fashionable admiration, and the popular wonder of the day.
>
> Animated by applause, stimulated by success, her genius seemed almost to rise above itself; the happiest, the most original poetic flights, soon obtained her a distinguished rank among the first *improvisatori* of fashion. (III.270)

Later, suffering disillusionment and shame from an overly public life, Imogen returns to France. Her return to virtue requires that she abandon improvisation. Although Imogen's troubadour-lover recognizes her virtuosity and innovation ('you, at least, are no imitative musician, but the foundress of a new style of music' [IV.57]), the novel asks us to resist that charm, citing 'the danger of sudden innovation in every system' (III.329). In *The Novice*, improvisation surfaces fleetingly and only as a symptom of modern Italy's decadence. It comes linked to extreme radicalism (which produces 'sudden innovation') rather than Staëlian moderation.

That Owenson, soon to receive *Corinne* warmly, portrays improvisation as dangerously self-indulgent illustrates how powerfully Staël transformed the existing perceptions of some readers.[22] Others, however, continued Owenson's initial line of attack against improvisation, arguing the larger point that cultural differences in female conduct represented not legitimate differences of opinion but deviations from a single real standard: that of British Protestant domesticity. Caroline Gonda has noted this tendency in *The Corinna of England* (1809), for instance, and in a later example, at the end of Joanna Baillie's *The Legend of Lady Griseld Baillie* in *Metrical Legends of Exalted Characters* (1821), the narrator wonders whether a modern woman reader will recognize the virtues of her heroine. She does so with a sarcastic appeal to English women who imitate Corinne:

> Will she such antiquated virtues prize,
> Who with superb Signoras proudly vies:
> Trilling before the dear admiring crowd,
> With out-stretched straining throat, bravuras loud,
> Her high heaved breast press'd hard, as if to boast
> The inward pain such mighty efforts cost? (256–7)

Baillie's narrator has no problem with female accomplishment, but she does object to standards of female conduct, in an improvisatory model, working differently in different countries. By alluding to *Corinne*, Baillie's narrator opposes a politics of improvisation including unconventional gender roles as well as poetic production.

Though emphasizing Staël's associations with France rather than Corinne's (half) Italianness, Hannah More's *Moral Sketches of Prevailing Opinions and Manners, Foreign and Domestic; with Reflections on Prayer* (1819), published two years before *Metrical Legends*, builds a more sustained attack on Staël from a position similar to Baillie's.[23] More's argument illustrates the mix of insular English patriotism and borderless religious certainty necessary to counter the myth of Corinne. More deplores excessive contact between the English and the Continent: 'For is it not worthy of remark, that we only refuse to imitate our continental neighbors, in the very point in which they are really respectable? *They stay at home*' (xv–xvi, emphasis original). More invokes the old notion of Italy as the corrupt, emasculated state that England must avoid emulating: 'It was from the land of polished arts that ancient Rome imported the poison of her sturdy morals, the annihilation of her masculine character' (17). More uses the Reformation to break the parallel between the Roman and British empires:

> England has a palladium for her protection, which Ilium, which Rome never possessed…Our palladium is the Christian, the Protestant Religion. It cannot be taken by storm; but, like that of Ilium, it may be taken by stratagem. The French are to us as much more formidable than the Greeks were to Rome, as we have much more to lose…
>
> In making our country an island, Divine Providence seems to have made a provision for our happiness as well as for our security. As that circumstance has protected us from the sword, it should also protect us from the manners of our continental neighbours. (17–18)

From this general xenophobia, More moves to a specific offensive against Staëlian performance, what More calls the French 'talent, in which they must be allowed to excel all others – the talent *se faire valoir*' (31), the talent of putting oneself forward, or of showing off.

Responding to Staël's remarks in *Considérations sur les principaux événements de la Révolution française* (1818) about the conversational reticence of English women, More reduces female performance to a selfish diversion: 'If, indeed, we were only sent into this world to be entertaining; if we had nothing to do but talk, nothing to aim at but to shine, nothing to covet but admiration; we should more readily coincide in opinion with this sprightly lady [Staël]' (33). After re-emphasizing English domesticity ('Perhaps this lady did not know that the English educate, or rather *did once* educate, women of fashion for *home*' [35, emphasis original]), More dismisses the notion that women travel 'from the desire of escaping from the restraint on their manners' (37). Then, in the key internationalizing turn of her argument, More counters Staëlian cultural relativism by moving back to religion, now generalized as 'Christian':

> The essence of the worldly code of ethics is selfishness; that of the Christian is disinterestedness . . .
>
> In the society of Christians, every man does not so much look on his own things as on the things of others. Christians do not make conversation a theatre for dispute or display. (40)

The Englishwoman is Christian, argues More, and the Continental woman theatrical; ne'er the twain shall meet, if the argument has its way. This anti-theatrical More had once participated actively in theater, as we see in a letter to her sister about a performance of More's *Percy, a Tragedy* in 1777: 'Nothing was ever more warmly received,' she wrote.[24] 'I went with Mr. and Mrs. Garrick; sat in Mr. Harris's box, in a snug dark corner, and behaved very well, that is, very quietly. The prologue and epilogue were received with bursts of applause; so indeed was the whole; as much beyond my expectation as my deserts!' (quoted in Roberts I.123). If More had changed her mind about the theater, however, she had not wavered from her commitment to the British domestic virtue represented by the Percy family. The Percy name linked the much admired Bishop Percy to More's dramatic hero and to the antiquarian tradition (propagated by Bishop Percy himself as well as Scott and others) of celebrating the current Percys. As much as any other family, the Percys connoted ancient, virtuous Britishness extending into modern times.

The Percy name resurfaces in a later, allusive addition to anti-*Corinne* literature, Maria Jewsbury's *History of an Enthusiast* (1830). Jewsbury locates educated English virtue in a pair of Percys, father and son, the father-in-law and husband that Julia, the novel's performing heroine, loses because she comes too late to say, 'I am cured of ambition' (127). Julia's reading includes not only Staël but also Shelley, Byron, and other writers who tempt her with Continental contamination. The younger Percy warns that 'an intellectual fountain of emotion, of which Goëthe and Schiller, Petrarch and de Staël, and Shelley, and a dozen others, are the presiding spirits, will be productive of more loss than gain' (66), and the novel's plot bears his prediction out. Jewsbury's *History* deploys a much more extensive set of literary references than do either Baillie's or More's attacks on Staël, but its logic works much like More's.[25] London corruption, in which a high society room becomes 'quite an Italy' (174), lures Julia from a moral center in the English countryside.

In Cecil, the younger Percy, Jewsbury adds another layer to the inversion of Corinne-like wanderlust: Cecil Percy wants to travel overseas, but not to Italy and not to perform. With a chaplaincy in the West Indies, he wants to save 'the heathen part of the world', which he says 'may indeed be said to lie in wickedness' (142). When he tells this to the nearly reformed Julia, he mentions the 'glorious realities of the inner life'; 'Ah!' she responds, 'how well I know what you mean – you mean emotion' (142). He means no such thing, of course – he means 'the life of faith' (142) – and the novel characteristically encourages us to think of Julia's sufferings as chosen, not inevitable. She wishes she had heard Percy's words 'when my mind was blank paper' (143). Remarkably, the novel's closing pages endorse male dislike of female intellect by shifting the grounds of the dislike from jealousy to honorable domesticity: 'Man does not secretly dread and dislike high intellect in woman, for the mean reason generally supposed – because it may tend to obscure his own regal honours; but because it interferes with his implanted and imbibed ideas of domestic life and womanly duty' (150). The anti-improvisatory female countertradition that Owenson foreshadowed and More fully established here becomes a negative image of *Corinne*.

Conclusion: reconstructing improvisation

In her study of Letitia Landon, Glennis Stephenson argues that 'improvisation is the core of [Landon's] declared female poetics and the feature which most clearly distinguishes her from the male Romantics' (*Letitia Landon* 5). To support the historical association of women with improvisation, she uses George Bethune's colorful 1848 stereotype of the woman writer:

> They [women] write from impulse, and rapidly as they think. The strange faculty, which women have, of reaching conclusions (and, in the main, safe conclusions) without the slow process of reasoning through which men have to pass; the strong moral instincts with which their nature is endowed...their keen and discerning sensibility...render them averse to critical restraints . . . Scarcely any of them seem to have inverted their pen. As the line came first to the brain, so it was written; as it was written, so it was printed. (quoted in Stephenson *Letitia Landon* 10)

Stephenson notes Bethune's 'immense satisfaction in that notion of female intuition and female improvisation which naturalises the poetess and marks her work as the spontaneous, confessional outpouring of emotion' (*Letitia Landon* 11).

Bethune's link between women and improvisation would have made much less sense when *The Improvisatrice* was published in 1824, however, than it did in 1848. Bethune uses a broader sense of 'improvisation' than was current when Landon wrote, and he applies the term to English writers with no apparent sense of incongruity. He cites women who themselves wrote of *improvvisatrici* and who identified themselves with Corinne: 'Mrs. Hemans's melody was as much improvisation as Miss Landon's' (quoted in Stephenson 'Victorian Improvisatrice' 4). He omits contrary evidence, including women who defined themselves against improvisation and men who described themselves as improvising (Byron, Shelley, and Hans Christian Andersen) or as writing rapidly and without revision (Scott, Hogg, and many others). Choosing different writers to represent their genders would allow Bethune's terms to be reversed with little loss of sense: 'Scott's melody', one might say in paraphrase, 'was as much improvisation as Byron's'. In fact, Scott's relationship to improvisation was a matter of interest at least until 1886, when *The Athenæum* contended that 'in the deepest and truest sense, Scott, often called the most improvisatorial, is the least improvisatorial of writers' (*OED* 'improvisatorial').

Bethune's passage, in other words, is bad literary history as well as bad psychology. By offering women writers a new way to write positively about female performance, Romantic-era improvisation rewrote the gender assumptions of a well-established tradition of British minstrelsy.

Table 3.1 Selected chronology of (what we now call) improvisation

Year	Writer	Work	Quotation/Description
1753	Joseph Spence	*The Works of Virgil, in Latin and English*	'This seventh eclogue, as the third before, seems to be an imitation of a custom among the shepherds of old, of vying together in extempore verse. At least 'tis very like the *Improvisatori* at present in Italy; who flourish now perhaps more than any other poets among them, particularly in Tuscany. They are surprisingly ready in their answers (*respondere parati*) and go on *octave* for *octave*, or *speech* for *speech* alternately (*alternis dicetis amant alterna Camenae.*) . . . At Florence I have heard of their having even *Improviso* comedies . . . They were Tuscans too who brought this method to Rome' (quoted in Warton n. 121).
1766	Tobias Smollett	*Travels through France and Italy*	Smollett calls 'the improvisatore' 'one of the greatest curiosities you meet with in Italy' (*OED* 'improvisatore'). This is the first *OED* citation of any variant.
1789	Hester Lynch [formerly Thrale] Piozzi	*Observations and Reflections Made in the Course of a Journey through France, Italy, and Germany*	Piozzi writes that 'Giannetti . . . is the justly-celebrated improvisatore, so famous for making Latin verses *impromptu*, as others do Italian ones' (I.275).[26] Later in her narrative, Piozzi describes the 'powers of improvisation' (I.320) of Corilla and remarks that 'the Capitol will long recollect her being crowned there' (I.320). Piozzi then refers to 'the present improvisatrice, the charming Fantastici' (I.321). Piozzi thus uses 'improvisation' in this sense and 'improvisatrice' before the *OED* documents either usage.
1797	Ann Radcliffe	*The Italian*	The novel contains a passing reference to an *improvvisatore* (273).

1801	Robert Southey	Preface to *Thalaba the Destroyer*	Southey writes, 'Verse is not enough favoured by the English reader: perhaps this is owing to the obtrusiveness, the regular Jews-Harp *twing-twang*, of what has been foolishly called heroic measure. I do not wish the *improvisatorè* tune, but something that denotes the sense of harmony, something like the accent of feeling; like the tone which every Poet necessarily gives to Poetry' (I.ix).
1803	Isaac D'Israeli	*The Carder and the Carrier*	A footnote refers to 'the numerous Improvisatori, the Minstrels of modern Italy' (1).
1804	Matilda Betham	*Biographical Dictionary of the Celebrated Women of Every Age and Country*	Betham mentions 'the poetess (improvisatrice) D. Maria Maddalena Morelli Fernandez' (*OED* 'improvisatrice'). This is the first *OED* citation of 'improvisatrice'.
1805	Sydney Owenson (later Lady Morgan)	*The Novice of St. Dominick* (working title: *The Minstrel*)	'Animated by applause, stimulated by success, her [Imogen's] genius seemed almost to rise above itself; the happiest, the most original poetic flights, soon obtained her a distinguished rank among the first *improvisatori* of fashion' (III.270).
1807	Germaine de Staël	*Corinne ou l'Italie* and English translations thereof	See Table 3.2 below.
1818	Lord Byron	*Beppo, a Venetian Story*	In stanza 33, Beppo's rival is described as a 'perfect cavaliero': 'He patroniz'd the Improvvisatori, / Nay, could himself extemporize some stanzas' (*CPW* IV.139).
1820	The Abbate [Francisco] Furbo	*Andrew of Padua, the Improvisatore: A Tale from the Italian of the Abbate Furbo*	This is an Italian novel dramatizing the theatrical career of an *improvvisatore*. *Andrew of Padua* deals much more with the economics and personal intrigues of Italian theater than *Corinne* had.

Table 3.1   (Continued)

Year	Writer	Work	Quotation/Description
1821	Percy Bysshe Shelley	*Hellas*	Shelley calls the poem 'a mere improvise' (*CW* III.7). Shelley had earlier begun a review of the *improvvisatore* Sgricci, but he did not finish it.
1821	Thomas Lovell Beddoes	*The Improvisatore, In Three Fyttes*	An *improvvisatore* story in name only, the poem is a British minstrel story that never uses the word 'improvisatore' or any variant of it.
1824	Lord Byron	*Don Juan*	The narrator says, 'I feel the "Improvisatore"' (canto XV, stanza 20).
1824	L.E.L. [Letitia Elizabeth Landon]	*The Improvisatrice*	Landon's well-known poem, perhaps a response to Beddoes, re-established the Italianate and female improvisatory tradition. The publication of *The Improvisatrice* is perhaps the point at which 'improvisatrice' becomes a widely recognizable term in English, although the word had been used a few times before, and the readers of the French-language *Corinne* would have recognized it.
1827	Samuel Taylor Coleridge	'The Improvisatore, Or, John Anderson My Jo, John'	As it had been for Beddoes, the name 'Improvisatore' is here something of a joke, a 'nick-name' obtained by 'perpetrating charades and extempore verses at Christmas times' (*PW* I.1057).
1833	Isabel Hill and L.E.L.	New Bentley edition of *Corinne*	See Table 3.2 below.
1835	Hans Christian Andersen	*The Improvisatore; Or, Life in Italy*	A novel translated by Mary Howitt, Andersen's *Improvisatore* ran through at least 13 printings in the 1800s. The English edition of 1845 uses 'improvise' in its modern sense (I.70).

Table 3.2 Naming improvisation in *Corinne*

Phrase in French-language Corinne ou L'Italie (1807)	*Translation in the first, anonymous English edition (1807)*	*Translation in Lawler's second English edition (1807)*	*Translation in Isabel Hill/L.E.L. edition (1833)*
Corinne	Corinna	Corinna	Corinne
Improvisatrice[27]	'composer of extempore rhymes' (I.51–2). Footnote: 'The *improvvisitore* [sic], or art of composing extempore verses, is an accomplishment peculiar to the Italians' (n.I.52).	'improvisatrix' (I.54). Footnote: 'A succeeding note of the translator's will explain the meaning of this appellation' (n.I.54).[28]	'improvisatrice' (18)
Talent d'improviser[29]	'talent for extempore effusions' (I.67).	'talent for extempore poetry' (I.69). Footnote: 'For that particular species of poetry here alluded to, called, in Italian, *Improvisatore*, the translator can find no English denomination' (I.69).	'talent as an improvisatrice' (23).
Improvisation[30]	'Extempore Effusion' (I.75)	'extempore Effusion' (I.78).	'Chant' (25)
Talent d'improviser (twice)[31]	'talent for extempore composition' (I.124)	'talent for extempore poetry' (I.130)	'talent for improvisation', then 'faculty of extemporising' (43)

However, Romantic-era literature that describes or invokes improvisation encompasses much more than that. It was a mode of revision and reversal, of sympathetic adaptation and hostile takeovers. In England, the combination of the familiar conventions of minstrelsy and a pointedly unfamiliar mode of composition only increased the potential for a wide range of adaptations. Negotiating allusion and innovation, national allegiance and subjectivity, social duty and genius, the wide-ranging corpus of writing adopting and commenting on improvisation resists universalizing and teleological readings. Like Corinne's improvisations, such texts present themselves as responding to their immediate contexts, with literary revision and the rewriting of history at the core of their method. As Staël described it, improvisation retained minstrelsy's responsiveness to an audience but added a new emphasis on creativity arising from adverse circumstances. Through *Corinne's* blending of genius and praxis, Staël made improvisation into a new minstrelsy of artistic and ideological flexibility.

4
The Minstrel and Regency Romanticism: James Beattie and the Rivalry of Byron and Wordsworth

When he first met Walter Scott in 1803, William Wordsworth saw him in the process of shaping the minstrel mode for the early nineteenth century. Scott had turned his attention from the largely editorial enterprise of *Minstrelsy of the Scottish Border* (1802–3) to the original verse romance of *The Lay of the Last Minstrel*. During the visit, Scott 'recited parts of the first four cantos ... and when [*The Lay*] was published, in January 1805, it made him instantly famous' (Johnston *Hidden* 801). Scott built on the success of *The Lay* in the years that followed his meeting with Wordsworth. When Wordsworth prepared a series of new works for publication in 1814 and 1815, he was well aware of the contrast between the hostile reception of his own *Poems, in Two Volumes* (1807) and the reading world's enthusiasm for Scott and the newer poetic sensation, Lord Byron. As Peter Manning relates, 'On May 5, 1814, three months after the appearance of *The Corsair* – whose brisk sales relative to *The Excursion*'s would only intensify this rivalry – Wordsworth wrote rather enviously to Rogers to announce *The Excursion*: "I shall be content if the publication pays its expenses, for Mr. Scott and your friend Lord B. flourishing at the rate they do, how can an honest *Poet* hope to thrive?"' (*Reading Romantics* 207, emphasis original).

Wordsworth's self-presentation as 'an honest *Poet*' recalls his more general objections to representing writing through the popular trope of minstrelsy; in Wordsworth's view, writers who imagined themselves as minstrels sullied their honesty – in the most morally charged senses of the term – by pandering to patrons, the literary fashions of the day, or both. In fact, the Pastor of *The Excursion* casually associates minstrelsy

with economic and moral corruption as he describes a dissolute young
man buried in front of him:

> The City, too,
> (With shame I speak it) to her guilty bowers
> Allured him, sunk so low in self-respect
> As there to linger, there to eat his bread,
> Hired Minstrel of voluptuous blandishment;
> Charming the air with skill of hand or voice,
> Listen who would, be wrought upon who might,
> Sincerely wretched hearts, or falsely gay. (265–6)

Then, in one of Wordsworth's many statements of preference for plain
conversation over the songs and instruments of minstrelsy, the narrator
assures the reader that the Wanderer is one 'to whom the general ear /
Listened with readier patience than to strain / Of music, lute, or harp, –
a long delight / That ceased not when his voice had ceased' (386).

At this time, Wordsworth would have had good reason to associate
his rivals' popularity with their interest in representing minstrelsy, and
to hope that readers – like the Wanderer's listeners in *The Excursion* –
would receive his more naturalistic poetry with eagerness and patience.
Scott had built his career out of his self-presentation as a modern literary minstrel, and as I will further explain below, Byron's works to this
point explicitly announced their debts to Scott, James Macpherson, and
James Beattie, among other writers routinely invoked in the age's representations of minstrelsy. The works that Wordsworth published in 1814
and 1815 – *The Excursion* (1814), *The White Doe of Rylstone* (1815), and
the first collected edition of his *Poems* (1815) – constitute, among other
things, a sustained argument against literary minstrelsy, especially as
Scott and Byron practiced it.

Paradoxically, however, Wordsworth's opposition to literary minstrelsy
required him at this more than at any other time to allow the conventions of minstrel writing to guide his own work. *The Excursion's*
use of multiple characters who seem partly to speak for the author,
for example, takes Wordsworth as close as he ever gets to the playfully performative personae of Scott and Byron. And *The White Doe*
involves an undisguised attempt to inhabit and thereby transform Scott's
mode of historical romance. Manning has suggested 'that *The White
Doe*, however it may transform popular narrative, was at least in incep-
tion an attempt to capitalize on that genre, and that we should not
overlook the temptations to which Wordsworth, as an impecunious and
badly reviewed author, was subject' (*Reading Romantics* 165). I will argue

that in *The White Doe* and the other works of this stage of his career, Wordsworth was attempting to resolve the tension Manning identifies between transforming and capitalizing on popular narrative. That is, Wordsworth deploys the generic signals of popular narrative but only provisionally, as part of an effort to persuade readers away from the kinds of writing to which Wordsworth initially appeals.

This effort of persuasion involved a two-sided reliance on metaphors of development and maturation. In this period, Wordsworth created a myth of his own development as a poet, a myth drawing in important ways on James Beattie's *The Minstrel: Or, the Progress of Genius* (1771 and 1774). Wordsworth also described habits of reading in terms of human development, subtly positioning Byron's and Scott's works as the favorites of a youthful taste readers needed to outgrow. Wordsworth's approach probably arose partly as a reaction to Byron's minstrel-inflected first cantos (1812) of *Childe Harold's Pilgrimage*; as Kenneth Johnston has written, 'The Solitary is like a sarcastic Byronic hero suddenly stalking through the benignly paradisal Wordsworthian landscapes. Not content, like Byron, to represent magnificently the despair of his era, Wordsworth (like Goethe) takes the next, dangerously unattractive stop: he tries to overcome it' (*Wordsworth and* The Recluse 265). And it is easy to imagine the idea of the 'Wanderer' as a pointed response to Byron's controlling metaphor of a skeptical pilgrimage. Whatever the degree of Wordsworth's intentional antagonism here, *The Excursion* certainly provided fodder for Byron's later attacks on Wordsworth.[1]

Identifying an opposition between Wordsworth and Byron in nineteenth-century British reading culture is hardly new. For one recent example, Alison Hickey has described an 'identification of Wordsworth with the moral and religious informing of the British mind and with the "foundations of ... national greatness"' in which 'Wordsworth's admirers, usually committed to representing him as an unequivocal force for piety, moral good, and national virtue, latch onto the figure of Byron as a convenient repository of all that threatens these qualities' (168). I propose that Wordsworth's admirers were here following a playbook that Wordsworth himself had written in his publications of 1814 and 1815, which are carefully crafted to work at two levels. The poetry in those volumes is complex and often ironic; the elements of irony and uncertainty in Wordsworth's dramatic masks – what David Simpson describes as a 'sameness-in-difference' (188) connecting Wordsworth and his personae – have long been established.[2] At the same time, however, these works operate at a level of cultural iconography that encourages the bluntly moralistic reading that would solidify among Wordsworth's Victorian supporters but take root in some of the reviews of 1815: that Wordsworth offers a mature poetry that readers can take up as an alternative to the dazzling but immature work of Byron. To understand this process, we must first re-examine an old subject, Beattie's relationship to Wordsworth, in light of the specific context of the middle Regency.

'To doubt is to rebel': Beattie's *Minstrel* in wartime

It may seem strange that Beattie's *Minstrel* should have played a significant part in shaping major works of British poetry in Regency England, especially works as different as *Childe Harold's Pilgrimage* (1812–18) and *The Excursion* (1814). The initial heyday of Beattie's poem had long passed; by the time the first cantos of *Childe Harold's Pilgrimage* were published in 1812, *The Minstrel's* first book had circulated for more than 40 years, and its author had been dead for nearly a decade, since 1803. We have some evidence, however, that Beattie enjoyed a posthumous revival. After *The Minstrel's* early success – there were many separate printings from 1771 to 1775 – came a dry spell. Printings in 1776, 1779, and 1784 are the only ones between 1775 and 1793. In 1794 began a deluge: four new printings by the end of the century, five from 1801–5, six from 1806–10, and then, at a slower rate, seven more by 1825.[3] Though first published in the age of Johnson, Beattie's *Minstrel* may have enjoyed its widest circulation in the age of Wordsworth, Scott, and Byron.

Some of the interest in Beattie doubtless arose from the publicity occasioned by his death and two resulting memoirs, by Alexander Chalmers (1805) and William Forbes (1806). But the acceleration of editions of *The Minstrel* began earlier than that, in 1794, at the height of the Reign of Terror, when the optimism of the French Revolution's early years collapsed into reactionary disillusionment. As Britain turned to anti-Gallic and increasingly reactionary politics, that is, it also turned to *The Minstrel*, and to Beattie, the impeccably orthodox opponent of Hume. The *Edinburgh Review*, noticing Forbes's Life of Beattie in April 1807, describes Beattie's good standing among 'all the orthodox enemies of skepticism' (174). This standing came largely from the principles of Beattie's antiskeptical prose works, the principles of which *The Minstrel* explicitly and implicitly illustrates.

The poem gives to social inequality the force of natural law, arguing for simple piety as it portrays financial hardship as a condition to be patiently endured or even welcomed: 'Hail poverty!' (II.xxii) the protagonist, Edwin, exclaims. The poem's narrator, presumably Beattie *in propria persona*, tells us that 'Poverty's unconquerable bar' (I.i) is a bar to fame, not to happiness; Beattie's minstrel is relentlessly unambitious. For these and other reasons, by the time Beattie attached his name to the poem in 1774, it was received as part of his larger moral project, following his celebrated *Essay on Truth* (1770), a monument of earnest conservatism that had earned Beattie the praise of a wide range of literati and politicians, including King George III.

After Beattie died, the marketing of his poetry called readers' attention to Beattie's moral qualities, even at the expense of his purely poetical reputation. For example, *The Wreath*, a collection of elegant poetry that included *The Minstrel* in 1814 and 1815, includes a 'Sketch of the Life' of Beattie that praises his poetry but implies that Beattie's moral character was more perfectly polished than his verse:

> Had he continued to cultivate the Muses, his classical talents, and harmonious numbers, would have ensured him still greater fame; but there is reason to suppose he neglected the mountain of 'Olympus' for the hill of 'Zion,' and latterly had been more anxious to obtain the reputation of a *Christian Hero*, than that of the greatest of Modern Bards. (x, emphasis original)

The anonymous 'Critical Observations' prefaced to the 1816 and some later printings of *The Minstrel* similarly discount Beattie's poetic skill, saying that *The Minstrel* 'exhibits scarcely any power of invention'. 'Still', it adds, 'so beautiful are the sentiments ... that few poems in the language are more adapted to please, and by pleasing to exert over the mind of the reader a beneficial influence' (5). Broad as the appeal of Beattie's poetry remained, the Regency saw a renewed emphasis on the moral purity of his life and writing. So it was that the influence of Beattie and his Edwin increased, even as Beattie's reputation as a poet arguably declined.

The poem also held another appeal. *The Minstrel* was an especially appropriate text for wartime England because it anticipated the narrative of youthful exuberance being tempered into a more reasoned adult wisdom; that narrative, in broad strokes, is the 'Progress of Genius' to which the subtitle refers. Specifically, Edwin learns poetry as a youth only from a 'beldam' who tells wild, sentimental stories – 'Ah me!' says the narrator (I.xlv), lamenting Edwin's limited musical education.[4] We are assured, however, that though Edwin's 'infant Muse' is 'artless', 'some future verse' in the *Minstrel* will give him 'elegance' (I.lix). This assurance comes as part of the poem's more general optimism, linked to its rebukes of 'cold-hearted sceptics' (I.liii). '[L]et us hope', we are told; 'to doubt is to rebel: / Let us exalt in hope, that all shall yet be well' (I.xlix). Edwin's story is interrupted in midstream, as Beattie never finished his plan to have Edwin take up a more formal minstrelsy and engage in military service.[5] Nonetheless, we see enough to understand the nature of his 'progress': a wise hermit appears to take the place of the beldam and to tell Edwin that 'Reason ... learns, from facts compared, the laws to trace, / Whose long progression leads to Deity' (II.xlvi). In short, *The Minstrel* is a story of personal and political redemption, where a mildly prodigal youth is trained into a reasoned, devout adulthood. In the shape of that story lies its attractiveness to a British audience terrified of French invasion – as well as its more specific attractiveness to a Wordsworth interested in presenting his early, more radical poetry as part of just such a narrative.

The progress of Wordsworth's genius: making a proper modern minstrel

In 1838, in a playful pseudonymous letter to Christopher North in *Blackwood's Edinburgh Magazine*, Charles Neaves indicated the extent of Wordsworth's connection to Beattie by suggesting that Wordsworth had committed a kind of plagiarism. Neaves's letter suggests that Wordsworth had invited the 'censure of imitation' by borrowing many elements of *The Excursion* (1814) from *The Minstrel*. *The Excursion*, says Neaves, 'is not the first time that the development of intellect and imagination in an humble mountain boy has been made the subject of poetry'. He then catalogs points of resemblance between the poems:

> So closely has the idea of [Beattie's hero] Edwin been followed by Mr. Wordsworth ... [that] the two stories coincide in almost every particular. The country, Scotland – the locality, a mountainous district – the youth's profession, pastoral – the forms of nature represented as the means of exciting and spiritualizing his mind – and the aim of it all to illustrate 'the pursuit of knowledge under difficulties' ... [T]he Excursion is, in its general plan, a vindication of those very principles of hope and faith which Beattie so well inculcated in his Minstrel, before a French Revolution had occurred to frighten him into them ... (512–14)

Similarities between *The Minstrel* and *The Excursion* have also attracted the notice of modern scholars, who use them to argue for Beattie's importance in establishing what would become the conventions of Romantic autobiography. In Everard King's words, '*The Minstrel* indicated to Wordsworth the possibility of new concepts and new directions in poetry' (107). Such claims of influence, however, do not fully account for the nature or effect of Wordsworth's borrowings from Beattie, such as the fact that, as Neaves implies, Wordsworth borrowed from Beattie's poetry mainly when he came closer to sharing Beattie's politics. More than a case of simple influence and appropriation, Wordsworth's use of Beattie's work in *The Excursion* tells us about Romantic autobiography's roots in the literature and cultural politics of the middle Regency, especially how Wordsworth then positioned himself as the politically palatable foil to Byron.

To understand Wordsworth's self-fashioning in this period, we need first to see the extent to which reviewers addressed his poetry through the lens of his prose. The sympathetic reviewers of Wordsworth's works of 1814 and 1815 – most of them, that is, with the exceptions of Francis Jeffrey in the *Edinburgh Review* and John Herman Merivale in the *Monthly Review* – work on the poems with the tools that Wordsworth affords them. Those critics repeatedly structure arguments by ceding to Wordsworth the right to frame their responses: as the *British Critic* put it in 1815,

> Since [Wordsworth's] poetry is the shadow of his philosophy…its interest depends in a great measure on a right understanding of the process which formed it. But there are few who have music enough in their souls to unravel for themselves his abstruser harmonies: only let him sound the key-note, and the apparent confusion will vanish: let him make his tones well understood, and they will be to every ear delightful, to every soul elevating… (450)

The *Augustan Review* went so far in admiring Wordsworth's commentary on his poetry as to suggest that if Wordsworth would 'addict himself to good plain prose, his unceasing benevolence, and his turn of thought always so moral and religious, might render him a highly respectable essayist' (356). Many reviewers were willing to read past the subtleties of the poem's religious dialogues and accept Wordsworth as an ally of faith in general; an 'emphasis on a kind of religious note, however theologically unorthodox it might be, is an increasingly important dimension of the critical reception of *The Excursion*' (Mahoney 17–18).

It is well known that Wordsworth was turning to more religious verse at this time – *The Excursion* was 'his most evidently religious poem so far' (Gill 295) – and we have already noticed the striking debts of *The Excursion*, the poem that in many ways revived Wordsworth's reputation, to Beattie's *Minstrel*.[6] I propose additionally that Wordsworth turned strategically to Beattie's *Minstrel* in 1814 because the earlier poem provided him a ready-made cultural icon representing the cultural narrative he needed to construct: that of a poet moving beyond youthful exuberance to arrive at a mature dedication to God and country. In his treatment of the two poems quoted above, Neaves focuses on Beattie's prescience in describing the disenchantment of revolutionary sympathizers: 'the *Excursion* is, in its general plan, a vindication of those very principles of hope and faith which Beattie so well inculcated in his *Minstrel*, before a French Revolution had occurred to frighten him into them'. Neaves playfully overstates his case for effect, as *The Excursion* is hardly a simple recasting of *The Minstrel*, but the graver misrepresentation is one of tone rather than fact.

Rather than attempting a secret plagiarism, Wordsworth had deployed the conventions of *The Minstrel* to signal his own shift to something like Beattie's politics. Wordsworth even calls the semi-autobiographical Wanderer of *The Excursion* a 'lone enthusiast' (I.348), using the phrase that Beattie applied to Edwin and that friends applied to Beattie. And as Kenneth Johnston has noted, when the Wanderer 'represent[s] himself as "singled out . . . from a swarm of rosy boys . . . For my grave looks, too thoughtful for my years," he [is] adapting Beattie's words for Edwin' (*Hidden* 85). In accusing Wordsworth of borrowing from Beattie, Neaves catches a fugitive pleading to be caught.

In fact, *The Excursion's* relationship to minstrelsy goes well beyond its allusions to Beattie and *The Minstrel*. The opening of *The Excursion's* second book introduces the ancient minstrel as a prosperous wanderer opposed to his poorer modern counterpart: 'In days of yore how fortunately fared / The Minstrel!' (51), it begins, and then describes the ancient minstrel's prosperity. The mood changes quickly:

> Yet not the noblest of that honoured Race
> Drew happier, loftier, more impassioned thoughts
> From his long journeyings and eventful life,
> Than this obscure Itinerant [the Wanderer] (an obscure,
> But a high-souled and tender-hearted Man)
> Had skill to draw from many a ramble, far
> And wide protracted, through the tamer ground
> Of these our unimaginative days . . .

> What wonder, then, if I, whose favourite school
> Hath been the fields, the roads, and rural lanes,
> And pathways winding on from farm to farm,
> Looked on this guide with reverential love? (52)

The Wanderer later reinforces this message with a frontal attack on minstrelsy's tendency to celebrate wartime exploits rather than '[t]he good Man's deeds and purposes' in rural life:

> Noise is there not enough in doleful war –
> But that the heaven-born Poet must stand forth
> And lend the echoes of his sacred shell,
> To multiply and aggravate the din?
> Pangs are there not enough in hopeless love –
> And, in requited passion, all too much
> Of turbulence, anxiety, and fear –
> But that the Minstrel of the rural shade
> Must tune his pipe, insidiously to nurse
> The perturbation in the suffering breast
> And propagate its kind, where'er he may?
> – Ah who (and with such a rapture as befits
> The hallowed theme) will rise and celebrate
> The good Man's deeds and purposes; retrace
> His struggles, his discomfiture deplore,
> His triumphs hail, and glorify his end? (326–7)

Here, as in *The White Doe*, Wordsworth invokes the conventions of minstrel writing only to point his readers to a contrast: he marks Scott's brand of historical minstrelsy as an activity beyond the purview of his own poetic approach. As King has noted, Wordsworth, following Beattie's lead, 'rejects the "romantic" minstrel as the proper image of a modern bard and looks instead to a "poor villager" for inspiration' (99).

Even in *The White Doe*, where Wordsworth takes up the subject matter and form of historical verse romance, he does so to display his separation from the conventions of minstrel writing, to the extent that Geoffrey Hartman could call the poem 'still a lyrical ballad' (324). The battles and confrontation one might see in Scott's romances largely take place off-stage. The multitude of different historical perspectives *The White Doe* presents (Wordsworth in 1815, Wordsworth in 1807, the 'Rising of the North' in 1569, the ascension of Elizabeth in 1558, the implied edict of Henry VIII that destroyed Catholic abbeys, the War of the Roses, and others) breaks political and military history into series of fleeting images and fragments of stories. Wordsworth's notes replace that history with a narrative of the development of the landscape itself, dating its alterations and leading the reader from the time of the story back to Regency England: one note recalls Wordsworth's *Guide to the Lakes* (1810) by saying, 'I cannot conclude without recommending to the notice of all lovers of beautiful scenery – Bolton Abbey and its neighborhood' (164).

In fact, Wordsworth portrays the minstrelsy of Scott's historical romances as he does the life of the city in some other poems; that is, minstrelsy participates in the clamor of public life, away from which the writer finds the true stuff of poetry. The opening of *The White Doe's* second canto, for instance, describes something like a scene of minstrelsy, with characters singing to a harp, but in keeping with Wordsworth's poetics, the reader encounters only the narrator's second-hand description of the song, not (as in Scott or Byron) an inset poem of the song itself. And when fighters leave to enter the 'din of arms and minstrelsy' (II.417), the poem lingers to learn the thoughts of those left behind. As Theresa Kelley notes, 'Having hollowed out the sublime, heroic center of this Scottish romance, Wordsworth creates a space which the beautiful gradually inhabits' (152). To move away from 'the sublime, heroic center' of the romance is precisely to break the analogy between the poet and the minstrel.

The last of Wordsworth's major works of 1814–15, the 1815 *Poems*, uses more subtle means to align the poet with Beattie's minstrel myth, and it goes beyond the telling anecdotal engagement with minstrelsy in *The Excursion* and *The White Doe* to theorize Wordsworth's opposition to minstrel writing more fully. The Preface to the *Poems* creates a developmental narrative along the lines of Edwin's 'progress' to explain the relationship between Wordsworth's early and later works. While many reviewers accepted Wordsworth's prefatory premises, some did not. Merivale in the *Monthly Review*, for one, scoffed at the new collection being 'scientifically distributed by the author into classes' (225), contending that

> In a preface to the 'Poems' before us, which is not remarkable for clearness of idea nor for humility of tone, a fresh attempt is made to give that air of invention and novelty to Mr. W.'s writings which it seems to be his main object to claim ... We have here such a pompous classification of trifles, for the most part obvious and extremely childish, that we do not remember to have ever met with so 'Much Ado about Nothing' in any other author ... (225–6)[7]

But the ado is about something important, something that Merivale himself raises with this question concerning 'The Star-gazers': 'We are aware', he says, 'that we may be told by the admirers of Mr. Wordsworth that this is one of his *early* absurdities, and must not be brought forwards

[sic] as the test of his present improvement. Why, then, does he republish it?' (232, emphasis original).

One answer to that question is that Wordsworth republishes the poem, along with many other works, precisely to reveal them as early productions analogous to the songs and tales Beattie's Edwin hears in his youth. Like many of Wordsworth's poems, the Preface tells a story about Wordsworth's growth as a poet based on the collection's system of classification:

> the following Poems have been divided into classes; which, that the work may more obviously correspond with the course of human life, for the sake of exhibiting in it the three requisites of a whole, a beginning, a middle, and an end, have also been arranged, as far as it was possible, according to the order of time, commencing with Childhood, and terminating with Old Age, Death, and Immortality. (*Prose* III.28)

This story serves two functions: it positions his most radical published work such that his moralizing, philosophical poetry of 1815 becomes the end towards which his earlier works were tending. Moreover, it positions other writers of 1815, especially Scott and Byron, as mired in the gothicism and romance of Britain's national youth, and by extension minstrelsy, from which Wordsworth has emerged triumphantly mature.

The stakes of these developmental arguments become clearest in the 'Essay, Supplementary to the Preface' of the 1815 *Poems*, an extended attack on the judgement of poetry by its popularity that could hardly fail to call to mind Scott and Byron, Wordsworth's more marketable rivals. Here Wordsworth establishes a metaphorical maturity that does not correspond to chronological age; he speaks of readers who have grown old but not 'advanced in true discernment beyond the age of youth' (344). Shakespeare's work, by contrast, exemplifies a process of apparently various materials maturing into a coherent whole:

> that the judgement of Shakespeare in the selection of his materials, and in the manner in which he has made them, heterogeneous as they often are, constitute a unity of their own, and contribute all to one great end, is not less admirable than his imagination, his invention and his intuitive knowledge of human Nature! (352)

Having used the language of religious teleology ('one great end'), Wordsworth drops a strong hint at his own likeness to Shakespeare in this respect, characterizing Shakespeare's sonnets as a project anticipating Wordsworth's own: 'There is extant a small Volume of miscellaneous Poems in which Shakespeare expresses his own feelings in his own Person' (352). Using Shakespeare's 'own feelings in his own person' as a model of a larger unity encompassing even Shakespeare's 'miscellaneous' works helps Wordsworth seek to show, as James Chandler puts it, 'that what he did and wrote after the fall of Napoleon was continuous with what he did and wrote in his golden decade' (' "Wordsworth" after Waterloo' 98).

This identification with Shakespeare serves by contrast to exclude other writers. Though Wordsworth does not address his contemporaries directly, he pointedly omits Scott when praising Scotland for producing 'a Dunbar, a Buchanan, a Thomson, and a Burns' (365). And the increasingly scandalous Byron lurks in the culmination of the argument, where Wordsworth repeatedly likens the taste for inferior, popular poetry to the sexual appetites of youth – 'Men' pursue it 'as if urged by an appetite' (372) for its 'qualities which dazzle at first sight' (373). By the end, the opposition between popular and lasting poetry has become a deeply moral issue of the opposition between 'vicious poetry' (373) and the human share in 'divine infallibility' (374). The essay as a whole extends Wordsworth's claim to having achieved an artistic and moral maturity that has eluded his contemporaries. It maps a narrative of the great author's reception onto what M. H. Abrams describes as the linked, redemptive trajectories of 'Christian history and Christian psycho-biography' (46).

In this context, we can see why it became useful to Wordsworth to turn to Beattie's precedent at this point in his career, though Beattie's relatively weak reputation as a poet made him more useful as an implicit counterpart to the avowed model of Shakespeare. Alluding to *The Minstrel* in *The Excursion* allowed Wordsworth to invoke a celebrated, impeccably orthodox poet who had endorsed a similar kind of development. The subtlety of the allusions and references to Beattie's work enabled Wordsworth to make the connection while still claiming to follow the examples of only the greatest poets. Edwin's early training in, and affinity for, overly gothic and sentimental poetry provided a pre-existing myth through which Wordsworth could portray his own early work as a natural stage in his artistic and political development. Wordsworth aligned himself with Edwin so thoroughly, in fact, that one modern critic has taken Beattie's work as a kind of biography, before the fact, of Wordsworth: '*The Minstrel* is a prime source of information about the nature and scope of Wordsworth's early experiences, for...the poem captures the essence of the poetic life in the making' (King 62). Though obviously an extraordinary claim, this idea reveals the enduring effectiveness of Wordsworth's project in 1814 and 1815: by means of *The Minstrel*, he naturalized his potentially embarrassing youth into something appropriate or even *essential* to the mature poet: his youth became 'the essence of the poetic life in the making'.[8]

In other words, Wordsworth describes his own life, via Beattie, in ways that persuade his readers and critics to understand his lack of market success as a sign of artistic excellence. The 'game of "loser wins"' (*Field* 39) that Pierre Bourdieu describes as controlling the cultural field had not yet become a settled convention, but Wordsworth explains the rules of such a game and the promise of symbolic capital for his supporters, the 'disinterested investors' (Bourdieu *Field* 101) who would recognize the value of the Wordsworthian project before it enjoyed its afterlife of popular recognition. In fact, one way to appreciate the virtuosity of Wordsworth's cultural performance in this period – a performance largely separate from the complexity and craft of the poems – is to note how thoroughly Wordsworth capitalizes on what Bourdieu would identify as the structuring metaphors of the artistic sector, 'in which success is suspect and asceticism in this world is the precondition for salvation in the next' (*Field* 101). As Bourdieu explains in terms precisely applicable to Wordsworth, the artistic and popular spheres present 'two different ways in which firms, producers and products *grow old*' (*Field* 104, emphasis original). Connecting these metaphors of salvation and maturation, Wordsworth presented a map of his own cultural field that not only claimed a place for himself but also turned the popular success of Byron and Scott against them: loser wins, winners lose.

Taking Wordsworth's cue, sympathetic reviewers could endorse his sense of triumphant teleology as something that separated him from other poets of the day. In *Blackwood's*, for the most important instance, John Wilson used the opportunity of reviewing *The White Doe* in 1818 to comment on the Lake School. The essay identifies the three central poetic geniuses of its time as Wordsworth, Byron, and Scott, 'who may be said to rule, each by a legitimate sovereignty, over separate and powerful provinces in the kingdom of Mind' (369). These provinces may be separate, Wilson argues, but they are not equal. He prefers Wordsworth, who differs from Byron in being a 'Philosopher' as well as a Poet, as supported by the fact that

> His faith is unshaken in the prevalence of virtue over vice, and of happiness over misery; and in the existence of heavenly law operating on earth, and, in spite of transitory defeats, always visibly triumphant in the grand field of human warfare. (371)

That is Beattie's teleology, and Wordsworth enabled reviewers to make it his own as well; Wilson's support at this time was an important part of Wordsworth's rise in reputation. It must be noted that at its best, Wordsworth's poetry always complicated such simple teleologies, to the point where Jonathan Arac can persuasively argue through *The Prelude* that Wordsworth means to tell his reader, 'let the interruption be the end; overlook nothing that comes athwart your path. Such dislocations from the expected circuit are the true reward' (63). But that sentiment is, at most, subtly understated in the prose works of this middle period and entirely absent from the reviews that argued for their importance.

The negative reviews, too, reflect the cultural importance of Wordsworth's metaphors of maturation. It is no coincidence that Wilson presents the voice of *Blackwood's* as fulfilling a redemptive teleology for Wordsworth against the earthly, biased efforts of the Whiggish Francis Jeffrey in the *Edinburgh Review*. Jeffrey's attacks on Wordsworth repeatedly attempted to undermine precisely the model of benevolent teleology that *Blackwood's* found so attractive. *Blackwood's* is correct, in a way, to say that 'scarcely one syllable of truth – that is, of knowledge – has ever appeared in the Edinburgh Review on the general principles of Wordsworth's Poetry' (371). Indeed, Jeffrey only brings up those 'general principles' set forth in Wordsworth's prose apparatuses in order to speculate whether each new poem will finally prove that Wordsworth's system will not eventually triumph. The famous 'This will never do' (1) that opens Jeffrey's 1815 review of *The Excursion* is more than an idiomatic expression of strong disapproval; it is also one in a series of Jeffrey's direct challenges to Wordsworth's claim that future audiences will vindicate his approach. This, says Jeffrey, will *never* do, no matter how long Wordsworth insists on the teleology that allows him to ignore the trials of the short term.

The increasingly powerful Tory reviews could disprove Jeffrey's attacks on Wordsworth by throwing their full weight behind effecting the very change in public opinion that Jeffrey claimed was impossible. Wordsworth's rise to fame became a public demonstration that faith and patience in the face of suffering would be rewarded in the end. The Wanderer of *The Excursion* portrays this belief in the extreme terms to counter the skeptical Solitary's pessimism: 'I wait – in hope / To see the moment, when the righteous Cause / Shall gain Defenders zealous and devout / As They who have opposed her' (155). (Recall Beattie, a prototype of the Wanderer: 'Let us exalt in hope, that all shall yet be well.') Wordsworth's narrative of his own reception became tied to the new teleology he had created for his work; the notion of a redemptive afterlife for human beings became intertwined with that of a redemptive 'afterlife' for Wordsworth's poetry.[9] Wordsworth therefore became doubly useful to reviewers who wanted to resist Byron's skepticism and immediate popularity; through Beattie, Wordsworth established the link between poetic and religious afterlife that Byron would resist in *Don Juan*.

Byron's minstrelsies

Whereas Wordsworth sought to engage the content of minstrel writing only to persuade his readers to abandon the minstrel metaphor, Byron inhabited the minstrel mode by exploring and transgressing its limits. The customary semi-autobiographical personae of the minstrel writer became in Byron's works a profusion of masks, a means of serious play by which author, minstrel, and man reveal themselves as overlapping modes of performance. Byron also engaged Beattie's odd presentation of a minstrel who does not perform minstrelsy, though for reasons nearly opposite to Wordsworth's.

Byron's earliest published works prefigure his interest in and resistance to minstrel writing. *Hours of Idleness* (1807) reveals a persistent concern with the romantic Highlands as the subject of poetry, particularly in the Ossianic productions of James Macpherson. 'The Death of Calmar and Orla, an Imitation of Macpherson's "Ossian"', a close mimicry of Macpherson's content and style, includes Byron's telling note:

> I fear Laing's late edition has completely overthrown every hope that Macpherson's Ossian might prove the translation of a series of poems complete in themselves; but, while the imposture is discovered, the merit of the work remains undisputed, though not without faults – particularly, in some parts, turgid and bombastic diction. – The present humble imitation will be pardoned by the admirers of the original as an attempt, however inferior, which evinces an attachment to their favourite author. (*CPW* I.375)

We can plausibly imagine that Macpherson's Ossian became more interesting to Byron because of, not in spite of, the fact that 'the imposture [was] discovered'. The Ossian that Byron borrows here is an acknowledged mask. The character is Ossian and not Ossian, Macpherson and not Macpherson, an imitation of a translation of a vanished original. The voice of Byron's poem is at once Ossian's, Macpherson's, and Byron's – an anticipation of later works such as 'The Isles of Greece' in *Don Juan*, sung by the mercenary poet whose voice is his own, Southey's, and Byron's, according to the turns of the reader's perception.[10] That is, Byron's interest in Ossian is less a bardophilic exploration of the past than an experiment in the latter-day minstrel's self-conscious adaptations of that tradition.

Contrarily, the limits of Byron's engagement with minstrelsy become clear in *English Bards and Scotch Reviewers* (1809), which attacks the minstrel pose of Walter Scott: 'And thou, too, Scott! resign to minstrels rude / The wilder Slogan of a Border feud: / Let others spin their meagre lines for hire; / Enough for Genius, if itself inspire!' (*CPW* I.257). Byron draws a line between his own interest in the performative flexibility of minstrel writing and Scott's self-fashioning as a modern minstrel occupying a place of respectable service to powerful families and Tory governing interests. In his attack on Scott, Byron conflates the mode of minstrel writing with what he sees as the unwelcome dependence of Scott's minstrel personae. Byron's would always be a lordly minstrelsy.

Despite his resistance to Scott's deployment of minstrelsy, Byron had good reasons to return to the minstrel mode, chief among them what Jerome McGann calls his poetry's 'preoccupation with the social structure of its rhetoric':

> This preoccupation appears frequently as a problem in Byron's verse which can be phrased, in simple terms, in the following way: a writer must have an audience and hence must operate with certain specific sets of audience expectation, need, and desire (which will be more or less explicit or inchoate); at the same time, the writer cannot merely attend upon and serve audience. Rather, the audience's social character must be reflected back to itself so that it can 'reflect upon' that reflection in a critical and illuminating way. (*Byron and Romanticism* 38)

Based on the staging of poets and audiences, minstrel writing is extraordinarily well adapted to this project – or, to shift the emphasis slightly, many of the ways Byron's poetry creates 'the social structure of its rhetoric' arise from the presentations of minstrelsy by writers including Moore, Scott, and Staël. This is true especially in his earlier works.

As early as 1809, Byron had begun to develop an ambivalence about minstrel writing that created a challenge for his later poetry: that of fashioning a kind of minstrel writing that exploited its extraordinary capacity for playful self-representation without also activating the personal and political associations of the mode as it was presented by Scott, its most visible practitioner. The first canto of *Childe Harold's Pilgrimage* is, among many other things, an attempt to meet that challenge.

'nor fix'd as yet the goal': Beattie's minstrelsy and *Childe Harold's Pilgrimage* Canto I

One persistent issue in modern criticism of Canto I of *Childe Harold's Pilgrimage* has been Byron's use of archaic language obviously inappropriate to the contemporary action of the plot. As Andrew Rutherford points out, 'Byron cannot justify his archaisms as Beattie does his occasional use of "old words" in *The Minstrel*, by saying they are appropriate to his subject, for Childe Harold, though referred to as a pilgrim, is a contemporary figure, and there is no point in using pseudo-medieval jargon to explain his actions' (26–7). Jerome McGann counters in *Fiery Dust* that the archaisms provide insight into 'the narrator's self-consciousness: a tension is set up in the early stanzas of the poem between the narrator's use of his artificial Spenserian diction and his more normal declamatory-meditative-conversation language' (56). While my reading of the passage accords more with McGann's sympathetic assessment, I wish to return to Rutherford's initial comparison to Beattie's use of 'old words' in *The Minstrel*. In my view, Beattie's archaisms are the basis of a sophisticated joke Byron means to tell with the archaisms of *Childe Harold* I, a joke that explains much of Byron's early participation in the minstrel mode.

Byron's preface draws on Beattie's authority but also preserves the potential for ironic distance between the poets. The relevant paragraph reads in full:

The stanza of Spenser, according to one of our most successful poets, admits of every variety. Dr Beattie makes the following observation: 'Not long ago I began a poem in the style and stanza of Spenser, in which I propose to give full scope to my inclination, and be either droll or pathetic, descriptive or sentimental, tender or satirical, as the humour strikes me; for, if I mistake not, the measure which I have adopted admits equally of all these kinds of composition.' – Strengthened in my opinion by such authority, and by the example of some of the highest order of Italian poets, I shall make no apology for the attempts at similar variations in the following composition; satisfied that, if they are unsuccessful, their failure must be in the execution, rather than the design sanctioned by the practice of Ariosto, Thomson, and Beattie. (*CPW* II.4–5)

Byron's invocation of Beattie has been taken as praising 'Beattie's facility with the stanza' (King 165), but Byron's comment does not judge Beattie's poetry. His praise, if praise it be, rather concerns Beattie's cultural position: Beattie is 'successful', a man whose 'authority' can 'sanction[ ]' a new work.[11] These terms reflect the reading public's opinion, leaving Byron's critical evaluation an open question. In fact, *The Minstrel* in many ways becomes the target of the first canto's satire, as Byron comically imitates the eccentricities of Beattie's work to produce a modern, skeptical minstrelsy.

Apprehending the oddities of *The Minstrel* is crucial to understanding Byron's response. As Rutherford notes, Beattie had carefully justified his 'old words' in the preface of *The Minstrel*:

> All antiquated expressions I have studiously avoided; admitting however some old words, where they seemed peculiarly to suit the subject: but I hope none will be found that are now obsolete, or in any degree unintelligible to a reader of English poetry. (vi)

As Beattie's commitment to making Edwin a practicing minstrel faded, however, so did his commitment to keeping his poem in the past. The poem's ending – where the ostensibly ancient narrator suddenly mourns the death of Beattie's mentor John Gregory – completely dispels the fiction of the past-tense setting. The result is a poem whose very theme is 'progress' but which, in content and diction, implies a bizarrely self-contradictory chronology. In other words, like *Childe Harold's Pilgrimage* but without the later poem's ironic self-awareness, *The Minstrel* employs archaic language for reasons that evaporate as the reader becomes aware of the poem's contemporary autobiographical function. Byron's explanation for his 'old words' makes little sense when taken unironically because it is, among other things, a comic imitation of Beattie's own inconsistency.[12]

But this is not simply a joke at Beattie's expense. Rather, it is part of a larger exploration of time and progress in which Byron uses two additional reference points: Beattie's aborted project of describing the 'progress of genius' and Walter Scott's more recent historicizing of the minstrel mode. When Byron deploys Beattie's and Scott's conventions, he does so to undermine their constructions of border disputes, of narrative teleologies, and of the events of the Napoleonic Wars. In his third stanza, for instance, Byron describes the spotted lineage of his hero:

> Childe Harold was he hight: – but whence his name
> And lineage long, it suits me not to say;
> Suffice it, that perchance they were of fame,
> And had been glorious in another day:
> But one sad losel soils a name for aye,
> However mighty in the olden time;
> Nor all that heralds rake from coffin'd clay,
> Nor florid prose, nor honied lines of rhyme
> Can blazon evil deeds, or consecrate a crime. (I.3)[13]

Whereas Scott's commercial progressivism relies on enjoying the romance of a tightly sealed past, Byron's narrator refuses to separate past from present judgements, and he enacts that refusal with Beattie's mix of Spenserian and modern language. Byron's portrayal of Harold's improvised destination ('nor fix'd as yet the goal / Where he shall rest him on his pilgrimage' [I.28]) is the territorial analog to what Phillip Martin calls the poem's 'broad historical vision, which recognises the competing claim of the immediate and the contemporary within the great span of time and the judgements of the future' (84). The needlessly archaic diction of the passage reinforces its skepticism about poets' romanticizing of great families – the celebration of noble families being, of course, a chief function of the minstrel.

That is, by undermining the notion of pilgrimage itself, with all its religious and literary associations, Byron seeks also to undermine Beattie's sense of a national and religious journey to an assured happy ending, evident in passages such as this from *The Minstrel*:

> One part, one little part, we dimly scan
> Through the dark medium of life's feverish dream;
> Yet dare arraign the whole stupendous plan,
> If but that little part incongruous seem.
> Nor is that part perhaps what mortals deem;
> Oft from apparent ill our blessings rise.
> O, then, renounce that impious self-esteem,

> That aims to trace the secrets of the skies:
> For thou art but of dust; be humble, and be wise.
>
> Thus Heaven enlarged his soul in riper years. (I.lii–liii)

When Beattie offers this optimism in the narrator's voice, then shifts it to Edwin's 'riper years', we see again the merging of biographical and sacred teleology that Byron seeks to ironize. Byron stands Beattie's rhetoric on its head, moving from the 'whole stupendous plan' of Beattie's religion to a figure for the lack of such a plan – the aimlessness of a pilgrimage with no goal.

When Byron seeks to develop the political implications of his anti-teleological minstrelsy, however, he turns to the more explicitly political minstrelsy of his contemporary, Scott. One of Scott's crucial myths is that of England and Scotland, battling over an arbitrary border, growing into a mutually beneficial modern partnership. This notion allows Byron to link Scott's political teleology to Beattie's myths of personal and theological maturation. Scott's border wars are analogous to the minstrel's younger days in Beattie's myth of individual progress; they are the romantic youth of the British nation. Byron responds to Scott's myth by displacing the drawing and erasing of borders onto the Continent. When Harold arrives at the border between Spain and Portugal, he notes that only a small stream 'the rival realms divide[s]' (I.32). Where Scott had introduced border scenes to note the physical and psychological similarities of Scots and Southrons, however, Byron points to a psychological border that enforces national distinctions more strongly than a topographical landmark: 'Well doth the Spanish hind the difference know / 'Twixt him and Lusian slave, the lowest of the low' (I.33).

Byron's subsequent description of the battle at Talavera extends this logic to erase Scott's most important boundary, that between Britain and France. At Byron's Talavera, '[t]hree hosts combine', and an observer's perspective cannot discriminate among French, British, and Spanish soldiers:

> Three hosts combine to offer sacrifice;
> Three tongues prefer strange orisons on high;
> Three gaudy standards flout the pale blue skies;
> The shouts are France, Spain, Albion, Victory!
> The foe, the victim, and the fond ally

> That fights for all, but ever fights in vain,
> Are met – as if at home they could not die –
> To feed the crow on Talavera's plain,
> And fertilize the field that each pretends to gain. (I.41)

Scott had blurred the border of England and Scotland to reinforce a line between Britons and the French, but Byron describes a deep psychological border between Spain and Portugal, allowing war to overwhelm Scott's line. In McGann's words, '[w]ar, martial glory, Spain, France, and England all weigh equally (or nearly so) in the balance of his equivocal mind' (*Fiery Dust* 53). Two stanzas later, Byron takes one more step and attacks the effectiveness of martial minstrelsy itself, apostrophizing the soldiers of Albuera:

> Till others fall where other chieftains lead
> Thy name shall circle round the gaping throng,
> And shine in worthless lays, the theme of transient song! (I.43)

After undermining many of minstrelsy's conventions, Byron redeploys Scott's language of 'chieftains' and 'lays' to devalue martial minstrelsy. Here the stakes of the joke on Beattie's archaisms are clearest: the celebratory minstrelsy of the past is not a means by which military sacrifice becomes heroism. Instead, an unending series of 'worthless lays' collapse past into present, producing not permanent fame but a permanently self-serving machine of 'transient' military celebrations.

Later, Byron took an opportunity to extend this critique of antiquarians' romanticizing minstrelsy. Following the early reception of *Childe Harold* I (and II, with which it was published), including predictable criticism for portraying an immoral hero, Byron responded with an 'Addition to the Preface' that defends Harold against charges 'that besides the anachronism, he is very *unknightly*, as the times of the Knights were times of love, honour, and so forth' (*CPW* II.5). In his new comments, Byron sets aside the straightforward answer to such criticism – that Childe Harold is not a medieval knight – and gleefully debunks the idealized chivalry on which the criticism is based. Byron's response reads, in part,

> Now it so happens that the good old times, when 'l'amour du bon vieux temps, l'ámour antique' flourished, were the most profligate of all possible centuries. Those who have any doubts upon this subject may consult St Palaye, *passim*, and more particularly vol. ii. page 69.

> The vows of chivalry were no better kept than any other vows what-
> soever, and the songs of the Troubadours were not more decent, and
> certainly were much less refined, than those of Ovid...Whatever
> other objection may be urged to that most unamiable personage
> Childe Harold, he was so far perfectly knightly in his attributes ... – If
> the story of the institution of the 'Garter' be not a fable, the knights
> of that order have for several centuries borne the badge of a Countess
> of Salisbury, of indifferent memory. So much for chivalry. Burke need
> not have regretted that its days are over, though Maria Antoinette
> was quite as chaste as most of those in whose honours lances were
> shivered, and knights unhorsed. (*CPW* II.5–6)

This passage participates in the established tradition of countering conservative myths of British minstrelsy by invoking French troubadours, as
had Sydney Owenson and others. Byron, however, moves beyond those
earlier efforts by emphasizing the sexuality of troubadour songs and
alluding to Burke's regard for chivalry. With his characteristic light touch,
Byron connects chivalric minstrelsy to political and sexual naïveté. The
popularity of *Childe Harold's Pilgrimage* made it a more powerful plat-
form for Byron's position than, for example, Owenson's *Novice of Saint
Dominick* had been for her.

We can perhaps see the impact of Byron's comments in the anonymous
'Critical Observations' to the 1816 edition of *The Minstrel*, excerpts of
which were quoted above. For the writer of the 'Observations', Byron's
sense of the troubadour has entirely overtaken Beattie's notion of the
'sacred' minstrel. Quoting Beattie's intention 'to trace the progress of a
Poetical Genius, born in a rude age...till that period at which he may be
supposed capable of appearing in the world as a MINSTREL' (6), the writer
responds:

> We know not what advantage Dr. Beattie promised to himself in
> investing the ideal person of this EDWIN with the obsolete profession
> of the Troubadour, unless he proposed to employ him subsequently
> in that character, for some dramatic or moral purpose. The historical
> character of the Troubadour is, in all its essential features, utterly at
> variance with that of the ideal Minstrel...(6)

Even after quoting Beattie's description of his minstrel, the writer leaps
immediately to substitute 'Troubadour' for 'minstrel' and to use Byron's
logic in declaring his or her suspicion of that 'character'. Whether or

not the writer had Byron in mind, we see here that Beattie's legacy is suddenly complicated by a new concern with troubadour morality.

The writer goes on to defend Beattie by completing Beattie's own movement away from historical minstrelsy and suggesting a Wordsworthian reading of the poem. Here the figure of the minstrel is not simply neglected but actively rejected in favor of an allegorical reading that looks at the poem 'philosophically':

> We are inclined to view THE MINSTREL rather as a natural and beautiful allegory, in which the progressive development of the imagination and of the reasoning powers in a mind of native genius and sensibility, together with the influence of natural scenery and of solitude upon the heart, is philosophically illustrated. (6)

Though a minor document, the 'Observations' provide a microcosmic view of larger movements in Regency writing. Perhaps the end of the war lessened the need for historical minstrelsy in Scott's style. Perhaps Byron's skeptical internationalism made the fictions of minstrelsy difficult to sustain without irony, so writers began, in this critic's words, to translate historical minstrelsy into 'a natural and beautiful allegory'. In any event, as we shall see in Chapters 5 and 6, minstrel writing after *Childe Harold's Pilgrimage* I and II began to portray minstrels of many nations, to display an ironic awareness of its own conventionality, and to address the modern phenomenon of minstrel writing as a professional trade.

The Giaour, improvisation, and Byron's minstrel modes

In *The Giaour* (1813), Byron made a more original contribution to the minstrel mode with a largely unprecedented use of a minstrel narrator. As is often the case with *The Giaour*, this point is based on the poem's unusual textual history. Whereas Byron built *Childe Harold's Pilgrimage* and *Don Juan* largely by adding new segments to the end of an existing structure, he built *The Giaour* by interspersing new sections throughout the length of the poem. In 1813, Byron first published *The Giaour* as a poem of 684 lines, then added more lines to the next six editions until the wildly popular 'snake of a poem', as he called it (Marchand I.408), reached its full length of 1334 lines in its seventh edition later the same year.

Critics of *The Giaour*, from the earliest to the most recent, have for the most part accounted for the poem's expansion in one of two ways. Some surmise that Byron expanded the poem in order to sell more copies, offering products like a modern software company – a *Giaour* 3.0 with new features to attract the owners of *The Giaour* 2.1. More sympathetic critics simply treat the seventh edition as the authoritative version, the endpoint to which the earlier versions always tended. Scott Simpkins, for one contemporary example, says that the poem at that point 'had everything it needed' and thus finally fit into Byron's 'apparent overall plan' (204). Most critics do not state this view so directly; they imply it, however, by making passing mention (or no mention) of Byron's changes to the text and then speaking of its final incarnation as '*The Giaour*'. Jerome McGann has challenged this teleological approach to the poem in his *Critique of Modern Textual Criticism* by describing the difficulties of locating textual authority in conflicting versions of the developing poem.[14] McGann's insight allows a new way of reading *The Giaour* as a poem that grew and changed as Byron saw the responses of the poem's readers. Like Corinne at the Capitol – a model Byron seems often to have kept in mind – Byron could improvise, taking new information into account as he added to his poem. In fact, the poem itself begins to reflect on that process in Byron's later additions; in the process, *The Giaour* becomes a text about its own textuality, with layers of reading and perception building on each other as the poem neared its final state.

The poem's connection to minstrelsy begins with a note that Byron included even in its first and shortest edition. This note, which comes almost at the end of the poem, describes the source of the tale as a contemporary eastern minstrel:

> The story in the text is one told of a young Venetian many years ago, and now nearly forgotten. – I heard it by accident recited by one of the coffee-house story-tellers who abound in the Levant, and sing or recite their narratives. – The additions and interpolations by the translator will be easily distinguished from the rest by the want of Eastern imagery; and I regret that my memory has retained so few fragments of the original. (*CPW* III.423)

This account echoes myths of last minstrels, as it attributes the story to a dying oral tradition that he remembers only imperfectly. Byron even refers to himself as the 'translator' of the tale rather than its author – as James Macpherson had with his Ossian, Thomas Moore with the Thomas Little poems, and Samuel Rogers with *The Voyage of Columbus*.[15]

The assurance that the reader will 'easily' tell what parts of the tale come from the 'coffee-house story-teller' must be at least partly disingenuous. Unraveling the narrative voices of *The Giaour* and separating its component fragments has proved difficult even for careful critics, and to make matters still more complicated, the note appears only at the very end of the poem, where it would be useless in an unassisted first reading of the text.[16] In *Fiery Dust*, McGann proclaims this ballad singer 'the source of the work's final consistency precisely because he lets us know that he is assuming roles, that the poem is a virtuoso production' (144). As Byron expanded the poem, it became increasingly clear that the virtuosity of the ballad-singer was mostly or entirely of Byron's own making, which is to say, the poem took its place in the minstrel mode, being a representation of a minstrel performing for an audience – but with the performance displaced into a framing note.

The note takes minstrel writing's conventional semi-autobiographical personae to an extreme. The words of Byron the author become largely indistinguishable from those of the minstrel recounting a widely circulated oral tradition, in which the imperfect cultural memory of people in the Levant – the story is 'now nearly forgotten' – parallels Byron's own 'regret that [his] memory has retained so few fragments of the original'. The accretions of the poem render the note even more difficult to decipher, as many of the later textual additions introduce 'Eastern imagery' that Byron claims to be the signature of the Turkish storyteller. The multiplicity of authoritative variants that makes *The Giaour* such an editorial puzzle also served to create a shifting, impenetrable minstrel-persona lurking at the end of each growing edition. We see Byron and the Turkish minstrel-figure moving closer and closer together, approaching the point of full identification realized in the narrator of *Don Juan's* 'I feel the "Improvisatore"' (XV.20).

In the last major additions to *The Giaour*, those of the seventh edition, Byron added a telling image in the Giaour's description of Leila:

> She was a form of life and light –
> That seen – became a part of sight
> And rose – where'er I turned mine eye –
> The Morning-star of Memory! (*CPW* III.75)

Leila's 'form' creates a kind of improvisatory perception that reconstitutes not only 'Memory' but the very nature of 'sight' when she is 'seen'. The complexity of this image works much better than Byron's explicit note to explain the relationship between the poet and the Turkish story-teller. *The Giaour* in its growth shows '[t]he additions and interpolations by the translator', as Byron calls them, taking on the characteristics of the Turkish minstrel-figure. Rather than retaining a separate voice, the coffeehouse minstrel once perceived becomes a part of perception – once heard, a part of composition.[17]

In *Don Juan*, as mentioned above, the narrator's voice explicitly likens itself to an *improvvisatore*, and Byron's use of that figure has received a good deal of critical attention. Critics have documented the historical and literary sources of Byron's Italianate style, his specific interest in the *improvvisatore* Sgricci, and their respective implications for the 'desultory rhyme' of *Don Juan*.[18] The extended play with beginnings and endings in *Don Juan* and the use of the *improvvisatore* both extend Byron's earlier work that focused more narrowly on revising British minstrel writing. Where Wordsworth would excise the historical and martial content of minstrelsy, Byron could align himself with that side of minstrel writing, keeping his connection, as he put it in *Beppo*, with 'Men of the world, who know the world like men, / S[co]tt, R[oger]s, M[oo]re, and all the better brothers / Who think of something else besides the pen' (*CPW* IV.153, 1.602–4). After Childe Harold set down his harp, however, Byron abandoned straightforward presentations of minstrelsy, instead incorporating elements of the minstrel's, Turkish storyteller's, and *improvvisatore's* compositional styles into his narrative voices.

Endings: minstrelsy and teleology

I have proposed that Wordsworth and Byron debated a certain kind of political and religious optimism through their adaptations of James Beattie's cultural legacy and of the conventions of minstrel writing more generally.[19] Narrowly conceived, this exchange between the two poets illuminates a relatively minor point of literary history, the posthumous influence of Beattie on two later and greater poets. More broadly imagined, the exchange between Byron and Wordsworth connects to the more fundamental issues involved in writing public poetry during the Regency: the political question of whether society's aggrieved classes should rebel after the example of the French or bear their burdens with the patience of Edwin, the newly pressing question of the role of popularity in literary judgement, and the question of the fate of the human soul after death – the latter issue, of course, gaining new resonance with Beattie's death.

Byron understood the stakes of these issues as well as Wordsworth, and in *Don Juan*, Byron for the first time mustered a response as comprehensive as Wordsworth's set of arguments published in 1814 and 1815. Here Byron links Wordsworth's claim to posthumous glory and Christianity's promise of rewards in the afterlife in passages such as this one, which links skepticism about the two kinds of human afterlife:

> He that reserves his laurels for posterity
>   (Who does not often claim the bright reversion?)
> Has generally no great crop to spare it, he
>   Being only injured by his own assertion;
> And although here and there some glorious rarity
>   Arise, like Titan from the sea's immersion,
> The major part of such appellants go
> To – God knows where – for no one else can know. (Dedication 9)

To the linked ideas of literary, religious, and finally national happy endings, Byron opposes the wanderings of his hero and his narrator, who jokingly indulges in false ends and beginnings, likens himself to an 'Improvisatore', holds that 'the great *end* of travel ... is driving', and displays a self-assured skepticism about the ends of people, reputations, souls, and nations (IV.20, X.72). As McGann points out, in *Don Juan* 'the idea of a Divine Plan is itself represented as one of man's hypotheses' (Don Juan *in Context* 104), and Byron's Staëlian use of improvisation brings to the surface the improvisational principles underlying the internally accretive form of *The Giaour*.[20]

Byron weaves yet another thread into his argument with his ironic insistence that, in a formal sense, he is of the party of known endings and moral certainties:

> If any person should presume to assert
>   This story is not moral, first, I pray,
> That they will not cry out before they're hurt,
>   Then that they'll read it o'er again, and say,
> (But, doubtless, nobody will be so pert)
>   That this is not a moral tale, though gay;
> Besides, in canto twelfth, I mean to show,
> The very place where wicked people go. (I.207)

Of course, the wit of the passage in its original published form lies in Byron's having published only a fragment of his work, so readers have no access to the promised moral ending.[21] Byron confronts readers who judge literature by seeking endings that punish vice and reward virtue; to address *Don Juan*, they must respond to a tale without an ending.

This argument about endings – based in part on *The Minstrel*, itself a tale without its promised ending – is also an argument about beginnings, about childhood.[22] As we have seen, Wordsworth characterized the popular poetry of the day as work produced and consumed by metaphorical children. Byron responded to that characterization in the first canto of *Don Juan*, with the lovelorn hero's venture into nature that, as McGann writes, 'is a terribly witty attack upon Romantic Imagination and poetry, especially Wordsworth's poetry, as a fantasia of pubescent experience' (Don Juan *in Context* 119). Byron's attack is also a precise reversal of Wordsworth's own earlier attack on popular poetry 'as a fantasia of pubescent experience' at a time when readers could not fail to think of Byron as the time's leading icon of popular poetical success.

These mutual accusations of immaturity found a second life in Victorian critics' enduring preoccupation with Romanticism as a movement that never achieved a mature form. For Thomas Carlyle, as Andrew Elfenbein has noted, 'if Byron had been allowed to reach maturity, he would have accomplished great things. Since he did not, those who followed him, such as Carlyle, must achieve the greatness that he did not. In so doing, they would develop beyond Byron, whom they could associate with youthful immaturity' (94–5). And even for Matthew Arnold, who thought Wordsworth and Byron the greatest nineteenth-century English poets, the shortcomings of Romanticism resulted from a kind of prematurity: 'This was the grand error of the French Revolution; and its movement of ideas, by quitting the intellectual sphere and rushing furiously into the political sphere, ran, indeed, a prodigious and memorable course, but produced no such intellectual fruit as the movement of ideas of the Renaissance' (266). To an important degree, Romantic poetry gained lasting associations with youth, doubtless in large part because of the early deaths of many of its poets, but perhaps also because Wordsworth and Byron established relied so heavily on the trope of poetical immaturity while they lived.

Much of the poets' antagonism must have arisen from the underlying similarities of their undertakings, especially in the Regency. McGann writes of Byron's semi-autobiographical subjects that 'one has to read them – as Coleridge might have said – in terms of a "sameness with difference"' (*Byron and Romanticism* 106). And as noted above, David Simpson describes the protagonists of *The Excursion* in terms of their own 'sameness-in-difference' relative to Wordsworth. The poets shared a deep investment in sincerity balanced by explorations of dramatic masquerade, as well as a concern about the phenomenon of widely popular poetry that both associated with minstrelsy. As Byron puts it in a self-apostrophe in *Childe Harold's Pilgrimage* II, 'Soon shall thy voice be lost amid the throng / Of louder minstrels in these later days: / To such resign the strife for fading bays' (II.94). Even amid the poets' most intense antagonism, we can see in their Regency writings the underlying commonalities that signal Romanticism's extensive engagement with – and separation from – the minstrel mode.

5
The Minstrel Goes to Market: the Prizes and Contests of James Hogg, Letitia Elizabeth Landon, and Felicia Hemans

The natural desire of every man to engross to himself as much power and property as he can acquire by any of the means which might makes right, is accompanied by the no less natural desire of making known to as many people as possible the extent to which he has been a winner in this universal game. The successful warrior becomes a chief; the successful chief becomes a king: his next want is an organ to disseminate the fame of his achievements and the extent of his possessions; and this organ he finds in a bard, who is always ready to celebrate the strength of his arm, being first duly inspired by that of his liquor. This is the origin of poetry, which, like all other trades, takes its rise in the demand for the commodity, and flourishes in proportion to the extent of the market.

Thomas Love Peacock, *The Four Ages of Poetry* (4), 1820

Poetry, and the principle of the Self, of which Money is the visible incarnation, are the God and Mammon of the world.

Percy Bysshe Shelley (in response), *A Defence of Poetry* (*CW* VII.134), 1821

In his *Historical Memoirs of the Irish Bards* (1786), Joseph Cooper Walker equivocates as he speculates on the existence of ancient contests of bards or minstrels: 'We have good reason to believe, that the ancient Irish had MUSICAL CONTESTS; but, as we want the authority of history to support us, we will not venture to assert that they had' (98). Walker has more 'authority' to support a description of a modern contest, however, and he allows himself a long footnote on that subject. The note begins,

In the *Dublin Evening Post* of July, 1784, there appeared the following advertisement, which was re-published in July, 1785.

IRISH HARP.

To encourage the national music of Ireland, the following prizes will be given at Granard, on Monday the 1st of August next, to Performers on the Irish Harp, under the decision of Judges to be appointed by the Company then present.

> Seven Guineas to the best Performer
> Five ——— to the Second
> Three ——— to the Third
> Two ——— to the Fourth
>> Mr A. Burroughs,
>> Mr Connel,
>> Mr Edgeworth, Stewards.[1]

This advertisement naturally awakened my curiosity. (98)

Walker then reveals that the contest had been sponsored by a nationally-minded expatriate, a Mr Dungan from Granard, who had moved to Denmark. Mr Dungan's motive – to employ his fortune 'in charities to the country which gave him birth' – stems from Irish cultural nationalism, but his immediate inspiration is Scottish:

About two years since, he observed in an English paper, an account of a prize having been offered in Scotland to the best Player on the Highland Bagpipe. He was pleased with the idea, and immediately wrote to a friend in Ireland, empowering him to offer the parties specified in the above Advertisement, to the best performers on the Irish Harp. – The contest was held at the appointed time. The company was large and brilliant; but the performers were only *mediocre*, and the music common, and ill selected. (99, emphasis original)

Perhaps because news of previous *'mediocre'* performances had not reached him, Walker seems unaware that this was not the first Dungan-sponsored contest. The first had taken place in 1781, four years earlier (Tessier 2).

Walker, that is, saw one of a series of contests leading up to the more famous Belfast Harper's Festival of 1792, which was held in July to coincide with the anniversary of Bastille Day. In spite of occasional hints of nationalism in his own project – 'Nothing', he says in a note, 'can argue a greater insensibility to pure melody in the English, than their disrelish for Irish music' (91) – Walker's account of the Granard contest presents its international roots and specific economic incentives, both elements that would seem out of place in explicitly patriotic projects such as the later Belfast festival. As a result, Walker unwittingly lets us glimpse the potential of bard and minstrel contests to become a vehicle by which writers could point to tensions within nationalist and Romantic models of poetry's function, both of which downplayed or rejected the model of living poets competing for money. That is to say, Walker's account suggests but leaves untapped the potential for competing bards and minstrels to act as a figure for a competitive literary marketplace, something like Peacock's conception of poetic production rather than Shelley's in the passages quoted above. Later writers would follow Walker in discussing contests of bards and minstrels, but they would explore further the implications of the contest as a metaphor for modern writing.

Marketing disinterest: the university prizes

At roughly the same time the Scottish and Irish bardic contests gained visibility, another kind of poetry contest became more prominent: British universities and public schools began to publicize and promote their English-language poetry prizes on an unprecedented scale. Like the Irish contests, school prize competitions promoted the value of patriotic disinterest even as their development reflected an increasing attention to financial incentives for writing. Noting the degree to which public schools and universities functioned as 'one of the most important sources of the new [British] cultural identity', Linda Colley has pointed to the prize poems produced by these institutions as repositories of extreme patriotism and masculinity (167).[2] At once an extension of the classical curriculum and an expression of its 'constant diet of stories of war, empire, bravery, and sacrifice', Colley writes, '[s]chool and university prize poems and essays from this period creak under the weight of such themes, as well as exuding a lush appreciation of masculine heroism' (168).

I have found such 'lush appreciation of masculine heroism' abundantly evident in Oxford prize poems of the time. Cambridge prize poems, because of the terms of the Seatonian prize on which I will elaborate, emphasized the Anglican rather than the British side of Anglican Britishness. But Colley's larger point holds: prize poems of the time reflect one element of state-sponsored attempts to unify the British nation. The prize poem itself was also becoming a newly public literary genre, with new levels of funding and publicity. The Seatonian prizes, first awarded in 1750, included publication of the winning work as part of the prize. Oxford began publishing its collected prize poems in the 1790s, and by the 1810s, both Oxford and Cambridge were periodically collecting their prize poems for sale. In addition, poets from other schools had begun using the phrase 'prize poem' in subtitles and on title pages. During this time, the label 'prize poem' became a part of poets' and publishers' marketing strategies, much as 'prize-winning' still is; the notion of the 'prize poem' gained enough currency by 1830 that even a losing Cambridge entry came advertised as *'Byzantium, an unsuccessful prize poem by George Stovin Venables'.*[3]

As Venables or his publisher undoubtedly realized, participation in a prize contest itself signaled a poem produced in an exclusive environment, written by a man of some consequence, containing sentiments of unimpeachable patriotic feeling or religious devotion. The aforementioned Seatonian prize at Cambridge, for example, is so named because it was created by a Reverend Seaton's bequest to address

> a Subject, which Subject shall for the first Year be one or other of the Perfections or Attributes of the Supreme Being, and so the succeeding Years, till the Subject is exhausted; and afterwards the Subject shall be either Death, Judgment, Heaven, Hell, Purity of heart, &c. or whatever else may be judged by the Vice-Chancellor, Master of Clare Hall, and Greek Professor to be most conducive to the honour of the Supreme Being and recommendation of Virtue. (front matter of Smart)

So it was that Christopher Smart, who won the first five Seatonian prizes, did so with poems titled *On the Eternity of the Supreme Being, On the Immensity of the Supreme Being, On the Omniscience of the Supreme Being, On the Power of the Supreme Being,* and *On the Goodness of the Supreme Being.* (After George Bally won the next prize describing *The Justice of the Supreme Being,* Cambridge, apparently finding no more almighty attributes suitable for versification, gave the next prize to Beilby Porteus for *Death.*) Oxford's prizes varied more in subject matter, covering a range of topics – 'war, empire, bravery, and sacrifice for the state', in Colley's words – but thematic variation came with formal consistency: every Oxford prize poem through at least 1834 consists of heroic couplets (Oxford *Prize Poems*).[4] The newly public genre of the school prize poem represented the height of social exclusivity, religious orthodoxy, and traditional forms.

University poetry prizes were a kind of official credential that writers outside the Oxbridge sphere – women and Catholics, for instance – could never attain, no matter how well they supported the British cause in their work.[5] We know that Thomas Moore, for instance, bristled at his exclusion from prize competitions as a Catholic at Trinity College, Dublin, going so far as to take examinations to prove he could have won top prizes had he been allowed to compete for them (Clifford *Life* 11–12). Moore's case at Trinity suggests that there, the school's academic prizes had become a last line of defense for establishment Protestantism. In England, Catholics and Dissenters continued to be excluded not only from prize competitions but also from the entire system supporting those competitions – from teaching in the universities and older public schools and from attending the universities (Addison 9).

The classical curricula of those schools reinforced the patrician values underlying university exclusion, with educational capital reinforcing political dominance:

[T]he virtual monopoly of higher education which the upper classes possessed – and safeguarded – gave apparent validity to their rule. To the claims of blue blood, they could add superior education: it was, in the eighteenth century, a formidable combination. They were right to mistrust Dissenting Academies as threats to their position, and their determination to exclude Dissenters from Oxford and Cambridge suggests a recognition of the important part which educational privilege played in maintaining aristocratic supremacy. (Cannon 35)

Women were equally excluded, of course, and they had even less hope of access than Catholic or Dissenting men. Two centuries before Pierre Bourdieu analyzed French educational prizes, the example of Britain supported what would become his opening remark in *The State Nobility*: 'There is probably no object that could provide a clearer picture of the social structures and mental structures that govern academic verdicts than the system of statistical relations characteristic of a given population of academic *prizewinners*' (9, emphasis original).

To writers beyond the pale of the public schools and universities, the genre of the prize poem could easily have reeked of self-congratulatory hypocrisy. The poems' ideology of Roman and Christian self-sacrifice and disinterest was promoted by a machinery of aristocrats intent on defending its interests through exclusion and cash incentives. To some degree, we see here a tension that remains with us today, created by the uncomfortable border between ostensibly disinterested art that abhors mercenary urges and the capital (cultural and financial) generated for the recipients of prizes. The content of Romantic-era prize poems enforces even more strongly the tension James English describes within all artistic prizes:

> [T]here is at the very core of the prize a crucial ambiguity or duplicity. On the one hand, we tend to think of a prize – including the trophy or medal, the honor it signifies, and whatever cash award accompanies it – as a sort of gift... Yet on the other hand, 'prize' has its etymological roots precisely in money and in exchange... And of all the rituals and practices of culture, none is more frequently attacked for its compromising convergence with the dynamic of the marketplace than is the prize... (5–7)

This 'equivocality', says English, allows the prize to 'serve simultaneously as a means of recognizing an ostensibly higher, uniquely aesthetic form of value and as an arena in which such value often appears subject to the most businesslike system of production and exchange' (7). The tension English identifies in literary prizes mirrors that within military discourse, where the 'higher' value of patriotic disinterest likewise 'often appears subject to the most businesslike system of production and exchange'.

Such tensions created a strain of minstrel writing in which Romantic-era writers explored financial interest – or the lack of it – in military action, in writing, and in writing about military action. The remainder of this chapter will address one 'prize poem' written for public purposes rather than a university competition, *Wallace's Invocation to Bruce* by Felicia Hemans (1819), and then a series of contest poems: James Hogg's *The Queen's Wake* (1813) and Letitia Elizabeth Landon's *The Troubadour* (1825) and *the Golden Violet* (1827). As writers who could not afford a Shelleyan or Wordsworthian disdain of the marketplace, and as people without access to the literal and metaphorical prizes of the university system, Hemans, Landon, and Hogg used the institutions of the minstrel contest and the prize poem to explore the problems of competition and financial interest in literature by staging themselves on the selling block of the literary marketplace.

A prize poem: *Wallace's Invocation to Bruce*

In 1819, with the Napoleonic threat receding into memory, Felicia Hemans won a contest publicized by *Blackwood's Edinburgh Magazine* with *Wallace's Invocation to Bruce*. Funded by an anonymous donor, the contest supported the building of a monument to William Wallace. (Such a monument now stands in Stirling, though it was built decades after

Hemans wrote.) Hemans's acute understanding of market dynamics, of the literary incitement to patriotism, and of cultural competition produced a remarkable reinterpretation of the Wallace myth. Hemans's poem looks back on the national and literary dynamics of Napoleonic-era minstrel writing in a stance of tribute and critique, with a subtly ironic distance from her subject that would perhaps have been impossible five years earlier. In large part, the irony arises from the tension inherent in the very notion of a 'prize poem' written by a woman in a public competition advertised in a mass-produced periodical, circumstances that reversed the conventional associations of the phrase *prize poem*.

In 1819, the first edition of *Wallace's Invocation to Bruce* was published simultaneously in Edinburgh (by William Blackwood) and London (by Cadell and Davies). To get to that title, however, the reader had to pass through two presentations of the poem by another name: the first printed page reads, 'Mrs. Hemans's Prize Poem', and the second, 'Prize Poem'. Only after those pages does one come to the Wallace title on the customary title page, followed on subsequent pages by an advertisement and the text of the poem proper. In later collections, 'A Prize Poem' frequently appears as a subtitle to the work, and many include the text of the prize-centered advertisement, to which I will return. Relative to the first publications of the poem, then, the modern convention of calling it simply *Wallace's Invocation to Bruce* dramatically underplays its status as a 'prize poem'.

Hemans understood thoroughly the pressures of the literary marketplace. As Paula R. Feldman has shown, Hemans in her letters expressed candidly her desire to shape her work in response to market conditions. Writing to John Murray in 1817, Hemans asked him the favor of 'suggesting to me any subject, or style of writing, likely to be more popular' than her present work (quoted in Feldman 153). Doubtless aware of the power of minstrel-based historical writing to attract a mass audience, given Walter Scott's phenomenal success, Hemans had published a *Waverley*-inspired poem in Scott's *Edinburgh Annual Register* in 1815 (Feldman 152). After giving up work of 'sentiment or description' because of its limited public appeal, Hemans turned to history in 1819 with *Tales and Historic Scenes, in Verse*, which received good reviews and sold well.[6] When she wrote *Wallace's Invocation to Bruce* for a twenty-five-pound prize later that year, then, Hemans did so fully aware of the income and regard historical verse had brought her.[7] Winning twenty-five pounds with the Wallace poem only made explicit the terms of competition and economics to which she had already grown accustomed.

With *Wallace's Invocation to Bruce*, Hemans won a contest that asked poets to describe a touchstone moment in Scottish nationalist tradition: William Wallace confronting Robert the Bruce, who had betrayed the Scottish cause to form a pragmatic alliance of English and Scottish nobles. Like virtually all modern stories of military heroism, this one glorifies sacrificing mercenary self-interest for the good of the nation. As she presents the scene of Wallace's speech, Hemans dutifully reproduces the conventions of nationalist, masculine minstrelsy. Hemans's Wallace is a manly man from a manly land, and he utters statements such as, 'O'er softer climes let tyrants sway!' (16).[8] In persuading the Bruce to reverse his turn from the Scottish side to the English, Wallace appeals to a pride of nation stemming from their shared experience of Scottish manhood and from the Scottish land and air that call them to oppose England. Wallace tells the Bruce,

> The nurture of our bitter sky
> Calls forth resisting energy,
> And the wild fastnesses are ours,
> The rocks with their eternal towers;
> The soul to struggle and to dare,
> Is mingled with our northern air,
> And dust beneath our soil is lying
> Of those who died for fame undying.
> Tread'st thou that soil! and can it be,
> No loftier thought is roused in thee? (17)

Wallace, whom we understand to be the moral center of the poem, articulates a straightforward national logic: he and the Bruce share the experience of Scottish land and air, and Scotland itself '[c]alls forth' their opposition to England. As the poem's readers would have known, the invocation worked, with the Bruce taking over Wallace's cause after Wallace's betrayal and death. Even here, however, the poem's emphasis on the connection between Scottish 'nurture' and national feeling comes with a touch of ironic tension. If the feeling comes from men's childhood experience of Scotland's landscape, the English woman author of the poem should in all senses be foreign to it.

That tension becomes complicated and amplified by the variety of frames around Wallace's speech, all of which undermine the straightforward patriotism of the invocation. The tightest of those frames is that of the opening and closing of the poem itself, which surround the historical action with a present-day commentary. The poem begins by placing itself on 'Caledonia's classic ground, / Where the bold sons of other days / Won their high fame in Ossian's lays' (7). This formulation undermines itself, however, both syntactically and allusively: syntactically by placing the warrior's victories in Ossian's lays – in the realm of poetry – rather than on a battlefield; and allusively by choosing of all Scottish military verse that of Ossian, whose nationality was disputed and whose authenticity, always in doubt, had been discredited for most readers in 1805 by Henry Mackenzie's report on the poems' authenticity and Malcolm Laing's debunking edition.

A similar, even more complicated sequence forms the other book-end surrounding the historical narrative. At the end of his invocation, Wallace proclaims, 'My country shall forget me not!' (23). Hemans's narrator then moves the final lines of the poem back to the present time by asking, '*Art* thou forgot?' (23, emphasis original). That question begins the closing plea to Scots to remember their hero. What is striking about the question – '*Art* thou forgot?' – is its absurdity; thanks to the efforts of Robert Burns, Jane Porter, and many others, remembering Wallace by 1819 was less a cognitive process than a national industry. It is worth establishing more of the literary context of Wallace's story in this period before returning to the end of Hemans's poem.

Not only an important vehicle for historical romance, Wallace stories were also one of the most prominent tools for Unionist writers opposing Wallace-style Scottish nationalism. The medieval Wallace myth of 'Henry, the Minstrel', or 'Blind Harry', was frequently reprinted in the eighteenth century, in two translations.[9] In William Hamilton's widely circulated rendition of that story in couplets, 'Sir William Wallace' (Henry, the Minstrel *History* 25) is a gentleman, the son of a chief, who takes part in a political fight among nobles for the control of Scotland. Hamilton's introduction describes the years after Wallace's death as ones in which the Scots 'requited the harms received from them before, and enriched themselves with their spoil' (16). But the revisions of the Romantic era generally wrote out both the unapologetic desire for economic gain and the nationalist moral; when carefully recontextualized, Wallace's very nationalism made him a powerful symbol through which to argue that ancient Scottish nationalism could be converted to modern British Unionism.[10]

One of the earliest Romantic-era versions of the Wallace story, Henry Siddons's *William Wallace: or, the Highland Hero. A Tale, Founded on Historical Facts* (1791), sets forth the argument that Edward I's cruelty betrayed *Britain*, not Scotland.[11] It closes, 'Edward here [in executing Wallace] stained all his former glories; for he should have considered, that mercy and compassion for unfortunate merit are the true insignia of A BRITISH HEART' (176). No Wallace story questions Wallace's heroism or Edward I's faults. Many of them, however, join Siddons's in presenting Edward I's crimes not as a function of his Englishness but as a betrayal of it. Thus could Wallace become a hero fighting against Edward I and against aristocratic snobbery but ultimately *for* Britain – a Britain characterized by neighborly benevolence and Burkean liberty.

In 1809, the Wallace myth took a new turn, becoming the means by which Margaret Holford became the first woman to declare herself the 'minstrel' of a full-length romance in Scott's mode (iv). Holford's *Wallace; Or, the Fight of Falkirk; a Metrical Romance* (1809) celebrates unified Britishness from its dedication – 'Hail George the Good!' (v) – to its close, carefully moving between Scottish and English soldiers, portraying both as largely admirable but betrayed by internal villainy.[12] It comes as no surprise that Wallace is brought down by a mercenary betrayal: Edward I buys the services of Red Comyn, causing the narrator to exclaim, 'Oh! traffic foul!' (117). When the noble Stewart sees Comyn's treachery, he tells his men that hope is gone, but they must fight even so to avoid a specifically economic shame: 'Yon English lords shall tell their wives / How hunted lions sell their lives!' (168). The following year, the success of Jane Porter's *The Scottish Chiefs* (1810), also a Unionist story deploying nationalist conventions, reinforced the new sense of Wallace as a woman writer's subject, a sense so strong that Joanna Baillie in 1821 claimed to be aware of only four 'modern' Wallace stories: Holford's, Porter's, Hemans's, and her own *Metrical Legend of William Wallace* in *Metrical Legends of Exalted Characters* (1821).[13] *The Scottish Chiefs* musters the most direct attack on mercenary ideology in the Wallace line, as Wallace presents Edward I's use of mercenaries as a key to building a unified Scottish avenging force:

All have suffered by Edward; the powerful, banished into other countries or assassinated at home, that their wealth might reward foreign mercenaries; the poor, driven into the waste, that the meanest Southron might share the spoil. Such has been the wide devastation. Where all have suffered, all must be ready to revenge. (I.332–3)

Later, a hermit tells of Wallace's plans to galvanize national forces against a mercenary-tainted English opposition. As Edward I gathers his 'host of mercenaries', Wallace by contrast plans to 'infuse his own spirit into the bosoms of the chiefs of the numerous clans in this part of the kingdom' (I.343–4). And in 1822, Thomas Campbell, who himself had drafted a

Wallace poem decades earlier, could assume his audience understood the context when he opined that '[i]f an English poet under Edward III had only dared to leave one generous line of commiseration to the memory of Sir William Wallace, how much would he have raised our estimation of the moral character of the age!' (184). The British national myth of Wallace's legacy was thriving as Hemans wrote.

It is unlikely, then, that Hemans means the question '*Art* thou forgot?' to have any answer but 'no'. The poem's final lines reinforce that impression. The narrator proceeds to implore Scotland, now the '[l]and of bright deeds and minstrel-lore', to build a 'proud Cenotaph', the project supported by the patron of the poetry contest (25). The meaning of this monument, however, shifts in the last six lines. The narrator suddenly decides Wallace's name has not been forgotten and therefore needs no monument. Instead, the cenotaph becomes a monument of Scottish pride *itself*, mediated through the figure of Wallace. Hemans's poem closes with an address to Scotland:

> Not to assert, with needless claim,
> The bright *for ever* of its [that is, Wallace's name's] fame;
> But, in the ages yet untold,
> When *ours* shall be the days of old,
> To rouse high hearts and speak thy pride
> In him, for thee who lived and died. (25–6, emphasis original)

'[S]peak thy pride' mentions Scotland's ambiguous 'pride' for the second time in eight lines, in addition to the preceding description of the 'proud Cenotaph' itself. (Earlier, 'pride' had also described the face of the Bruce in his least sympathetic position, facing Wallace as part of the English host.) These lines, and indeed the whole poem, *can* appear straightforwardly patriotic; the poem did, after all, win the contest. Nonetheless, the opening and closing sections can also work in tandem to display the Wallace phenomenon – and, arguably, modern minstrel writing as a whole – as a project of questionable reliability fueled by the narcissism of its patrons. As Hemans presents the cenotaph, it is a marker of self-promotion rather than patriotic self-abnegation.[14]

The poem's first appearances in print complicated matters even further. In December 1819, *Blackwood's Edinburgh Magazine* printed the poem in one of its typical wide-ranging essays, called 'The Tent', with multiple characters commenting on literary and political matters. The essay includes an exchange between 'James Hogg', a caricature based on the writer, and the English Harry Seward; in that exchange, 'Hogg'

> recited to the Oxonian his wild lays of fairy superstition, and his countless traditionary ballads of the olden time – while the Christ-Church man, in return, spouted Eton and Oxford Prize Poems, – some of them in Latin, and, it was suspected, one or two even in Greek, – greatly to the illumination, no doubt, of the Pastoral Bard. Hogg, however, informed his gay young friend, 'that he could na thole [endure] college poetry, it was a' sae desperate stupid'. ('The Tent' 683)

The joke seems simple enough, with the humor stemming from the clash of cultures, so to speak, between the rough Scot and the polished Englishman, with 'Prize Poems' placed squarely on the side of the latter.

Without an explicit connection, however, the essay immediately offers its readers another sort of prize poem. The magazine's editorial persona introduces *Wallace's Invocation to Bruce*, a new poem by Felicia Hemans, explaining that it has won a prize of its own. In spite of the Scottish subject, generated by the specifically national project of the contest itself, *Blackwood's* calls attention to Hemans's Englishness. As an English-woman, she becomes a sign of separateness from Scotland but also part of a community of women's poets spanning Britain, each representing her own country: 'Scotland has her Baillie –' it says, 'Ireland her Tighe – and England her Hemans' (686).

Even before the poem proper begins, then, the university prize poems that signal Hogg's and Seward's inability to understand each other are transformed through Hemans into a prize-winning work that crosses borders: the national pride of England and Scotland come together as Hemans writes of Wallace and the Bruce. Equally excluded from Hogg's authentic Scottish rusticity and Seward's world of Eton and Oxford, Hemans enters the essay as both an outsider and a point of connection. *Blackwood's* introduces her poem as evidence of a community of women writers where national figures achieve the kind of mutual understand-ing that Hogg and Seward never will (in this fiction), given their cultural and economic differences. At the same time, however, Hogg and Seward introduce exactly the poles of exclusion marking Hemans's poem: the traditional school prize poem on one side, and authentic Scottishness on the other.

When published on its own, *Wallace's Invocation* came with an advertisement, exchanging the *Blackwood's* frame for yet another. The advertisement's first paragraph raises the stakes of the link, earlier only implied, between economic exchange and the discourse of nationalism:

> 'A Native of Edinburgh, and Member of the Highland Society of London,' with a view to give popularity to the project of rearing a suitable National Monument to the Memory of Wallace, lately offered Prizes for the three best poems on the subject of – that Illustrious Patriot inviting Bruce to the Scottish Throne. The following Poem obtained the first of these prizes. It would have appeared in the same form in which it is now offered to the Public, under the direction of its proper Editor, the giver of the Prize: but his privilege has, with pride as well as pleasure, been yielded to a Lady of the Author's own Country, who solicited permission to avail herself of this opportunity of honouring and further remunerating the genius of the Poet; and, at the same time, expressing her admiration of the theme in which she has triumphed. (Hemans front matter)

One can hardly overstate the rapidity of exchange between England and Scotland in this paragraph. A Scottish gentleman, who lives in England, supports a Scottish monument with an English poet's poem about a Scottish hero; then an English Lady buys control of the poem. The advertisement continues:

> It is a noble feature in the character of a generous and enlightened people, that, in England, the memory of the patriots and martyrs of Scotland has long excited an interest not exceeded in strength by that which prevails in the country which boasts their birth, their deeds, and their sufferings. (Hemans front matter)

This second paragraph equates the 'interest' – a highly ambiguous term – of Scotland and England in Scottish heroes, literally devaluing exactly the national connection that the poem's Wallace uses to reclaim the allegiance of the Bruce. If English and Scottish people have equal interest in the Wallace story, in other words, national origin has no value in the patriotic calculation. While the soldiers of the poem fought to 'buy their freedom with their blood' (8), a noble economy that would 'hallow minstrel's theme' (16), their latter-day counterparts operate through a literal economics of international exchange.

Taken together, the two paragraphs of the advertisement construct the production of Wallace stories as jumping national boundaries for economic and not patriotic reasons. The advertisement characterizes the project of Scottish minstrelsy as resembling the movement of the traitorous Bruce to the English side when the move serves its 'interest'. In producing a prize-winning text on Wallace, Hemans stages a conflict within Romantic-era literary nationalism: if nationalist conventions circulated widely enough to influence a pan-British audience, they also enabled the reproduction of those conventions. That reproduction, and the attendant commerce in texts among England, Scotland, Ireland, and Wales, enacted the very exchange that Unionists on both sides of the borders cited to demonstrate the economic value of union. Even as Hemans's poem produces the conventions of homosocial sincerity and personal connection – that is, Wallace's invocation works because his nationality and gender allow him to speak authentically to Bruce against the English – the advertisement's narrative of the poem's creation shows Wallace's story to be exchangeable across lines of gender and nation if the price is right. The text as a whole presents the literary *production* of nationalism, driven by international economics, eating away at the cultural *project* of nationalism, which held itself above economic interest. It presents Hemans as a new minstrel of the Unionist order, writing a different sort of poem for a different sort of prize.

Contesting minstrelsy I: *The Queen's Wake*

The delicate play with symbolic and economic capital that characterizes Hemans's prize poem becomes a more explicit investigation of the international minstrel market in contest poems. By allowing writers to adopt the characters of well-known minstrel types, contest poems served two functions: the rhetorical structure of the contest enabled writers to demonstrate their proficiency in a range of genres and tonalities, and the contests' competitive dynamics provided a means of examining the economics and authorial conventions of the book trade. I have argued in previous chapters that minstrel authorship frequently depended on a semi-autobiographical projection of the author as minstrel. In the contest poem, the single projection splits into a series of poetic personae, making the author a mimic or ventriloquist, often with a new kind of critical or ironic distance from the projected characters. This mechanism allows writers to present minstrelsy as a staged commercial endeavor, with inspiration and national character themselves the reproducible commodities of a literary market.

The Queen's Wake, which made James Hogg's reputation as a poet, narrates a minstrel/bard contest held before Mary, Queen of Scots on her arrival in Edinburgh. (A 'wake' in this sense has to do with local festivals in Britain, not death rites.) Whereas most minstrel writing before Hogg strove to reproduce the conventions of the author's own nation or region, *The Queen's Wake* splinters its minstrelsy into a din of competing voices. That characteristic has caused Peter Murphy to write of the poem that Hogg's frame narrative disrupts the 'unity' of the poem so dramatically that the reader can hardly tell whether it is one poem or a miscellany:

> The several poems Hogg has 'by him' compete for attention, and this creates a kind of cacophony, instead of a publishable book: so Hogg makes cacophony itself the subject of the story and in this way tames, or at least confines, his unruly talent... The result is typical of his career: a 'poem' that works well enough, but which is not quite all one thing. In his later life, Hogg divided his time between Ettrick and Edinburgh; just so his poems. Their lack of unity keeps them from succeeding as they might. (102)

Where Murphy sees flaws of disunity, others may well see a Chaucerian delight in the contest as a mechanism for displaying poetic flexibility. (The poem even plays with its disunity by calling one of its own episodes 'too varied' [280].) More important for present purposes is that Hogg exploits the contest structure to explore the dynamics of the minstrel market itself: the balancing of patronage and commercialism, sincerity and imitation, nationalism and internationalism that shaped the space of his literary career, especially in terms of Scott's dominance of the literary marketplace. Hogg stages his own relationship with Scott in the poem, but he puts that relationship in the context of broader concerns about minstrelsy and Britain's political position in 1813.

In thinking of a series of songs by different minstrels, Hogg could work with models that were for him close to home. Best known was Scott's series of minstrel songs in the final canto of *The Lay of the Last Minstrel* (1805). Far from competing with one another, Scott's singers specifically work to defuse the competitive tensions around them by entertaining their crowd; the minstrels sing 'lest farther fray / should mar the concord of the day' (*PW* 37). Such is the tendency of national minstrel writing: in battle or in private service to the gentry, a spirited competition for money would have been portrayed as unethical or militarily irresponsible. In many cases, such as Scott's, the minstrels enjoy and admire one another's work, downplaying any sense of competition a reader might be tempted to feel. Before Scott, James Macpherson in

Fingal had written of bards singing in turn: 'five bards advance, and sing, by turns, the praise of Ossian…The joy of Crona was great: for peace returned to the land' (253).[15] Here, too, the atmosphere is one of friendly celebration.

The Queen's Wake, on the contrary, stages intense competition, corrupt judgements of literary merit, and complicated national factionalism, including the unabashed prejudices of Hogg's narrative voice. Although the best singer, an Ettrick shepherd clearly meant to evoke Hogg himself, is a model of virtue, his environment seems irretrievably corrupt. Hogg's Ettrick bard, in contrast to the respectable minstrels of Scott's tradition, finds himself scorned by Edinburgh's nobility

> when the bard himself appeared,
> The ladies smiled, the courtiers sneered;
> For such a simple air and mien
> Before a court had never been. (106)

Hogg links his narrator (ostensibly the Hogg of 1813) to the Ettrick character by feeling as well as by geography; the narrator says he once gave up minstrelsy after being 'jeered by conceit and lordly pride' (3) as the shepherd had.

In the footnotes, Hogg adds still another persona.[16] Like the voice of the Ettrick shepherd and that of the narrator, the voice of the notes is also ostensibly that of Hogg himself, just as that of Scott's notes is conventionally called 'Scott'; the poem has no separate editorial persona. Combining a Scott-like editorial stance with the explicitly autobiographical Ettrick Shepherd character, however, produces an extraordinary effect: whereas Scott relies heavily on the separation of the (modern, rational) editor and (obsolete, superstitious) fictional world, Hogg collapses the two, repeatedly emphasizing the continuities between the world of the Wake and that of Hogg, as in an early note on superstitious traditions: 'Beside the old tradition on which this ballad is founded, there are some modern incidents of similar nature, which cannot well be accounted for, yet are as well attested as any occurrence that has taken place in the modern age' (345). In Hogg's work, the voice of modern editorial authority inhabits the same fairy-animated world that the featured minstrels do.

For Hogg, the border between England and Scotland (like Mary, Queen of Scots herself) becomes a subject not of productive connection but of mutual alienation: one of the two misfit bards in the contest 'seemed a courtier or a lord; / Strange his array and speech withal, / Gael deemed him southern – southern, Gael' (24). Other regional and national differences produce rancor as well: the poem presents vicious stereotypes of foreigners (the Italian and Irish poets are both simpering and effeminate; we can tell them apart because the Irishman is also drunk), and the Scots and Britons hardly come off much better. The contest degenerates into regional bickering in a final, 'worst dispute':

> 'Twas party all – not minstrel worth,
> But honour of the south and north
> ⋯⋯⋯⋯⋯⋯⋯⋯
> While Lowland jeer, and Highland mood,
> Threatened to end the Wake in blood. (309–10)

The passage obviously indicates a failure of Scotland to overcome regional divisions, but it also portrays that failure as something like an economic event, as a miscalculation of 'minstrel worth'. What connections do exist arise in uncomfortable places: a note likens King James V – a Stuart king – to Napoleon: 'King James V. acted on the same principle with these powerful chiefs, most of whom disregarded his authority, as Bonaparte did with the sovereigns of Europe' (349).

The content of the inset poems reinforces a sense of crumbling order. As they compete for the Queen's prize, the minstrels sing of madness, grief, dejection, rape, jealousy, and hate, with the editorial apparatus of the story only adding more layers of emotional chaos rather than containing the disturbing material. The inset poems show hierarchical orders producing a passive-aggressive death from a broken heart, in one case, or the active resistance of 'Young Kennedy', who rapes his master's daughter after smoldering in resentment:

> His master he loved not, obeyed with a scowl,
> Scarce smothered his hate, and his rancour of soul;
> When challenged, his eye and his colour would change,
> His proud bosom nursing and planning revenge. (49)

Whereas antiquarian collectors such as Scott had responded to child murder and other disturbing content in ballads by developing what Ann Wierda Rowland describes as an 'exemplary formal attention' that sidestepped the problems of content ('Fause' 237), Hogg here reproduces the violently disruptive content of the ballad tradition, but he does not use his editorial apparatus to establish a Scott-like critical distance between himself and that content.

Hogg's destruction of Scott's boundaries between ancient content and modern editorial practice allows Hogg to address another point of contact between ancient and modern poetry: patronage. Within Hogg's poem, of course, Queen Mary is the presiding patron; the poem itself is dedicated to a parallel contemporary figure, Princess Charlotte. Hogg dedicates the poem 'To Her Royal Highness Princess Charlotte of Wales' at the height of Scott's favor with the Prince Regent. (Scott was offered the Laureateship in 1813, although he respectfully declined it.) Also in 1813, Charlotte was inspiring rallying cries from opposition writers, who called attention to the Regent's mistreatment of Queen Caroline and emphasized that Charlotte could rule the nation (Behrendt 10).[17] The dedication to Charlotte, with its obvious parallel to Mary as the patron of the poem's wake, evokes a highly ambiguous set of associations. Within the poem itself, Mary inspires a bardic and military national allegiance:

> For such a queen, the Stuarts' heir,
> A queen so courteous, young, and fair,
> Who would not every foe defy!
> Who would not stand! who would not die! (8)

Hogg here cites Raphael Holinshed's history of Mary, saying she was raised in banishment but returned to 'the love of her faithful subjects' (332). So much is all that *The Queen's Wake* tells directly of Mary's biography, but the unstated culmination of her history – well known at the time – colors the story in darker shades: Mary had been betrayed by Scottish nobles and banished to her eventual captivity and death.[18] When the narrator asks rhetorically, 'Who would not stand! who would not die!' one reasonable answer is that Scotland itself would not.[19]

The poem's mention of the house of Stuart also omits a crucial side of the story. Mary's danger to Elizabeth stemmed not only from Mary's Stuart blood but also from her (and, eventually, her husband's) Tudor lineage. Mary thus represents a figure of potential pan-British connection, a symbol of reconciliation like so many of Scott's characters and like Elizabeth herself in Thomas Gray's 'The Bard: A Pindaric Ode'. The historical Mary, however, embodies not reconciliation but multidirectional alienation, not union but disintegration. When Hogg dedicates *The Queen's Wake* to Charlotte, he implies that she is to Hogg as Mary is to the Ettrick Shepherd of the Wake: an authorizing presence who will allow the poem's merit to be acknowledged, just as the poem's Ettrick Shepherd receives his earned applause only after '[f]air royalty approve[s] and smile[s]', thus overcoming the prejudice that has defeated the shepherd in front of noble audiences before (130). Hogg, in other words, portrays royal favor not as an unusual bias or advantage – like the favor conferred by the partisan squabbling of the other observers – but as a mechanism by which real esteem is allowed to emerge. He thus combines the economic reality of patronage with a justifying marketplace ideology. However, Mary's history necessarily lurks behind the optimism of that portrayal. By analogy, Charlotte's situation points to the partisan rancor that threatens to undermine both national unity and the system of compensating minstrel worth by putting mercenary self-interest over national duty. Furthermore, although the poem includes a prophecy of a Scotland-led victory over Napoleon, that prophecy comes in a context of celebrations accompanied by ominous forebodings.

The much loved Princess Charlotte thus stands with Mary in the position of an ideal patron who can rectify the effects of a corrupt system simply by expressing her feelings. But Mary's eventual entrapment in the very factionalism she seems to transcend haunts the story. In what now, with the knowledge of Charlotte's 1817 death, seems an uncannily prescient maneuver, Hogg thus gives Charlotte a sense of doomed glory captured before a fall. In opposition to Scott's narratives of progressive enlightenment, Hogg portrays moments of celebration trying vainly to ward off inevitable ruin. Scott's myths rely so heavily on their progressivism – it lets his stories contain the bitter rivalries and mercenary action of the border in a modern, properly commercial context – that Hogg's sense of deterioration signals a broad ideological departure from his mentor.

That departure manifests itself most clearly in the poem's characterization of the history of minstrelsy itself. At the beginning of the poem, Hogg's extended footnote on the word 'wake' separates Scottish wakes from their English counterparts, using that difference as a basis for explaining the state of modern minstrelsy. Hogg's emphasis on the failure of minstrels' audiences extends beyond that moment. In a revision of the ubiquitous 'last minstrel' myths, Hogg offers an unusual explanation for the decreased visibility of the modern minstrel. Minstrels still exist, says Hogg. They have simply been forgotten and impoverished by a system that has not supported them:

The minstrels, who, in the reign of the Stuarts, enjoyed privileges which were even denied to the principal nobility, were, by degrees, driven from the tables of the great to the second, and afterwards to the common hall, that their music and songs might be heard, while they themselves were unseen. From the common hall they were obliged to retire to the porch or court; and so low has the characters [sic] of the minstrels descended, that the performers of the Christmas wakes are wholly unknown to the most part of those whom they serenade. They seem to be despised, but enjoy some small privileges, in order to keep up a name of high and ancient origin. (330)

Wakes, like the minstrels themselves, are 'now scorned by all'; they 'Were first begun in courtly hall, / When royal MARY, blithe of mood, / Kept holiday at Holyrood' (5–6). After decades of competing theories explaining the death of minstrelsy, Hogg intervenes with a simple new explanation: minstrelsy is alive but not well, rendered invisible not by its own decline but by the neglect of its audience consisting of 'the principal nobility'.

A decade earlier, in *Minstrelsy of the Scottish Border*, Scott had offered a very different explanation of the fall of minstrelsy, saying that the quality of minstrelsy itself degenerated, not the willingness of the nobility to patronize it:

If they [artists] exhibit paramount excellence, no situation in society is too high for them which their manners enable them to fill; if they fall short of the highest point of aim, they degenerate into sign-painters, stone-cutters, doggerel rhymers, and so forth – the most contemptible of mankind. The reason of this is evident. Men must be satisfied with such a supply of their actual wants as can be obtained in the circumstances, and should an individual want a coat, he must employ the village tailor, if Stultze is not to be had. But if he seeks for delight, the case is quite different; and he that cannot hear Pasta or Sontag, would be little solaced for the absence of these sirens by the strains of a crack-voiced ballad singer. Nay, on the contrary, the offer of such inadequate compensation would only be regarded as an insult, and resented accordingly. (quoted in Ross 280)

As Marlon Ross notes, in this passage 'Scott distances his good minstrels from the reality of competition...Market competition is both at work and not at work in his explanation' (280), which pushes aside the existence of working minstrels and 'reinvest[s] the minstrel with Percy's chivalrous qualities' (281). Hogg, on the other hand, answers Scott by putting 'the reality of competition' and the failure of aristocratic support at the center of *The Queen's Wake*.

At other points in the text, Hogg draws out his engagement with Scott more explicitly. For instance, Hogg's editorial voice speaks of the loss of

Scottish fairies, emphasizing the separation between the haunted past and rational present, much as Scott might: 'The fairies have now totally disappeared, and it is pity they should; for they seem to have been the most delightful little spirits that ever haunted the Scottish dells' (336). The poem also contains contrary movements, however, as when Hogg as editor says that Scotland still has its witches. This note relates tales of the witches, including one of Michael Scott, which occasions a jab at Walter Scott's collecting practice: 'Mr Walter Scott has preserved [the tale], but so altered from its original way, that it is not easy to recognize it' (330). A later note ends with a suggestive comment about 'the too powerful Scotts, who were not noted as the best of neighbors' (350). After seeming at first to reinforce Scott's sense of history, this note ends by suggesting that Scott's method has its blind spots. The juxtaposed accusations of Scott's editorial deficiency and his family's lack of neighborliness suggest personal as well as professional differences between the two writers, but Hogg for the moment does nothing more than suggest them.

As the contest ends, however, the present-day conflicts become more explicit. The Ettrick bard of Hogg's poem wins a second prize of a 'harp of magic tone', which we understand to be more precious than the more elaborate but less sonorous harp given for first place. Hogg uses the harp to bring Scott onto the poem's stage explicitly. The harp makes its way from ancient bards to modern, finally passing to 'Walter the Abbot', and then from Scott to Hogg himself when Scott 'wonder[s] at [Hogg's] minstrelsy' and gives him the harp. In a passage that he omitted after the first two editions of the poem, however, Hogg says that Scott has tried to take his gift back after Hogg began his own work:

> But when, to native feelings true,
> I struck upon a chord was new;
> When by myself I 'gan to play,
> He tried to wile my harp away. (323)[20]

According to the poem, then, Scott has not only created a self-serving theory of minstrelsy's reception, in that the enormously popular Scott links market success to artistic merit, but he has also participated actively in the suppression of his former protégé and present rival. Scott's failure to support Hogg mirrors the failure of the nobility to support the poem's shepherd before Mary's arrival. That parallel suggests an analogous link between the political factionalism of Mary's court and the troubled British situation of 1813. This sudden invocation of Scott as a critical authority places him in the poem's chain of patrons, linking the minstrel theories of the poem to its equally suggestive theory of patronage. Whereas Scott had argued for a meritocracy of minstrelsy, with instinctive taste rewarding deserving performers, Hogg presents a network of obstacles facing own poetical aspirations – obstacles including the disfavor of his own patron, Scott himself.

The happy ending of the poem's prize contest thus stands out as a brief moment of justice in the midst of what Hogg portrays as a corrupt, mercenary system. *The Queen's Wake* portrays transhistorical minstrelsy as a darkly comic mirror of the Scottish tradition's respectable genealogies. Hogg's past and present minstrels are connected not through venerability but through common experiences of snobbery, virulent national and regional prejudice, and even the experience of British oppression. Offered as a tribute to a patron, Charlotte, and a mentor, Scott, the poem treats both of them with unsettling ambiguity. Although *The Queen's Wake* does not move beyond the boundaries of the British masculine minstrel tradition (as Landon's contest poems would), it troubles that tradition by claiming to move more deeply to its center – to a meaner, more disorderly place than Scott's minstrels visit – and by refusing to separate the troublesome world of the minstrels from the Scotland that Hogg and Scott both inhabit. Hogg thus created the genre of the minstrel contest poem as a means of exploring the underbelly of the literary marketplace. Twelve and fourteen years later, Letitia Elizabeth Landon would adapt the contest structure to her own purposes, extending the metaphor to explore women's place in the business of minstrelsy.

Contesting minstrelsy II: L.E.L.'s contest poems

> A man of sense will desire to find in his domestic associate, good taste, general information, and a correct judgment. In the course of their literary pursuits and conversation together, he will take pleasure in refining and improving her mind; but he would not delight in a wife who will always be introducing subjects for debate, who will be always disputing the palm of victory. Competition and emulation do not contain the elements of domestic happiness. He married for a companion, not a competitor.
>
> Hannah More, *Moral Sketches of Prevailing Opinions and Manners, Foreign and Domestic; with Reflections on Prayer*, 1819 (35)

Letitia Elizabeth Landon's two long poems following *The Improvisatrice* (1824) were *The Troubadour* (1825) and *The Golden Violet* (1827). Both build their plots around minstrel contests in Toulouse offering the prize of a golden violet. Hannah More's opinion that wives must not be 'competitor[s]', quoted above, illustrates the way that the dynamics of the contest poem could take on additional layers of complexity in a woman's hands. While male minstrel writers negotiated delicate mores of gentlemanly behavior when they portrayed competition, women writers had also to allow for the additional impropriety of addressing competition at all. Exploring that impropriety became Landon's primary engagement with the development of the minstrel contest poem.

In both of her contest poems, Landon makes her central minstrel figure a troubadour, which itself signals an important revision. As Sydney Owenson had before her in *The Novice of Saint Dominick* (1805), Landon routinely describes troubadours as a subcategory of 'minstrels' rather than as something separate. Troubadours had functioned differently from bards and minstrels because British nationalist antiquarians generally kept their minstrels as free as possible of French contamination. By the mid-1820s, however, troubadour literature had become an important part of minstrel writing, sparked in part by Byron's assertion of troubadours as a precedent for the immorality of *Childe Harold's Pilgrimage*.[21] Landon attributes her own source story to Jean-Charles-Léonard Simonde de Sismondi, and other writing about troubadours accessible to a British audience included Susanna Dobson's 1779 translation of Sainte-Palaye's *History of the Troubadours* and Joseph Ritson's troubadour-centered attack on Percy's minstrel history.[22] By 1825, troubadours had connotations of being like the British figures celebrated in minstrel writing but more politically and morally suspect than proper minstrels.

Landon's first extended portrayal of a minstrel contest comes in *The Troubadour*, where the contest controls only the end of the poem, as it allows the leading man's triple qualities of warrior, bard, and lover to intersect through a troubadour disguise. In allowing that to happen, the contest performs a critical role in the poem, but it does so only through an isolated contest scene at the end, and without portraying any other participants in the contest. The poem does, however, provide the profusion of self-contained stories typical of contest poems. *The Troubadour's* many episodes and nested stories build a network of overlapping conventions, generally concerning physical memorials of loss or separation. One can hardly read a page of the poem, for example, without encountering a commemorative flower, jewel, or tree. The poem reminds us constantly that all of its many stories share structures of affection, loss, and mourning.

Of course, such repetition is the basis of traditional objections to sentimental verse: that it is predictable, that all its stories sound the same. *The Troubadour*, in fact, proclaims itself to be derivative, not only by its internal repetitions and but also with its opening footnote about Walter Scott: 'The foundation of this tale was taken from the exquisite and wild legend in the Bride of Lammermuir. It is venturing on hallowed ground; but I have the common excuse for most human errors, – I was tempted by beauty' (323). The explicit borrowing from Scott – one that goes out of its way *not* to point out the extent to which Landon's version revises Scott's – acts as a microcosm of the larger patterns of the work. *The Troubadour* in many ways tells the same story repeatedly, but the very extremity of that repetition takes the subject matter across generic lines. The hunts and battles so typical of Scott's minstrelsy function through the same cycles and rituals that the love stories do, and one of the most important links between the stories of violence and love is a universal emphasis on the primacy of the first feeling of a given kind; for two examples, Raymond's first battle and Eva's first love give them emotions that can never be duplicated.

Yet even as the poem establishes the primacy of those first experiences, it reminds us constantly that the vast majority of human experience must necessarily be derivative, a sentiment that culminates in a final autobiographical lament for the father of the narrator (ostensibly Landon):

> 'Twas the first time I mourn'd the dead; –
> It was my heaviest loss, my worst, –
> My father! – and was thine the first! (253)

This relationship with the father, we are told, can never be duplicated or replaced by other loves, which must be derivative and therefore inferior: 'Never dear father, love can be, / Like the dear love I had for thee!' (254). This repetition creates an aesthetic of the derivative as the fundamentally human, even as it appears to be glorifying the original, and it creates a sense of sameness among stories of romantic love, familial love, battle, hunting, and killing. The specter of incest constantly hangs over the love stories, for instance, and the relationships between warrior men are frequently likened to heterosexual romantic relationships. Through the implications of its parallel structures, the poem uses minstrelsy's conventional mechanism of the story collection to explore the consequences of extreme sentimentalism, where all emotion starts to function in the same way.

For present purposes, the most important parallelism is that between the roles of 'both knight and bard' (236) in Raymond's character; although many earlier texts featured warriors who could act as minstrels, or minstrels who could help a battle along, *The Troubadour* gives Raymond the conventional biography of both the warrior and the bard simultaneously. When we first meet him, for instance, he enters as the 'last of a proud race / Who left him but a sword and name' (9), but only five lines later, the warrior becomes a fully conventional Beattiean minstrel boy, living the

> loveliest part
> Of a young poet's life, when first,
> In solitude and silence nurst,
> His genius rises like a spring
> Unnoticed in its wandering … (10)

We learn immediately, however, that this happy pastoral minstrelsy will come to a dark ending:

> Mocking will greet, neglect will chill
> His spirit's gush, his bosom's thrill;
> And, worst of all, that heartless praise
> Echoed from what another says. (11)

The narrator thus dooms Raymond to a derivative, melancholy future, with both his poetry and its reception only 'echoe[s]' of earlier, better versions. This premonition is easy to forget at the end of the poem, many pages later, when the narrator thanks her own readers for their praise when she was young and gives Raymond a happy ending; the readers' praise and Raymond's happiness have been devalued from the start.

The Troubadour shares many elements of Hemans's and Hogg's prize and contest poems. The contest story itself, the investigation of parallels between warriors and bards, and the concern with the price of an audience's approval hint of a cynical view of minstrel writing's mercenary side. But the poem only begins to make use of the structure of competitive performance that the minstrel contest offers, and *The Golden Violet* (1827) enacts explicitly what *The Troubadour* often only implies. Here the minstrel contest takes center stage, and Landon for the first time takes full advantage of the contest's ability to generate a profusion of poetic personae. The contest story controls the structure of the poem as Hogg's Wake story had *The Queen's Wake; The Golden Violet* is a full-scale imagining of women's entry into minstrel contests.[23] And as minstrel poems so often do, *The Golden Violet* works on two historical tracks. In the poem's historical world, we see a minstrel contest actively controlled by a woman – as opposed to Hogg's, which is performed for a largely passive Queen Mary – with female minstrels as full participants in the contest and in more private singing apart from the contest. In the present-day narrative frame of the poem, the narrator poses as L.E.L., the lovelorn woman writer who can only write of women's subjects, even as the same narrator reminds us that the contest poem we are reading belies that pose. In short, L.E.L. tells us that she should not be able to write the poem we are reading, according to her own and others' conventions of melancholy sincerity in women's poetry, and the poem explores the consequences of that problem.

From the beginning, *The Golden Violet* concerns itself with gender, economics, and their relationships to poetic production. The opening pages display Clemenza, the presiding patron of the poem's minstrel contest, and her annual festival. Although men are present at the festival, they are incidental; the scene illustrates both a 'lady's rule' (3) and a natural world dominated by female images: April, for instance, is figured as a nurse and mother bringing her daughters, the roses, into May. What seems at first a straightforward mirror image of the male-dominated minstrel scene (even *The Queen's Wake* portrays a passive queen in the midst of a swarm of male minstrels and courtiers), however, quickly complicates itself, as the poem's perspective moves from a benevolent panoramic view to a focus on the bleaker image of Clemenza herself.

We see Clemenza first in a Byronic pose of melancholy solitude at the fringe of a bustling crowd, then moving to a beach on which to sit and think. She chooses a shaded beach because 'the rest [that is, of the beaches] / Bared to the open sky their breast' (11), whereas the shaded one enjoys the protection of 'two old patriarch chestnuts' (11), making it a fit habitat for 'moralist in pensive mood' (11). These lines work against the opening of the poem by transforming nurturing images into ones of vulnerability, with even Clemenza's controlling presence in need of 'patriarch[al]' protection. The poem soon connects the beaches' bared breasts to the vulnerability of the passionate poet in the public sphere: Clemenza thinks of 'Some bard, who died before his fame; / Whose songs remain'd, but not his name' (15), then reflects that the poet's 'heart too fond, too weak / Lies open for the vulture's beak' (16).

The emphasis on the vulnerability of the public poet may seem odd in a poem about the public celebration of poetic merit, but this moment marks the beginning of a larger pattern: *The Golden Violet* deploys the conventions of the minstrel contest only to dismantle them. Clemenza holds the contest with the express purpose of preserving the minstrels' names, but the poem records few such names and pays very little attention to the character of individual minstrels. The minstrels come from many countries, moving beyond the standard types to include a Spanish Minstrel, a Moorish Bard, and a Norman Knight, among other unusual characters, but the poem takes very little care to differentiate them. Although the minstrel stories' names and geographic details sometimes vary according to the national origin, Landon's characteristically emblematic flowers, commemorative gifts, and melancholy tone link the tales, drowning particularities of national character in a sea of sentimental-narrative similarities.

The same narrative conventions also link the storytelling of the minstrel contest to what happens in the contest's interval. *The Golden Violet* is the first minstrel contest poem to show a detailed domestic scene during the break between the contest's songs; in her private singing room, Clemenza sings a lament, then hands the lute to a female friend who does the same. A third woman, Isabelle, then sings a mirthful song, only to catch the eye of Vidal (as Corinne catches Oswald's at the Capitol) and switch to a more somber key. The only difference between this private singing and the public affair of the contest seems to be the formal competition itself, as men's and women's songs move closer together as the poem progresses.

Even that difference falls away at the end of the poem, when the narrative collapses at the point of prize-giving. Clemenza unbinds the golden violet from her hair, and Landon lets suspense build for a few lines: 'Many a flash from each dark eye pass'd, / Many a minstrel's pulse throbb'd fast, / As she held forth the flower' (234). But Landon simply ends the story at that point:

> The dream is past, hush'd is my lute,
> At least, to my awaking, mute;
> Past that fair garden and glad hall,
> And she the lady queen of all.
> Leave we her power to those who deign
> One moment to my idle strain:
> Let each one at their pleasure set
> The prize – the Golden Violet.
> Could I choose where it might belong,
> Mid phantoms but of mine own song? (234)

By reclaiming all the minstrels' songs as Landon's own, the end of *The Golden Violet* breaks the conventional play between author and persona fundamental to literary minstrelsy: suddenly, a poem that has developed on the customary borders of minstrelsy – between collection and fiction, national sincerity and international projection – erases all ambiguity, asserting the control of a single author and establishing the many singers of the poem as *mere* imagined personae, with no supporting narratives of historical or national authenticity.

Even that reversal does not end the poem entirely, as Landon reserves one more rhetorical trick. Immediately after stating that she has created all the minstrel-poems of *The Golden Violet* (tales of battle, chivalry, romance, and so on), the narrator suddenly retreats into a pose of conventional feminine helplessness.

> How can I tell of battle field,
>   I never listed brand to wield;
> Or dark ambition's pathway try,
>   In truth I never look'd so high;
> Or stern revenge, or hatred fell,
>   Of what I know not, can I tell?
> I soar not on such lofty wings,
>   My lute has not so many strings;
> Its dower is but a humble dower,
>   And I who call upon its aid,
> My power is but a woman's power,
>   Of softness and of sadness made. (237–8)

'[B]ut a woman's power' indeed. Landon falls into self-deprecation at precisely the point when it makes least sense to do so: she has just reminded us – in a poem that includes a dramatic beheading in combat, for instance – that she can do everything she here claims to be beyond her.

Glennis Stephenson has noted the collapse of gendered authorship that Landon engineers in this sequence; she writes,

> The strict boundaries [between men's and women's singing] initially established are confused, and while the surface text continues to offer the conventional definitions of male and female art, the subtext repeatedly seems to warn against any hasty conclusions and to indicate that such definitions are, after all, ultimately constructs, the product both of the social context and the art of the

> poetess... While the apparent message here may be one of feminine modesty, the subtext can be seen as one of self-assertion, a not so subtle reminder that, despite the apparent division between man/art/narrative/imagination and woman/nature/lyric/feeling set up for the characters, in fact, a woman has written the whole lot. (*Letitia Landon* 70)

Reading this passage in the context of earlier minstrel poems extends the point even further, showing the dissolution of other oppositions upon which British minstrelsy built itself: notions of publicity and privacy, commercial and confessional authorship, Britishness and foreignness. Here the very building blocks of the traditional male minstrel contest crumble into the sand of Clemenza's quiet beach.

More than any of its minstrel-poem predecessors, *The Golden Violet* systematically reduces the basis of minstrel characterization – the assumptions of national and sexual character that drove minstrel plots from the beginning – to the status of stage masks. As the controlling actress of the poem, like Clemenza but with far more rhetorical power, Landon's narrator takes us through a new sort of minstrel show, and then strips away every pleasurable illusion at the end. Burke's lament that 'the age of chivalry is gone', which becomes the epigraph to *The Troubadour*, takes an ironic turn in Landon's hands; she ensures that her readers' transport into another age cannot survive, even within the poem itself. The passing of chivalry's age is here a matter of a rhetorical flourish, a quick shake that wakes the reader from a dream of the past. That sudden transition waves away the chivalric distinctions that had supported the minstrel stories of Percy and Scott – the distinctions of past and present, man and woman, operating in a benevolent chivalric system. Landon's poem draws back the curtain of minstrel productions, moving her audience past the staged competitions of gentlemanly minstrelsy to the present-day marketplace where Landon must compete without even admitting she has entered the contest.

Conclusion

The writer of a prize poem cannot, like William Wordsworth, declare poetry to be addressing an audience that will come to appreciate it later. In fact, Wordsworth's 1815 'Essay, Supplementary to the Preface' of his *Poems* presents an imaginary 'formal contest' in a discussion of the degrading influence of 'the gratification of the many':

Had there been a formal contest for superiority among dramatic Writers, that Shakespeare, like his predecessors Sophocles and Euripides, would have often been subject to the mortification of seeing the prize adjudged to sorry competitors, becomes too probable when we reflect that the Admirers of Settle and Shadwell were, in a later age, as numerous; and reckoned as respectable in point of talent as those of Dryden. At all events, that Shakespeare stooped to accommodate himself to the People, is sufficiently apparent; and one of the most striking proofs of his almost omnipotent genius is, that he could turn to such glorious purpose those materials which the prepossessions of the age compelled him to make use of. Yet even this marvellous skill appears not to have been enough to prevent his rivals from having some advantage over him in public estimation; how else can we account for passages and scenes that exist in his works, unless upon a supposition that some of the grossest of them, a fact which in my own mind I have no doubt of, were foisted in by the Players, for the gratification of the many? (I.350–1)

Similarly, a participant in a minstrel contest cannot afford, like Percy Bysshe Shelley, to think of the 'unacknowledged' impact of the poet. In contests, poets do not have the luxury of dictating the terms of their acceptance; the pleasure of an immediate, opinionated audience must rule the day if a prize is to be won, and the poet cannot afford to announce a negative judgement of that taste. Minstrel writing had traditionally celebrated the minstrel's ability to inspire listeners directly, with an oral performance appropriate to the moment of composition. Hemans, Hogg, and Landon saw the strings attached to that model of performance: that a patron's favor must come with a patron's control, that the privilege of celebrating a clan or nation turns quickly into an obligation to do so, that disinterested service lies close to mercenary servitude. To examine literal and imaginary poetry contests of the Romantic period is to explore what Walker's account of a contest only begins to suggest, a world of economic and competitive pressure that Romanticism separated from art by definition.

6

The 'Minstrel of the Western Continent': *The Last of the Mohicans* and Transatlantic Minstrelsy before Blackface

In *The Last of the Mohicans* (1826), James Fenimore Cooper writes the following about David Gamut, the Connecticut Puritan who accompanies the protagonists of the Leatherstocking Tales in this novel:

> He was, in truth, a minstrel of the western continent – of a much later day, certainly, than those gifted bards, who formerly sang the profane renown of baron and prince, but after the spirit of his own age and country; and he was now prepared to exercise the cunning of his craft, in celebration of, or rather in thanksgiving for, the recent victory. (133–4)

In describing Gamut as 'a minstrel of the western continent', Cooper assumes his reader's familiarity with minstrels of the *eastern* continent – primarily, the context implies, those of Britain and Ireland.[1] This assumption allows Cooper to portray those minstrels as the ground against which readers can see the minstrelsy of Gamut's 'own age and country', the American colonies of the 1750s. Cooper's interest in imagining an American alternative to British minstrelsy is not surprising in the context of Cooper's literary debts to Walter Scott and Scott's routine deployment of minstrels. As often as Scott's influence on Cooper has been noted, however, this novel does not figure in most genealogies of minstrelsy in antebellum America.[2] Scholars of blackface minstrelsy routinely mention the influence of song collections by Scott, Thomas Percy, Robert Burns, and Thomas Moore, but they do not convey the existence of a transatlantic literary conversation about minstrelsy in novels and other kinds of poetry throughout the early nineteenth century. These omissions add up to a missing generation in our genealogies of minstrelsy, a period lasting roughly from the first publication of Moore's

Irish Melodies in 1808 to T. D. Rice's Jim Crow dancing in the 1830s and the founding of Daniel Decatur Emmett's Virginia Minstrels in 1843.[3]

In proposing to fill a gap in the transatlantic genealogy of minstrelsy, I choose, as I have throughout this book, to emphasize the words *minstrel* and *minstrelsy* and to explore ways in which those terms crossed national and generic boundaries.[4] That emphasis becomes unconventional in a context that includes blackface performance. Only recently have scholars of blackface minstrelsy begun to address the implications of treating, for example, Scott's and Emmett's minstrelsies as two parts of a transatlantic phenomenon – the necessary first step in making a meaningful genealogy of their minstrelsies rather than treating their common terminology as little more than mere coincidence.[5] This investigation of common terminology raises by contrast the question of how to treat blackface performance before it was called minstrelsy.[6] Dale Cockrell has pointed to this problem of anachronism in *Demons of Disorder* (1997). Cockrell breaks with established conventions of commentary on blackface minstrelsy by arguing that 'words and names mean everything in this case' (152), referring specifically to Emmett's use of 'minstrels' to align his group's performances with those of the Tyrolese and German minstrels (and others) who had gained popularity on respectable American stages in the 1830s and 40s.[7] By claiming the name *minstrels*, Cockrell contends, Emmett's group advertised its pretensions to middle-class respectability.[8]

Cockrell's argument applies almost exclusively to the American context, hinting at a transatlantic connection only through those European ethnicities claimed by Emmett's predecessors in American stage minstrelsy.[9] Maureen McLane has recently addressed the early transatlantic uses of minstrelsy directly, recognizing in nineteenth-century writing about blackface minstrelsy 'an attempt to pour the songs of African slaves and their descendants into the literary-historical molds that British antiquarians had made for English, Scottish, Irish, and Welsh poets and traditions' ('Figure' 430). Like Cockrell, McLane relies on the importance of terminology: '[i]n British discourse, *minstrelsy* had long denoted the popular, vernacular poetry of a nation' ('Figure' 430). She analyzes the process by which minstrelsy first became 'alive to historicity' in the work of Walter Scott ('Figure' 438) and then carried its 'oscillat[ion] between the poles of impersonation and curation, ventriloquization and conservation' ('Figure' 449) into American blackface minstrelsy.[10]

I will add three related claims to existing commentary on early American blackface minstrelsy: first, that 'Negro minstrelsy' constituted one outgrowth of an under-appreciated internationalization of literary minstrelsy in the first part of the nineteenth century; second, that a new usage of the term *minstrel* to signify a kind of printed text complicated representations of orality and textuality in writing about minstrels; and, finally, that *The Last of the Mohicans* is part of a larger American literary effort, led by Cooper and then Henry Wadsworth Longfellow, to create a self-consciously American literary minstrelsy largely separate from the blackface stage.

'[T]he white warrior sang his death song': the growth of comparative minstrelsy

When he describes David Gamut's comic minstrelsy in the midst of battle, Cooper draws on a new comparative minstrelsy that had fully developed in the early nineteenth century:

> 'If the Jewish boy might tame the evil spirit of Saul by the sound of his harp, and the words of his sacred song, it may not be amiss,' [Gamut] said, 'to try the potency of music here.'
>
> Then raising his voice to its highest tones, he poured out a strain so powerful as to be heard even amid the din of that bloody field. More than one savage rushed towards them, thinking to rifle the unprotected sisters of their attire, and bear away their scalps; but when they found this strange and unmoved figure riveted to his post, they paused to listen. Astonishment soon changed to admiration, and they passed on to other and less courageous victims, openly expressing their satisfaction at the firmness with which the white warrior sang his death song. (206)

This passage involves two analogies between songs performed in different cultural situations. First, Gamut decides to sing in imitation of the biblical King David, who is Gamut's namesake, as Cooper points out repeatedly. Second, '[m]ore than one savage' resists attacking Cora and Alice Munro, 'the unprotected sisters', out of respect for Gamut's performance of what they perceive as their own genre of the death song. I will return to the notion of the death song and focus first on the context of minstrel writing newly concerned with analogies between cultures and nations. The development of this comparative minstrelsy is the most striking new characteristic of the minstrel writing of the early nineteenth century.

As I have mentioned, existing commentary on minstrelsy tends to pass over this period without comment. The convention of saying little or nothing of texts published later than Moore's *Irish Melodies* in discussing the British and Irish sources of blackface minstrelsy seems to stem from groundbreaking histories of American popular music dating back to 1970s foundational works. William W. Austin called attention to Scott, Moore, and others in his book-length analysis of Stephen Foster's songs in 1975. Four years later, Charles Hamm argued at length that Moore's songs 'became, quite simply, a cornerstone of English life and culture for the entire century' (45). For these writers and virtually all subsequent scholars of blackface minstrelsy, the importance of Scott, Moore, Thomas Percy, Burns, and other British writers lies in their contribution of ballads and songs whose texts became the raw material of American popular song, especially via Foster's work.

This approach leads to an emphasis on songs of a collector's local culture. For Percy and Burns, and in the early works of Scott and Moore, the figure of the minstrel assists primarily in the exploration of one's self-identified place of geographical origin. When Percy discussed his motivation for compiling his *Reliques of Ancient English Poetry* (1765), he defined his project as one in which he and his readers would learn about their 'own country':

> the Editor hopes he need not be ashamed of having bestowed some of his idle hours on the ancient literature of our own country, or in rescuing from oblivion some pieces (tho' but the amusements of our ancestors) which tend to place in a striking light, their taste, genius, sentiments, or manners. (I.xiv)

The same introspective impulse drove the self-presentation of most minstrel writing for decades after Percy's work appeared.[11] Modern literary minstrelsy implied a separation of the author from the represented folk culture of the region; the figure of the minstrel, partly an authorial persona and partly a fantasy of displacement to another time, linked a nation's ostensible folk history to its modernity.

As I have argued in previous chapters, some of the most important early breaks with this tradition appear in women's novels such as Sydney Owenson's *The Novice of Saint Dominick* (1805) and Germaine de Staël's *Corinne, or Italy* (1807), which established for a British audience ways of portraying women's performance through the minstrelsy of other places (in these cases, primarily France and Italy, respectively). Because *Corinne* takes place in a near-contemporary environment, its example is especially important here. Though she maintains minstrel writing's traditional structure of comparing the author or editor's culture to another, Staël replaces comparison of past and present with a comparison of synchronic national environments: one naïve and music-loving culture (Italy) and another (England or Britain) more politically advanced but less musical.

In the years following those early landmarks of comparative literary minstrelsy, more writers who had played minstrel of their localities began to present the minstrelsy of many nations: in the 1810s and 1820s, local minstrelsy turned international. Part of this turn was driven by the vogue for oriental tales such as Byron's *The Giaour* (1813), ostensibly the creation of a Turkish coffeehouse minstrel, and Moore's full-length Eastern minstrel tale *Lalla Rookh* (1817). Some writers also produced texts that merged religion and the minstrel mode, including Moore's *Sacred Songs* (starting in 1816) and Byron's *Hebrew Melodies* (1815). (Recall Cooper linking Gamut's modern minstrelsy to the singing of King David; by the time Cooper wrote, the construction of King David as a precursor to modern minstrels had already created a subgenre of Hebraic literary minstrelsy.) Moore also began developing a more comprehensively comparative approach in *National Airs*, whose publication began in 1818.[12]

Both of Moore's new series maintained the emphasis on first-person lyricism that, according to Hamm, had set Moore apart from his song-writing contemporaries (51). Given Moore's eventual importance to blackface songwriters, it is especially significant that his works make a distinct turn from the cultural nationalist representation of first-person voices of his native country towards assuming the characters of singers of many other places – the *National Airs* include songs based on French, Swiss, Venetian, Sicilian, Indian, Swedish, Portuguese, Hungarian, Mahratta, Highland, Russian, Neopolitan, Savoyard, Italian, Old English, Scotch, Languedocian, Cashmerian, Catalonian, German, Maltese, and Welsh tunes. Minstrelsy's new internationalism included other single-author collections of songs such as the 'Lays of Many Lands' series by Felicia Hemans (1825) and, as discussed in Chapter 5, the contest poems of James Hogg (*The Queen's Wake* [1813]) and of Letitia Elizabeth Landon (*The Troubadour* [1825] and *The Golden Violet* [1827]), which allowed their authors to take on many national voices as they presented the entries to the poems' represented contests. Novels representing minstrels, including those by Owenson and Scott, also described a wider range of geographical settings for minstrelsy.

Though this internationalization of minstrelsy was based in part on anthropological exploration of comparative national song traditions, it also involved the domestication of those traditions not only into English but also into the established poetic forms and sentimental conventions of the earlier works of more local minstrel writing. As Austin writes about the case of Moore,

> Moore's 'national airs' still showed little concern for the values that his German contemporaries were exalting in the name of the *Volk*. His poems were not, like many of Burns', classic versions of verses that had long circulated in variable forms. Moore knew nothing of the original words to most of the tunes that he used. In particular he knew no Gaelic. He knew little of peasant life . . . when he sang of rustic virtue, it was from the point of view of city people to whom rural life was almost as exotic as *Lalla Rookh*. (132)

Writers such as Moore and Hemans doubtless sought to capitalize on the marketability of their early song collections by expanding the imaginative scope of the genre to new geographic areas, with each author's name functioning as a kind of brand ensuring the quality and consistency of the verse. The movement from local to international minstrelsy created a tension between exoticizing and domesticating foreignness that came to be especially important in Cooper's and other writers' treatments of Native American music.

But this anthropological exploration had its limits. In spite of this increasing geographic exoticism in minstrel writing and the simultaneous popularity of abolitionist representations of African slaves, very few texts at this stage combined the language of minstrelsy with representations of Africa or Africans. An exception is the anonymous narrative poem *Yuli, the African: A Poem, in Six Cantos*, published in London in 1810.[13] An abolitionist work borrowing Scott's characteristic six-canto structure, *Yuli* portrays a sentimentalized minstrelsy as a sign of doomed happiness shared by African slaves and their British supporters. When a good master dies near the beginning of the poem, a 'panting minstrel' plays a 'bandore' (27), and a note explains the parallel between this instrument and those of European minstrels: 'Bandore, a musical instrument with strings, resembling a lute, much used by the Negroes'.[14] An African prince after the example of Aphra Behn's eponymous Oroonoko, Yuli later finds temporary solace in England from a man who sings a 'lay divine' on a 'magic harp' (61). The author of *Yuli* clearly intends to parlay readers' sympathy with the people represented in Scottish and

Irish minstrel writing into a similar sympathy with African, a strategy repeated occasionally in later abolitionist works. But *Yuli's* straightforward application of minstrel writing's conventions to an imagined Africa is remarkable for its rarity. In spite of the dramatic new internationalism of minstrel writing at this time, there is remarkably little foreshadowing of the coming vogue for 'Ethiopian' or 'negro' minstrelsy. The more prominent and more important treatments of race and minstrelsy before blackface arise in works that treat the subjects less directly, as Cooper does through the motif of the death song in *The Last of the Mohicans*.

Cora Munro's death song

One function of the title of *The Last of the Mohicans* is to assure readers that the inchoate romance between Cora Munro and Uncas, finally made explicit in their death songs but suggested throughout, will not result in miscegenation and thus the potential continuation of Uncas's family line. The title enters the novel when Uncas's father, Chingachgook, who will himself become 'the last of the Mohicans' when Uncas dies, declares early on that 'there will no longer be any blood of the sagamores, for my boy is the last of the Mohicans' (29). Without explanation, Cooper asks the reader to forget one of the first principles of novelistic plots: that young men at the beginning of novels are potential fathers. The reader's ability to sympathize with Chingachgook and Uncas as representatives of a doomed line depends on these early, improbable assurances that the Mohicans themselves understand their extinction to be inevitable. To preserve this sense of fatality, Cooper takes away Chingachgook's ability to hope for grandchildren, in spite of the novel's otherwise persistent focus on such matters of lineage and inheritance.[15]

By removing Uncas from marriage plots, the novel allows the reader to see him as the subject of nostalgic minstrelsy even as he lives. His situation recalls McLane's formulation that 'minstrelsy is always immediately obsolete; thus it requires endless revival and equally relentless burial' ('Figure' 450). Doomed on the title page not to attain the marriage and family life of other novels' heroes, Uncas is himself 'always immediately obsolete', and the narrator celebrates his masculine virtues throughout as in a death song, as the death-like obsolescence of Uncas allows the unapologetic sentimentalization of the warrior to begin well before he dies.

Because the book's title strips him of the potential for sexual reproduction, especially as it would continue his patriarchal line, Uncas is effectively emasculated even as the novel celebrates his strength and courage; sexually, he is 'as harmless as the tooting we'pon of the singer!' (313), to borrow a phrase from Natty Bumppo. Though my quotation takes the words out of context – Natty refers to the impossibility that his rifle, Killdeer, will be rendered as powerless as David Gamut's pitch-pipe – this connection is not merely coincidental. The novel associates song with an inability to preserve and reproduce oneself and one's line. Though Uncas, Gamut, and Cora are all admirable in different ways, they are also unable to maintain the patriarchal lines of their families. They are all the last of their houses; as a rule, the characters of *The Last of the Mohicans* make their posthumous impact in either song or progeny, but not both.

Cora's associations with song are less obvious than those of Uncas and Gamut, who both sing in the novel. But Cora is a derivative character, easily recognizable as the descendant not only of Scott's dark women such as *Waverley*'s Flora Mac-Ivor, as critics have often noted, but also of an earlier and similarly important female minstrel, Stäel's Corinne.[16] Flora and Corinne are both touchstones in writing about female minstrelsy, as their singing inspires the admiration of their British lovers: Flora enacts 'Highland Minstrelsy' (the title of *Waverley*'s twenty-second chapter), and Corinne performs an adapted version of Italian improvisation along with Scottish songs. Placing Cora in the context of her literary type reveals how Cooper connects her even more closely to Uncas than he already does within the novel's plot. The two characters' associations with music and their shared premature obsolescence come together in their death song sung by Delaware women, which Cooper describes at length:

[O]thers again, in due succession, spoke to the maiden herself [Cora], in the low, soft language of tenderness and love. They exhorted her to be of cheerful mind, and to fear nothing for her future welfare. A hunter would be her companion, who knew how to provide for her smallest wants; and a warrior was at her side who was able to protect her against every danger... Then, in a wild burst of their chant, they sang with united voices the temper of the Mohican's mind. They pronounced him noble, manly and generous; all that became a warrior, and all that a maid might love. Clothing their ideas in the most remote and subtle images, they betrayed, that, in the short period of their intercourse, they had discovered, with the intuitive perception of their sex, the truant disposition of his inclinations. (405–6)

This dual death song, shaped for Cooper's novelistic purposes, both draws on and departs from established conventions of literary death songs. The death song for Uncas draws on the literary conventions of Indian warriors' death songs that Tim Fulford has shown developing in the eighteenth century (17). Later, as an extension of the Sapphic melancholy that characterized much women's poetry in the early nineteenth century, the death song became a mode by which women writers portrayed a moment of sincere, sad poetry emanating from a speaker about to die, generally by suicide or because of a hopeless military situation. The subject of the death song generally speaks of some kind of collective as well as individual powerlessness: the plight of the woman writer (sometimes Sappho herself) or neglected female lover, in many examples including that of Shakespeare's Ophelia, or a child's helpless appeal to paternal authority, as in one of the most famous of death songs, Hemans's 'Casabianca'.[17] Implicitly or explicitly, death songs often protest the actions of powerful men, as the imminence of death provides an excuse for candid criticism ordinarily unavailable to the author.

British and American writers applied the death song's general theme of powerless protest to 'Indians' (both South Asian and Native American), often women, who voiced feelings of self-pity or resistance safely contained by the imminent death of the speaker. One remarkable example arises in Letitia Elizabeth Landon's *The Improvisatrice* (1824), where the unnamed main character attends a festival 'garbed as a Hindoo girl' (50) and then performs 'The Hindoo Girl's Song', a 'light strain' (52), followed by 'The Indian Bride', a third-person account of a widow who dies by performing *sati*, or immolating herself in her husband's funeral pyre. That is, Landon, writing in the persona of 'L.E.L.', creates a heroine who, in turn, plays the role of a Hindoo girl who then sings of an 'Indian bride'. The many steps of representation that separate Landon from that bride create contrary feelings of exoticism and solidarity. Landon links the stories and appearances of her female characters through parallel descriptions and plots even as the cultural specificity of the Indian bride's suicide ritual seems to separate her from Landon's world.[18]

Similar dynamics appear in Hemans's 'Indian Woman's Death Song', in which a spurned woman carries an infant daughter with her to the brink of a killing cataract. As in Landon's works, a tension exists between the poem's appeal to solidarity among women of many cultures on the one hand – the poem was published as part of the cross-cultural *Records of Woman* (1828) and features a pair of epigraphs, one conspicuously featuring Staël's name (as translator of *The Bride of Messina*) and the other from Cooper's *The Prairie* – and, on the other, the seeming primitivism of the

Native American woman's suicide and infanticide.[19] However a reader interprets the tone of the representation, the power of the woman's protest is contained by her impending drop over the falls. She may not be the last of the Mohicans, but she is ending her life and genealogical line.

The epigraphs by which Hemans connects her 'Indian woman' to Cooper and Staël brings us back to Cora's role in *The Last of the Mohicans*. For Cora's connections are as much to Staël's Corinne as to Flora Mac-Ivor; Cora's name combines Corinne's and Flora's, and the name of Cora's blond half-sister Alice echoes that of Corinne's blond half-sister Lucille. (Both sets of names fittingly come from the Latin for *heart* and *light*.) Moreover, Cora and Corinne both see their 'dark' ancestry (African and Italian, respectively) as a sign of their fated incompatibility with American and English societies that more easily accept their less forceful half-sisters. In the logic of their novels, both women, like Cora, are doomed to die rather than marry, being too passionate to adapt to conventional married life.

There is, however, a crucial difference between Cora and Corinne: Cora does not sing. Until Corinne decays from lost love into watching her own 'last song', a kind of death song, singing makes her attractive, famous, and politically formidable. Without song, Cora retains Corinne's tendency to self-destruction and little else. Cooper's novel celebrates Cora's courage, but that courage manifests itself only in a series of attempts to give up her life for her sister that cease only when one of Magua's henchmen lets her complete the sacrificial transaction; after he kills her, Cora becomes the passive object rather than the creator of her own death song.

Corinne's performances recur for Cooper not in Cora's character but in that of Uncas, who shares Cora's defiant courage but also displays a more effective eloquence and engages in minstrel-like vocal performance. The fates of Cora and Uncas are linked not only in the joint death song that they inspire, but also in their mutual connection to blackness. Cora uncharacteristically invokes her African blood ('the curse of my ancestors has fallen heavily on their child' [361]) soon before she dies, and shortly thereafter Uncas prepares for his final battle by singing a war-song 'with one-half of his fine features hid under a cloud of threatening black' (376). When the last Mohican seems most like a last minstrel, he blackens his face for his performance.

The precedent of *Corinne* provides a way to make use of the tensions in the longstanding critical argument over whether Cooper allows his readers to imagine a union between Uncas and Cora – whether the novel asks its readers at first to encounter them as generically tragic or comic characters. Critics have frequently commented on Cora's African heritage and its implications for reading her thwarted romance with Uncas. Many see Cora's blackness as a sign that Cooper means the reader to understand that the author 'denies any future to the romance', in Terence Martin's words, so Cora is 'made partly – but unrecognizably – Negro to placate the social requirements of Cooper's imagination' (63). Others, however, emphasize ways in which the novel allows the reader to spend hundreds of pages contemplating a connection between Uncas and Cora. As Nina Baym points out, the novel 'stridently assert[s] Cora's moral purity on every possible occasion', thus undermining any reading that posits an equivalence between Cora's African heritage and some moral flaw (74). From this point of view, '[a]n obvious outcome toward which this second plot might be tending is that Cora will marry Uncas after he has killed Magua' (Baym 75). Proponents of these two perspectives have been contending with each other from the time of the novel's earliest reviews to the present.[20]

Cooper's use of his audience's familiarity with Corinne and other dark heroines makes Cora a test case: could the new American context provide happiness for a dark heroine by breaking from the constraining British social order that could not contain a Flora Mac-Ivor or a performing Corinne? Scott and Staël had emphasized that their dark heroines' fates stem from their social contexts; the heroines cannot be happy because their specific worlds cannot accommodate their passions. Corinne, for example, cannot happily confine herself to English social norms, and England cannot expand its norms to accommodate Corinne, so, the story goes, Corinne loses her lover and dies. Corinne's willingness to step aside for Lucile enriches and complicates the ensuing match between her former lover and her half-sister; as in Ian Duncan's description of Scott's later dark heroines, Corinne is 'a figure not of dalliance but of passionate moral rectitude, [who] submits to the historical type (fair, mild) of domestic submission: in effect, donates her own magic to the domicile' (71).

By using her mixed heritage, her name, and other cues to associate Cora with Corinne, Cooper invites the reader to spend much of the novel considering whether a marriage between Cora and Uncas can exist within the nascent American republic. When Cora's death demonstrates that shifting Corinne's story to America has not allowed the dark heroine to find happiness, the implication is inescapable: for Cora, America has become a second England. The new nation has created its national identity by building on the blandly conventional and quietly racist model of Duncan Heyward and Alice rather than on the more nobly selfless heroism of Uncas and Cora. Instead of improvising a new situation that can allow Uncas and Cora to thrive, America is presented as pushing them through their deaths into the song that will become the soundtrack of the slaveholding Heyward's marriage to Cora's helpless sister. Jane Tompkins captures the bleakness of this plot in her argument that the novel is 'a meditation on *kinds*, and more specifically, as an attempt to calculate exactly how much violation or mixing of its fundamental categories a society can bear' (106). The recapitulation of Corinne's fate in Cora's is Cooper's sign of the New World's self-casting into the very societal roles from which the revolutionary nation had sought to break free.

However, even if Cooper cannot allow Uncas and Cora to marry, the novel's nearly comical proliferation of masks and disguises seems to offer other transgressive possibilities. The blackening of Uncas's face is one instance among many of masking and disguise in the novel, including many cases of the book's white characters taking on the guise of Native Americans.[21] Recent critics of the novel have sometimes read the success of these disguises as a sign that the novel presents race as a malleable social construction, in spite of the characters' essentialist rhetoric. It seems contradictory for race to be simultaneously essential and performable; hence, for instance, Shirley Samuels's argument that 'the disguises and substitutions of the novel indicate a more fundamental uneasiness about the constructedness of identity' (98) than the characters' rhetoric implies. By this logic, Cooper seems to be developing something like Margaret Fuller's position (following Staël's writings on translation) that 'what suits Great Britain, with her insular position ... does not suit a mixed race, continually enriched with new blood from other stocks the most unlike that of our original descent' (quoted in Boggs 51). For Fuller, writes Colleen Glenney Boggs, '[i]nherently, internally multiple, American culture overlaps with global national communities' (52).

But Cooper's position is not Fuller's. Even more than those of Landon and Hemans, Cooper's gestures in the direction of intercultural similarity are undercut by boundaries left uncrossed. Cooper's deployment of transgressive cross-dressing is susceptible to a critique analogous to Michael Rogin's argument that '[b]lackface buffoonery varied widely in content but was flawed fundamentally in form, for the color line was permeable in only one direction' (37).[22] (Recall that the British minstrel tradition includes frequent tales of kings dressing as minstrels to infiltrate enemy territory, but common minstrels do not imitate kings.) This is what Samuels's argument about *The Last of the Mohicans* neglects: the stability of naturalized racial difference persists in the face of performative transgressions because, in terms of the novel's categories, the imitations involve more civilized subjects imitating less civilized ones. Duncan Heyward disguises himself as a Native American healer, Bumppo a bear, Chingachgook a beaver, Alice Munro a Native American woman, and so forth. Even among Chingachgook, Uncas, and Natty Bumppo, only Bumppo can transform himself in their counsel to persuade the other two by 'suddenly assum[ing] the manner of an Indian, and adopt[ing] all the arts of native eloquence' (233). A similar logic leads not only to Tompkins's assertion that '[n]one of the lines of race, tribe, nationality, or calling which the disguises had seemed to obliterate had been erased in fact' (115), but also to the insight that Cooper's characters are not allowed, even temporarily for play or strategy, to cross those lines in ways that raise them in the novel's hierarchies of social standing.

In this light, the black face of Uncas can be read as an unwitting anticipation of the elements of blackface minstrelsy that still occupy its critics. Cooper presents Uncas as a uniquely civilized Native American, so the half-blackened face is the consciously decivilizing gesture that allows Uncas, singing his war-song, to partake directly of the musical and rhetorical gifts that the novel attributes to Native American culture. Such a moment is one where Cooper's presentation of race in America partakes most explicitly of what Rogin describes, using a phrase from James Snead in reference to blackface minstrelsy, as ' "exclusionary emulation," the principle whereby the power and trappings of black culture are imitated while at the same time their black originators are segregated away and kept at a distance' (25). Exclusionary emulation is also a broader structural problem in minstrel writing that addresses the writer's contemporary world. Any writer's representation, written or performed, of another culture's minstrelsy activates exclusionary emulation.

In *Corinne*, for example, the eponymous heroine encounters an Italian folk culture of poetic improvisation. She then becomes famous by performing an altered version of that improvisation for audiences that variously include common Italians and representatives of a pan-European higher class, including the novel's British hero. The reality of folk Italian improvisation is twice removed from the reader, who not only reads a foreigner's novelistic account of improvisation but also reads the words of Corinne's self-consciously adapted version of folk performance. If, in Eric Lott's words, '[t]he blackface performer is in effect a perfect metaphor for one culture's ventriloqual self-expression through the art forms of someone else's' (92), that metaphor is based on conventions established in the ventriloquizing practices of Percy, Moore, Scott, Staël, and many others. The fact that those authors and their readers saw themselves as celebrating rather than denigrating the ventriloquized peoples must have contributed to the attraction of some American abolitionists to early forms of 'Negro minstrelsy'. The cultural effects of minstrelsy could and did differ in context, of course; deploying exclusionary emulation to support the enslavement of Africans is hardly the same as deploying it, for example, for supporting or resisting the Union between England and Scotland. Nonetheless, the mechanism remains notably similar as the idea of the minstrel passes from generation to generation across the Atlantic at this time. Singing his war-song in a half-black mask, Uncas stands uncomfortably between the minstrel singers of Moore's *Irish Melodies* and Stephen Foster's *Ethiopian Melodies*.

Gamut's book: the minstrel as anthology

In minstrel writing, unlike stage minstrelsy, the principle of exclusionary emulation generally depends on a separation between, on one side, the oral culture of the people portrayed as surrounding a minstrel and, on the other, the evidently written text of the author. The fact that Gamut, Cooper's most explicit minstrel, carries a printed text marks him paradoxically as excessively modern and also obsolete – modern because his minstrelsy relies on the novelty item of an American-published book, obsolete because the minstrel's power traditionally stems from a connection to an oral culture that places his performances above the necessity of print.[23] Gamut's own words about his book convey a fetishistic attachment to the material object:

> I never abide in any place, sleeping or waking, without an example of this gifted work. 'Tis the six-and-twentieth edition, promulgated at Boston, Anno domini 1744; and is entitled, *The Psalms, Hymns, and Spiritual Songs of the Old and New Testaments; faithfully translated into English Metre, for the Use, Edification, and Comfort of the Saints, in Public and Private, especially in New England.* (20–1)

Gamut's immoderate concern with the text of this title page corresponds to his lack of other kinds of proportion. Cooper's initial description of Gamut's 'ungainly' body, closes, 'The same contrarity in his members seemed to exist through the whole man' (9). Gamut contains comic multitudes, perhaps most importantly in his contradictory status as a bookish minstrel.

Cooper's choice to signal Gamut's odd minstrelsy by attaching him to a book may have reminded readers how much the celebration of orality in minstrel writing had become an increasingly bookish matter in Cooper's lifetime.[24] The word *minstrel*, in fact, had come to stand for a certain kind of book: a collection of poems, usually songs – an anthology. I know of no dictionary that accounts for this usage, but it came about following the emergence of minstrel writing in the late eighteenth century and persisted on both sides of the Atlantic. An anonymous work called *The Minstrell; being a new and select collection of…English songs, duets, and cantatas, etc.* was published in 1780. In 1782 in Boston, the musician William Selby 'propose[d] a publication to be called *The New Minstrel*, a collection of secular pieces' (Hamm 94). Many other examples followed. Some were collections of secular pieces organized by region, most notably James Hogg's *The Forest Minstrel; a Selection of Songs, Adapted to the Most Favourite Scottish Airs* (1810), but also including many edited and anonymous collections. Others were collections of sacred pieces such as the anonymous *The Minstrel. A Collection of Moral and Religious Poems…* (1808) and James Edmeston's 1821 *The Cottage Minstrel: or Hymns for the Assistance of Cottagers in their Domestic Worship*. At least one of these anthologies exhibits the potential for 'minstrels' to become transatlantic collections: '*The Minstrel* (Baltimore, P. Lucas, 1812) has eighteen of [Moore's *Irish*] *Melodies* among its hundred-odd songs' (Hamm 45).

By the 1820s and 1830s, this kind of 'minstrel' would generally go by the name 'songster'. Books by that name still included material associated with the various kinds of minstrelsy, as in the example of *The United States Songster: A Choice Selection of about One Hundred and Seventy of the Most Popular Songs* (Cincinnati: U. P. James, 1836), which presents a good deal of Scottish and Irish material alongside 'The Star Spangled Banner' and John Hill Hewitt's 'The Minstrel's Return'd from the War'.[25] The collection also includes 'The Racoon [sic] Hunt, or Setting on a Rail', a song in full 'Negro' dialect ('Oh! den says I to Mr. Coon, / I'll hab your skin dis arternoon' [39]). That song is followed immediately by 'I'm Going to Fight Mit Sigel' in full German dialect ('I goes mit regimentals. / To schlaunch dem voes of Liberty / Like dem old Continentals' [42]). These books, from the earliest 'minstrels' to the later 'songsters', offer perhaps the clearest record of the expansion of comparative minstrelsy to include new, and often uglier, comic forms such as that of 'The Racoon Hunt'.

By the time Cooper wrote, then, a 'minstrel' could be many things: a performer of original or borrowed poetry celebrating a particular clan, geographic area, or religious musical tradition; a collector of such poetry for written publication; the printed collection itself; or a printed collection of poems of many geographic areas. In usage current for Cooper, though not for his characters, David Gamut is a minstrel with a minstrel. The slippage between performance and compilation in these varieties of minstrelsy illuminates an 1845 passage by James J. Kennard, Jr. in the *Knickerbocker Magazine*, 'Who Are Our National Poets?' After asserting that slave culture produces America's most 'national' poetry because slaves are free of the cosmopolitan experiences of other Americans, Kennard writes of the productions in which 'white men have blacked their faces to represent them':

> These operas are full of negro life: there is hardly any thing which might not be learned of a negro character, from a complete collection of these original works. A tour through the south, and a year or two of plantation life, would not fail to reward the diligent collector; and his future fame would be as certain as Homer's. Let him put his own name, as compiler, on the title-page, and (the real author's being unknown) after a lapse of a few centuries the contents of the book will be ascribed to him, as 'the great American Poet,' the object of adoration to the poetical public of the fiftieth century! What was Homer but a diligent collector? Some learned people *say* he was nothing more, at any rate. Thou who pantest for glory, go and do likewise! (45)

Kennard here reverses the convention of seeing the compiler of minstrel songs as modernity's poor substitute for the immediate efficacy of original oral performers. He posits the future 'great American Poet' as a 'diligent collector' whose nameless sources in 'plantation life' will be forgotten.

Kennard's vision of the collector-poet, involving a willfully perverse collapsing of the received distinctions between the original genius and the minstrel, captures tensions within American adaptations of minstrelsy that also underlie Cooper's novel. David Gamut's minstrelsy is an evidently debased, latter-day form. Unlike the many militarily savvy minstrels in the British tradition, Gamut does not understand the ways of warfare. Having lost connections with cultural tradition, he is ludicrously dependent on print culture, as his recitation of his hymnal's title page demonstrates. Even as Cooper uses Gamut to imply the absurdity of translating British representations of minstrelsy into the American wilderness, however, he presents the power of the Native American characters' eloquence and song as the authentic, native alternative to Gamut. Gamut is a mock last minstrel, a distorted mirror image of the last Mohicans. The usual ironies attendant on writing about oral minstrelsy arise in full force here: Cooper's valorization of Native American oral performance necessarily reaches his readers in a printed text under Cooper's name. The mockery of Gamut's impotent minstrelsy (in spite of Gamut's courage and good intentions) partly serves to obscure the fact that in writing the Leatherstocking Tales, Cooper plays a role much more like Gamut's than those of his more rugged heroes.

This link between Cooper and Gamut accords with the rare readings emphasizing Gamut's importance, such as Robert Lawson-Peebles's argument that Gamut offers a glimpse of music's potential to provide an 'antidote to the barbarity of the whites and the decline of the Indians' (129). As Lawson-Peebles points out, Cooper presents Gamut's song as analogous but inferior to those of the novel's Native Americans: 'In the episode at Glens Falls, David's song had to rise above "the miserable travesty" of the Puritan words. In contrast, the Indians have music embedded into their language' (133). The inherent musicality of other languages such as Italian and Gaelic had long been a staple of British minstrel writing.

The difference between discussing the power of music generally, as Lawson-Peebles does, and unearthing the specific resonance of minstrelsy is that minstrelsy was perceived as an obsolete form of music. That obsolescence, in fact, is the basis of W. H. Gardiner's attack on Cooper in the *North American Review* of 1826. Cooper has failed to maintain realism in presenting a minstrel, writes Gardiner, because

> [Gamut] is and does nothing more than the queen's dwarf and the king's jester were wont to be and do of old; which concomitants of royalty, like many more important jewels of prerogative, have long since ceased from the face of the earth, and become extinguished in the progress of civilization. (Dekker and McWilliams 109)

But Cooper knows this; the novel takes up the challenge of transforming the obsolescence of European minstrelsy into a new American textuality based on the alteration of oral forms. Part of Gamut's obsolescence stems from his being so obviously a stock figure of British novels, one carefully drawn from models such as Scott's Davie Gellatly of *Waverley*. Hence Gardiner's withering attack on Gamut as a 'concomitant[ ] of royalty' out of place in a novel about America. The structure of *The Last of the Mohicans* draws on Gamut's implied ties to British political and literary models to anchor the reader's awareness of their transformation as the novel progresses. The book begins with the figure of Gamut, in all his awkward inappropriateness; it ends by replacing him with new, parallel American minstrelsies – the Native American story of encounter with white heroes, and the colonists' answer of *The Last of the Mohicans* itself.

The lay of the last Mohican

Cooper's project of transforming the self-consciously obsolete attention to minstrelsy into a new American form is an instance of what Robert Weisbuch sees as the 'Anglo-American contest' of 'a struggle between two distinct senses of cultural time, British lateness and American earliness' (109). By placing the comically print-oriented minstrel David Gamut at the beginning of *The Last of the Mohicans*, Cooper presents his reader one manifestation of 'British lateness' that is later joined by other allusions to British writing about bards and minstrels. For example, three chapter epigraphs come from Thomas Gray's 'The Bard: A Pindaric Ode' (1757), the most important earlier text producing the mythology of lastness underlying Scott's last minstrel and Cooper's last Mohican. Another epigraph – 'Land of Albania! let me bend mine eyes / On thee, thou rugged nurse of savage men!' – comes from *Childe Harold's Pilgrimage* and evokes Byron's uses of minstrelsy there.[26] Cooper's paratextual quotation of Gray, along with Shakespeare and other earlier British authors, reflects Cooper's sentiment that '[t]he authors, previously to the revolution, are common property, and it is quite idle to say that the American has not just as good a right to claim Milton, and Shakespeare, and all the old masters of the language, as an Englishman' (quoted in Weisbuch 17).

Cooper's emphasis, however, was on creating something newly American from that inheritance, and as Paul Giles has written, Cooper was vexed that '[t]he absence of any international copyright agreement at this time had the effect of flooding the American market with cheap reprints of novels by…Scott and his contemporaries' (191). In two 1826 letters, Cooper argued for granting royalties to foreign authors in part because copyright laws enabled England to maintain 'her moral dominion over us, so long after her political sovereignty had ceased' (*Letters* I.172). By removing the competitive advantage of British works in the copyright system, Cooper wrote, the American government could help 'create a set of received opinions which may be suited to our institutions and to the state of our society'. 'A moral tie of this description', he added, 'will bind the Union together stronger than a thousand enactments or party-coloured constitutions' (*Letters* I.181).[27]

Cooper enacts this American literary Unionism in the structure of *The Last of the Mohicans*. The first part of the novel evokes the tradition-bound conventions of British minstrelsy and suggests their obsolescence. By the end, Cooper encourages the reader to envision America producing a minstrelsy of the future based on the mythologized history presented in *The Last of the Mohicans*. 'Years passed away', Cooper writes, 'before the traditionary tale of the white maiden, and of the young warrior of the Mohicans, ceased to beguile the long nights and tedious marches, or to animate their youthful and brave with a desire for vengeance. Neither were the secondary actors in these momentous incidents forgotten' (412). This minstrelsy of encounter among Cooper's Native Americans, an analog to Cooper's own project of remembering and retelling, ends with a crucial reassertion of American earliness: 'But these [tellings of the "traditionary tale"] were events of a time later than that which concerns our tale' (413). A handful of paragraphs from the end of the novel, Cooper transforms its action into the content of an American minstrelsy of anticipation. In a way, *The Last of the Mohicans* is here presented as parallel to but different from the Native Americans' oral tradition in the making. The plot ends with the Native American death song for Cora and Uncas, but Cooper's writing is the colonists' death song for the Mohicans.

One problem with making a new American literature out of a death song for the Mohicans was that when Cooper wrote, as critics now note routinely, the Mohicans were not dead.[28] In the contexts of transatlantic minstrel writing, we can see the special character and perniciousness of American minstrelsy, meaning not only blackface but also the relatively refined imaginings of Cooper and Henry Wadsworth Longfellow. Unlike the European peoples who sought a Herderian self-fulfillment in each nation's genealogical history and language, the American colonists faced an obvious separation between the histories of their bloodlines and their geographical location. Therefore, Herderian folk nationalism, which modern critics of blackface minstrelsy routinely cite as a precursor, could not function straightforwardly in the American context.[29]

In fact, Herder often argued against colonial projects such as the settlement of what became the United States. Although Herder made then-conventional comparisons of Native American cultures to what he described as the earlier, ballad-based stages of 'cultivated [*gebildet*]' societies (147), he argued vehemently against European colonial enterprises and any kind of national self-congratulation for imposing an invader's culture on a native one. In his 'Letters for the Advancement of Humanity' of the 1790s, Herder wrote in a characteristic passage,

What, generally, is a foisted, foreign culture, a formation [*Bildung*] that does not develop out of [a people's] own dispositions and needs? It oppresses and deforms, or else it plunges straight into the abyss. You poor sacrificial victims who were brought from the south sea islands to England in order to receive culture – you are symbols of the good that Europeans communicate to other peoples generally! (382)

To create American minstrelsy, writers and performers needed to adapt Herder's valorization of national folk cultures to a situation in which 'a foisted, foreign culture' had all too clearly violated Herder's sense that a nation must arise from a deep and long-developing linguistic heritage.[30]

American writers responded to this problem by celebrating the multiplicity of national histories as a benefit to the new nation, thus substituting for Herder's linear folk history what we might call an internalized version of Staëlian relational nationalism, in which national cultures define themselves as part of an ongoing process of translation and comparison. Boggs writes that for Fuller, Staël's foremost American disciple, 'cultural identity was not solipsistically original but intimately relational, and translation was the linguistic equivalent of that contingency' (32). The United States offered an extraordinary opportunity to conceive a self-contained community of 'intimately relational' identities.

So it was that Walt Whitman called the United States a 'teeming nation of nations' (quoted in Thomas 63). In this view, the nation was a Europe in itself, like the English language as Whitman described it, 'chock full with so many contributions from the north and from the south, from Scandinavia, from Greece and Rome – from Spaniards, Italians, and the French' (quoted in Thomas 63). But Whitman was not especially interested in creating American literature as a mode of minstrelsy; Henry Wadsworth Longfellow was, and his comments make clear that the requisite 'classic ground' of minstrelsy results directly from the extinction of 'our native Indians':

when our native Indians, who are fast perishing from the earth, shall have left forever the borders of our wide lakes and rivers, and their villages have decayed within the bosoms of our western hills, the dim light of tradition will rest upon those places, which have seen the glory of their battles, and heard the voice of their eloquence: – and our land will become, indeed, a classic ground. (quoted in Thomas 64)

For the purposes of constructing Herderian national myths, Longfellow's logic here creates a problem: if 'places' have 'heard the voice of [the dead Indians'] eloquence', the genealogical connection between the nation's ancient and modern peoples will be broken. Finding a way to restore that connection and thereby make Native Americans into the colonists' mythical ancestors is Longfellow's project in *The Song of Hiawatha* (1855), the last major work of transatlantic literary minstrelsy.[31]

In fact, *The Song of Hiawatha* opens with its narrator's direct claim to the authority of Native American oral tradition: 'Should you ask me, whence these stories?' says the narrator, the answer will be 'I repeat them as I heard them / From the lips of Nawadaha, / The musician, the sweet singer' (141). Longfellow addresses the poem to an audience already familiar with the conventions of cosmopolitan minstrelsy – 'Ye who love a nation's legends, / Love the ballads of a people' (143). This is the fundamental transformation of American minstrelsy: the bardic genealogy of Native Americans is mimicked and reproduced not for an audience that shares their language and ancestry (in the Herderian mode) but rather for a literary audience that understands the abstract conventions of minstrelsy, an audience of people who love *a* nation's legends, as Longfellow puts it, rather than their own ancestors' stories.

Longfellow's poem authorizes the colonial takeover of Native American lore in two ways. One is obvious: the poem ends with Hiawatha, on the authority of the Great Spirit, endorsing newly arrived white settlers and Christianity to his people. The other is more subtle: in the poem's section on 'Picture-Writing', Longfellow presents Hiawatha's people worrying that 'From the memory of the old men / Pass away the great traditions' (227) and therefore preserving them by painting 'songs' (230). Thus, Longfellow presents the Native Americans themselves authorizing writing as a legitimate outgrowth of their native tradition. They do so in a way that bridges the linguistic gap between them and speakers of English: if their pictures are transparently legible to European readers as 'songs', they can constitute a Herderian genealogy connecting the ancient songs and modern texts of the nation. Longfellow's own 'Song of Hiawatha' can make its paradoxical claim to be both a genuine piece of native folklore and a unifying national myth of white America.[32]

Conclusion

In this light, we can see the British and Irish vogue for minstrel writing not only as a genealogical predecessor to American conceptions of

Native American or African-American minstrelsy, but also as a continuing, visible part of the transatlantic rhetoric of minstrelsy throughout the period in which 'Negro minstrelsy' was born. As Lott has written, referring to approving statements about some aspects of blackface minstrelsy by Whitman, Fuller, and W. E. B. Du Bois, 'We ought ... to know how such positive assessments of the minstrel show were possible as well as wrong' (17). Such knowledge comes partly from understanding the transatlantic rhetoric of 'minstrelsy' as well as the development of blackface theatricals. The ability of minstrelsy to become a justification for slavery raises questions about the consequences of literary appropriations of oral performance in other incarnations of literary minstrelsy. At the same time, the widespread cultural nationalist affection for those other forms of minstrelsy helps explain the perplexing abolitionist affection for plantation melodies.[33]

To argue that the study of minstrelsy can still benefit from a transatlantic perspective is not to downplay the uniqueness of American blackface minstrelsy, especially its performative aspects and the extent to which it became a means of justifying and then pining for slavery. In fact, attention to the varied uses of minstrelsy throughout the nineteenth century clarifies the ideological maneuvering necessary to adapt minstrelsy as imagined by British and Irish writers to the ends of 'Negro minstrelsy'. Carol McGuirk has shown, for example, how Foster borrowed heavily from Burns but crucially tamed the rebellious sentiments of Burns's peasantry in transporting his verse conventions to the American South.[34] More generally, minstrel writing's split authorial personae of performer and editor transformed into the famous sheet music iconography of blackface artists in and out of costume. The gratitude to political and literary patrons in Percy's and Scott's minstrel writing transformed into slaves' appreciation of kind masters. The nostalgia for a politically independent Ireland in the work of Moore and Owenson are reincarnated in longing for antebellum dependence of slaves on their masters. And most fundamentally, the European emphasis on comparing varieties of European culture transformed into an opposition between black and white that served the purposes of white assimilation and political dominance.[35] While the works of European minstrel writers raise questions about the legitimacy of their authors' representations of other voices, blackface minstrelsy, in the words of David Roediger, 'did not steal Black material stealthily. It did so brazenly' (117).[36]

Nonetheless, the dynamics of love and theft that Lott describes – in his words, 'minstrelsy's mixed erotic economy of celebration and exploitation' (6) – are meaningfully present throughout the long period of minstrel writing's transatlantic popularity. That currency explains why a writer such as Cooper, struggling to separate his work from that of his British predecessors while writing to an audience sated with their works, would structure a novel such as *The Last of the Mohicans* to begin and end by addressing the implicit question, 'What would minstrelsy look like in America?'

That question persisted even into the twentieth century in ways we are only beginning to understand. In 1928, Dailey Paskman and Sigmund Spaeth remarked that 'the most distinctive form of native entertainment should bear a name charged with all the romance and glamour of medieval minstrelsy' (quoted in Mahar 182). This statement captures the balance between asserting the 'distinctive' nature of blackface while simultaneously claiming its value through its connection to 'the romance and glamour of medieval minstrelsy' – that is, the transatlantic cultural capital of minstrelsy that the performers and supporters of blackface minstrelsy sought to cash in. The recurring American interest in claiming novelty through minstrelsy, a practice centrally concerned with tradition and inheritance, involves the same irony by which minstrelsy was constantly pronounced dead and also found to be the source of a new American literary art in the early nineteenth century. For all minstrelsy's trappings of obsolescence, its transformation into a distinctive American style of singing or writing was also perpetually underway. Minstrelsy is dead, declare generations of nineteenth-century American writers; long live minstrelsy![37]

This American remaking of minstrelsy, though newly charged with racial arguments unique to the American context, did continue one strand of British Romantic-era writing. Minstrelsy's adaptations of Romantic sincerity emphasize the self-conscious theatricality of self-revelation through masking. 'Man is least himself', wrote Oscar Wilde, 'when he talks in his own person. Give him a mask and he will tell you the truth.' To that Jerome McGann adds, 'Perhaps no English writer, not even Wilde himself, executed the theory of the mask so completely as Byron' (*Byron and Romanticism* 141). Perhaps that is so – but before and after Byron came other authors who also helped create this theatrical Romanticism under the sign of the minstrel, from the French revolutionary sympathizers who used the minstrel mask to articulate otherwise inexpressible political truths to the late nineteenth-century performers who used comic minstrelsy to overtly reactionary, racist political ends. The minstrel mask in this broad sense was worn for a large range of literary and political purposes; the literary conversation about minstrelsy was a hotly contested one. But for many decades and in many influential forms, the practice of writing about and then performing minstrelsy persisted. To an important degree, in literature and song, the minstrel mask was the social face of the nineteenth-century poetic imagination.

Notes

1   The Minstrel Mode

1. Maureen McLane has noted that 'Wordsworth lauded the almost mystical connection between the first bards and their audiences' ('Ballads' 423) in his 1802 'Appendix on Poetic Diction'. In that appendix, part of Wordsworth's project is to assert that this 'almost mystical connection' was produced by 'language which, though unusual, was still the language of men' (*LB* 318). By insisting on the ancient and modern poets' shared attachment to common language, Wordsworth here downplays the importance of the shift from oral to print culture by emphasizing the primacy of diction. If the reader accepts Wordsworth's arguments, the fantasy of minstrelsy becomes unnecessary, as modern poets can recapture the connection between bard and audience through diction, thus rendering obsolete the need to imagine minstrels with live audiences. This explains why Wordsworth's deep interest in a bardic tradition, which Richard Gravil has documented thoroughly in *Wordsworth's Bardic Vocation*, does not lead Wordsworth to employ the conventions of minstrel writing.
2. In using and extending the metaphor of 'two-faced' writing, I have in mind Jerome McGann's comments stemming from this same passage in Mill. McGann writes that 'Romantic truth is inner vision, and Romantic knowledge is the unfolding of the truths of that inner vision' (*Byron and Romanticism* 115). McGann goes on to point out that '[h]ypocrisy is the antithesis of sincerity' and continues,

   > One can be sincere and yet speak incompletely, or even falsely, but it appears a patent contradiction to think or imagine that one could be sincere and at the same time speak deliberate falsehoods or develop subtle equivocations. To do so is to declare that one is 'two-faced,' and hence lacking the fundamental quality of the sincere person: integrity. (*Byron and Romanticism* 115)

   McGann argues that Byron wrote in genres such as satire that 'have an exchange going on between the writer and the reader' and therefore resist Romantic poetry's paradigmatic valorization of the 'overheard' (*Byron and Romanticism* 136) – or even, I would add by way of Keats, the unheard.
3. Historically, minstrels could legally travel only when authorized by attachment to a master or by holding their own land: 'the Vagabond Act of 1604, continuing earlier statutes, includes players of interludes, fencers, bearwards, minstrels, begging scholars and sailors, psalmists, fortune-tellers, and others. If the vagrant could not show he had land of his own or a master whom he was serving, he was tied to a post and publicly whipped' (Greenblatt *Will* 88).

4. In *The Bridal of Triermain*, Scott offers an amusing reversal of Boyer's revision, where Scott's narrator rejects 'harp' as too *modern* for his present taste:

> My Harp – or let me rather choose
> The good old classic form – my Muse,
> (For Harp's an ever-scutched phrase,
> Worn out by bards of modern days,)
> My Muse, then – (Stanza V of the Introduction to Canto III, *PW* 288)

5. Any discussion of Romantic-era harps must call to mind the Aeolian harps that pervade Romantic poetry and literary theory. Whereas the Aeolian harp responds to nature, whether or not an observing human mind is present to hear it, the minstrel's harp responds only to plucking, and writers frequently figure the minstrel as participating in a dialogue with the 'responsive' or 'knowing' harp that understands the emotional needs of a given situation.

6. This is not to say that Beattie and Gray had exactly the same sense of the poet's audience. As Linda Zionkowski has noted, Gray 'constantly stated his intent to write above the heads of the vulgar' (341), which was hardly Beattie's goal. Nonetheless, the eponymous 'Bard' of Gray's ode embodies a concern with poetry's public function and its interaction with historical process similar to Beattie's early conception of his minstrel's role.

7. This Advertisement, with some revisions, was called a Preface in later editions. Unless otherwise noted, I cite *The Minstrel* by book and stanza based on the 1771 and 1774 first editions of the first and second books, respectively.

8. Beattie's indecision about whether to portray an English or Danish invasion is a choice between two then-prominent models (as well as many older ones): Percy's *Reliques*, with its stories of border skirmishes between Scots and the English as well as the tales of English–Danish conflict quoted above, and John Home's *Douglas* (1757), which features a Danish invasion that calls its hero to action.

9. Scott had reviewed William Forbes's memoir of Beattie, so he presumably knew of Beattie's plan from the letter quoted above.

10. This is not to mention the similarities between Wordsworth and Beattie in their approach to diction. King has noted those similarities in his book (for example, in footnote 4 on 211 and following of *Origins*) and in many articles. Beattie addresses *The Minstrel* to a specifically English audience and trumpets the plainness of his diction: 'antique expressions I have avoided', he writes; 'I hope [no "old words"] will be found that are now obsolete, or in any degree not intelligible to a reader of English poetry' (vi). In one of the relatively sparse notes to the poem, Beattie calls attention to the difference between the diction of Percy's poems and his own. Beattie introduces Edwin's region with a rare gesture to ballad diction – 'But he, I ween, was of the north countrie' (I.xiii) – and the first note of the poem explains 'of the north countrie' to be an overused convention of the old ballads, explicitly referring the reader to Percy (7).

11. When one measures with the blunt instrument of publication frequency, at least, Percy's *Reliques* appears to have gained its prominence over *The Hermit of Warkworth* in the later nineteenth century, when the former was reprinted far more often than the latter. Before 1830, however, we have records of

more printings of *The Hermit* than of the *Reliques* – my count based on RLIN, the ESTC, and other catalogs puts the numbers at approximately fifteen and twelve, respectively. *The Hermit* enjoyed more printings between 1791 and 1807, whereas the *Reliques* became by far the more frequently printed work in the later nineteenth century. Wordsworth's praise of the *Reliques* and scathing critique of *The Hermit* in his 1815 'Essay, Supplementary to the Preface' (361–2) may have contributed to the growing emphasis on the *Reliques* in nineteenth-century publication and reception.

12. For example, any reader of Scott's poetry will recognize the blend of present-day geography and antiquarian interest in Percy's Advertisement, present at least by the 1772 third edition:

> Warkworth Castle in Northumberland stands very boldly on the neck of land near the sea-shore, almost surrounded by the river Coquet, (called by our old Latin Historians, Coqueda) which runs with a clear rapid stream, but when swoln with rains becomes violent and dangerous.
>
> About a mile from the Castle, in a deep romantic valley, are the remains of a Hermitage; of which the Chapel is still intire. This is hollowed with great elegance in a cliff near the river; as are also two adjoining apartments, which probably served for an Antechapel and Vestry, or were appropriated to some other sacred uses; for the former of these, which runs parallel with the Chapel, is thought to have had an altar in it, at which Mass was occasionally celebrated, as well as in the Chapel itself...
>
> But what principally distinguishes the Chapel, is a small Tomb or Monument, on the south-side of the altar: on the top of which, lies a Female Figure...(vi)

13. See Leith Davis for an analysis of Scott's effort to balance the value of historical authenticity with a suggestion of 'the importance that even an inauthentic work can have on the literary canon' (146).

14. Joseph Cooper Walker, for instance, writes of 'Bards of an inferior rank, or rather minstrels, strolling in large companies amongst the nobility and gentry' (204). On the other hand, Walker himself describes Irish bards in part via examples from writing about English and Scottish Border minstrels. Most strikingly, in a passage about the education of the old bards, Walker suddenly and uncritically weaves Beattie's *Minstrel* into his own narrative:

> Sometimes the young Bard, in order to relieve his mind from the severity of academic duties, 'essay's the artless tale,' as he wandered through his groves, obeying the dictates of his feelings, and panting from the rude scenes around him. –
>
> > Whate'er of beautiful or new,
> > Sublime or dreadful, in earth, sea, or sky,
> > By chance or search was offer'd to his view,
> > He scann'd with curious and romantic eye. (11)

The quotation of Beattie leaps out from the surrounding citations of Irish historians and classical sources.

15. The paradox of acted sensibility thus became a source of dramatic double entendre and of conservative anxiety. John Home's *Douglas* attracted the fire of Presbyterian critics in 1757, for instance, partly because they objected to the seemingly sincere portrayal of religious piety. The better the performance of Douglas's mother, in a literary sense, the more problematic it was for physiognomic readings of sincere emotion. Drama had long reveled in such paradoxes, but Home's critics wanted nothing to do with them.

    Catherine Burroughs has argued, on the other hand, that women writers

    > theorized an approach to theater practice that allows, indeed encourages, an appreciation of the theatricality of [closet theater as well as London playhouse performances]. This seeming unwillingness to discriminate against performance spaces bespeaks a flexibility and imagination that may in part be tied to women's experience of performing femininity on social 'stages'... (11)

    Judith Pascoe's work extends a similar sense of theatricality to non-dramatic writing, finding 'a propensity in romantic era verse that is directly at odds with Wordsworth's advocacy of a plain style' (3). I see a similar dynamic at play in minstrel writing, especially but not exclusively in minstrel writing by women.

16. Arguably, the ambiguously autobiographical narrator of *Peter Bell* would have constituted an important exception to this statement had Wordsworth followed through on his plan to include *Peter Bell* in *Lyrical Ballads*. Even the later, published version of *Peter Bell* carries some of the first version's ambiguity. Other characters in Wordsworth's poetry – the Solitary of *The Excursion* is one prominent example – have long been read as possessing autobiographical aspects, but Wordsworth ensures that any analogy between author and character is understood *as* an analogy. The Solitary (or the leech-gatherer, or any of a number of other characters) do not speak as 'Wordsworth' in the way that the speaker of 'Tintern Abbey' does.

17. See Averill, especially chapters 5 and 6 on *Lyrical Ballads*, for a closely argued analysis of Wordsworth's use of, ambivalence about, and framing of conventionally sentimental material.

18. Unlike the passage above, this one had been part of the 1800 Preface as well.

19. For further comment on Wordsworth's emphasis on the delay between inspiration and composition, see Angela Esterhammer's discussion of *The Prelude* in 'The Cosmopolitan *Improvvisatore*: Spontaneity and Performance in Romantic Poets' (153–4).

20. The texts of Wordsworth and Coleridge provide the most dramatic contrasts with minstrel writing, but a comparison to Shelley is also instructive. Shelley thought a great deal about the value of inspired moments in the creation of poetry, as in this passage from the *Defence of Poetry*:

    > The toil and delay recommended by the critics, can be justly interpreted to mean no more than a careful observation of the inspired moments, and an artificial connexion of the spaces between their suggestions by

the intertexture of conventional expressions; a necessity only imposed by the limitedness of the poetical faculty itself: for Milton conceived the Paradise Lost as a whole before he executed it in portions. We have his own authority also for the muse having 'dictated' to him the 'unpremeditated song'. (*CW* VII.136)

As much weight as Shelley places on the moments of inspiration, he separates those moments from the process of composition. Like Wordsworth and Coleridge, Shelley separates the composition of a poem from its inspiration and the audience from the inspired poet.

21. Page numbers in *Corinne* refer to the Goldberger translation unless otherwise noted.

22. This kind of annotation by other writers led Byron to quip to Lady Blessington that he had written his memoirs 'to save the necessity of their being written by a friend or friends, and have only to hope that they will not add notes' (quoted in Soderholm 145).

23. Jack Lynch deftly analyzes the work of Swift, Sterne, and many others in the context of the larger debate about editorial practice. Lynch reminds us of the debt of modern academics to the Moderns – or the Dunces – in the Battle of the Books: 'The ultimate victors in the annotation wars are evident to anyone in academia, where commentaries that outweigh the texts they presume to elucidate are no longer radical experiments, but the norm in scholarly publishing' (382). In my thinking about Augustan annotation, I am indebted to Lynch's essay and to his comments in correspondence.

24. *Tristram Shandy*'s footnotes, though subtle and few, illustrate the ironic possibilities of an editorial persona opposing directly the authorial one: 'The author here is twice mistaken' (164), proclaims one note. Of course, the novel also includes much broader satires on the urge to annotate in the character of Tristram's father. Sterne's novel is one of the three texts (with *Tom Jones* and *Finnegans Wake*) that Shari Benstock examines in 'At the Margin of Discourse: Footnotes in the Fictional Text'. Benstock's article offers a persuasive reading of footnotes in those texts, but it imagines that the footnote convention in fiction is an 'aberration' (205) confined to a very small number of works. (Benstock is 'intrigued by the . . . practice among writers . . . that may occur in fewer texts than can be counted on one hand: the use of footnotes in literary texts to extend, explain, or define the fictional premises of the work' [204].) While taking nothing away from the specific readings of Benstock's article, the much larger field of annotated fictions that I am discussing complicates its claims about the distinctions between scholarly and fictional footnoting practices.

25. There were some precedents for Macpherson's self-annotation. One with obvious connections to scholarly annotation of classical works is that of Ben Jonson's notes to his Roman plays and classicizing masques. Another, which is less important but interesting for other reasons, is Gabriel Nisbet's *Caledon's Tears: or, Wallace. A Tragedy* (1733). Nisbet does annotate his own play, as in the note explaining the Firth of Forth: 'A famous River that divides *Scotland* into South and North, and is joyned by an Arm of the *German* Ocean, which flows North-east from the Entry thereto, upon whose Banks there has been many memorable Battles fought, fatal to all Forreigners' (1). But even here,

Nisbet portrays himself as the *collector* of the play, heedless of the distinction between original work and collection that Percy, Scott, and others would later observe (or claim to observe). Nisbet also uses notes for that most traditional of purposes, the explication of Classical words, as in '*Cupid* ushering *Bellona*, imports, That Love to Liberty is an Introduction to a Just War' (2).

26. At least three other self-annotated genres developed alongside that of minstrel/bard romances: the Gothic novel, in which Walpole's fraudulent first preface provides a counterpart to Macpherson's work; the annotated satires documented by Gary Dyer (28–9); and the pedagogical/scientific works of Erasmus Darwin, Charlotte Smith, and others.

27. I use *genealogy* to describe the collection of minstrel texts I examine for many of the same reasons that Robert Miles favors the term: like the Gothic, minstrel writing is 'not . . . a single genre, but . . . an area of concern, a broad subject-matter, crossing the genres: drama and poetry, as well as novels' (4). I also find useful Miles's formulation (following Foucault) of the genealogy as operating outside of evolutionary models of literary history, instead recognizing that 'One text does not necessarily build upon a predecessor. On the contrary, it may initiate a "dialogue" with it, extending, or opening, a previous text, or texts, but also, at times, imposing closure upon it or them' (4). Additionally, I have been guided by Eric Lott's use of Fredric Jameson's suggestion that 'The virtue of genealogy . . . is that it defamiliarizes the cultural object, revealing from a diachronic perspective, as in an X ray, functional elements in forms such as minstrelsy that probably seem transparent enough' (Lott 22).

28. Walker's statement applies only to bardic practice in a strict sense. He does see a place for women in ancient Irish music with an important political function:

> But though women, during the heroic ages, held no rank in the order of Bards, yet it appears, that they cultivated music and poetry, whose divine powers they often employed in softening the manners of a people, rendered ferocious by domestic hostilities. What an unbounded influence must those arts, united with the irresistible sway of female beauty, have given the women of those ages! Accordingly, we often find them guiding in secret the helm of state, and proving the primary cause of great revolutions. (20–1)

29. Percy makes this comment in reference to a story he tells about a woman using a minstrel's costume to deliver a message to King Edward II. This story may well have provided some of the inspiration for later women to imagine women in minstrel dress as a way of breaking down the exclusive masculinity of ancient minstrelsy. Owenson's *The Novice of Saint Dominick* (1805) makes extensive use of this device.

30. The tradition of women's writing about William Wallace, one prominent example of this mode, will be addressed in Chapter 5.

31. Charlotte Brooke's *Reliques of Irish Poetry* (1789) is an exception that illustrates the rule. Brooke pursues a project of Ossianic antiquarianism and includes a bardic tale of her own. The preface to the volume apologizes

for the usurpation of a man's antiquarian role, asking 'where, alas, is this thirst for national glory? when a subject of such importance is permitted to a pen like mine! Why does not some *son of Anak* in genius step forward . . . ?' (iv). More complicated is the Introduction to Brooke's 'Irish Tale' in which she writes of 'Craftiné', a 'bardic sage', appearing to her and infusing her with the national spirit 'to the eye of Britain's Muse / [to] Present a sister's charms' (327). Brooke never calls herself a bard or represents a female bard, but she does take a clear step in that direction by linking herself to Craftiné's inspiration.

32. In *Marmion*, his first work after *The Wild Irish Girl*'s publication, Scott shows us Lady Heron performing as a domestic female minstrel. This performance, we are led to understand, is a debasement of the noble minstrelsy we see elsewhere in the poem; Lady Heron is a minstrel not for high purposes but with 'The pride that claims applause's due' (Canto V, 1.369). The episode may be part of a long, indirect conversation between Owenson and Scott; see Chapter 2.

33. One way of putting this is to say that Byron recognized the potential of minstrel writing's semi-autobiographical personae to create the 'romantic irony' described by Anne Mellor, in which, '[i]n Schlegel's terms, the ironic artist must constantly balance or "hover" between self-creation (*Selbstschöpfung*) and self-destruction (*Selbstvernichtung*) in a mental state that he calls *Selbstbeschränkung*, a rich term variously translated as self-determination, self-restraint, or self-restriction' (*English* 14).

2 The Minstrel in the World

1. Brendan Clifford addresses this gap directly. He opens the Introduction to his recent edition of Moore's *Political and Historical Writings on Irish and British Affairs* by describing a space in narratives of Irish history following the Union:

> Thomas Moore is one of two writers who exercised a profound influence on the course of Irish affairs during the generation between the Act of Union and Catholic Emancipation (1829). The other is Walter Cox. There is a high probability that, if neither Moore nor Cox had lived, Ireland would be substantially different from what it is. And yet Cox does not figure at all into our history books and Moore is doing well if he makes it into a footnote.
>
> With Moore and Cox thus deleted, real history in the period following the Union becomes a vacuum. And that vacuum is filled by O'Connell.
>
> But O'Connell is much too slight a presence in the first fifteen or twenty years of the century to account for the turn of events immediately following the Union. For better or worse, he filled the public life of the country in the 1820s and 1830s, but not before. (6)

I would clear a space for Owenson in Clifford's account. She preceded Moore as a writer of Irish 'national' materials and even as a collector of 'Irish Melodies', and like Moore, she became one of the most influential and well-compensated professional writers of the day, Irish or otherwise.

But Owenson, like Moore, Cox, and even the very period of their greatest influence, has tended to recede into the margins of Irish history.

2. The first numbers of the *Irish Melodies* presented them as William Power's project, with music by John Stevenson and lyrics to be composed with 'assistance from several distinguished Literary Characters, particularly from Mr. Moore . . .' (Moore *Irish Melodies* 113). Only gradually did they become known as 'Moore's *Melodies*'.

3. The epistolary narrator, in fact, explains in a letter that the novel's circumstances will *not* provide much distinctive information about Ireland:

> I am sorry I must disappoint your expectations . . . But the fact is, the general intercourse of nations in the present day, and universal promulgation of knowledge, leave the mind of a modern traveller but little scope for the due exercise of its penetration, in the discovery of national character: that of the Irish we have both read a thousand times, and were it otherwise, on my own observation, I should hazard little, as those whose aggregate constitute the people, and may be supposed best to preserve the national stamp, I have no opportunity of mingling with; and the people of fashion here are like the people of fashion every where else. (15–16)

4. Although the events of 1798 and 1802 must have changed Napoleon's thinking about the specifics of invading Britain, the broader objective remained, even as the primary objective of the French, after the rebellions: 'From 1798 to 1805, the conquest of Britain was Napoleon's primary strategic objective' (Colley 286).

5. Ian Dennis writes, 'This little piece of self-praise is quoted with surprising credulity by nearly every writer on Owenson. What indeed were the hazards and dangers, especially for a female writer? Probably, as Owenson herself points out, the biggest risk was that such writing would not be published at all' (183). Owenson may put her economic danger in more heroic terms than necessary, but I think Dennis's dismissal of her sense of the situation too strong. Dennis may be correct that Owenson herself did not face a bigger risk than being silenced (though her publisher did). However, 'that such writing would not be published at all' strikes me as a large risk indeed for Owenson in 1806. She was a professional writer, after all, one who relied on her work to support herself and her father. Silencing – whether through censorship or scandal – could have cost her the labor of producing her novel and perhaps her future earning power. Furthermore, the very real and recent atrocities committed on both sides of the rebellions could well have justified additional fears in 1806.

Fitzpatrick also gives us an anecdote of earlier state interference:

> In the Autobiography of A. Hamilton Rowan, there is an authentic conversation reported between Lord-Chief-Justice Clonmel and Mr. P. Byrne, Bookseller of Grafton Street, curiously illustrative of the unconstitutional terrorism which the executive of that day systematically exercised over the publishers of books having a patriotic or liberal tendency. Mr. Byrne having advertised the Trial of Hamilton Rowan for publication in 1793,

> was accosted non-officially by the Lord-Chief-Justice and informed, 'If you print or publish what may inflame the mob, it behoves [sic] the judges of the land to notice it,' and again, 'Take care, Sir, what you do: I give you this caution, for if there are any reflections on the judges of the land, by the eternal G– I will lay you by the heels.' The publisher replied, 'I have many thanks to return to your lordship for your caution!'

Fitzpatrick continues, 'Such grossly irregular interference of the Irish executive, soon reduced the publishing trade of Dublin to a state of almost utter prostration . . .' (110)

6. Stevenson explains:

> As well as arousing this general curiosity and sympathy, the attacks also indirectly brought her unexpected patronage. Several ladies of the vice-regal circle, particularly the Countess of Harrington and Lady Asgill, had taken a fancy to the quaint little writer, and wanted to help her. It happened, too, that the Whig Government, having begun to introduce a policy of conciliation in Ireland, had advised the Lord-Lieutenant, the Duke of Bedford, to modify the extreme anti-nationalism previously in vogue at the Castle. The persecution of *The Wild Irish Girl*, being a literary and social squabble which yet had political implications, presented itself as an opportunity for gratifying the liberals with a minimum of actual commitment. The power therefore made discreet inquiries as to a method of showing publicly their approval of Miss Owenson and her works; and by good luck they could provide just what she wanted. Her comic opera was ready, and the Viceroy's patronage would ensure its success. (85–6)

7. Byron's praise of *Italy* has become a standard component of Owenson biographies and criticism. For example, Fitzpatrick reports that Byron laughed at the idea of Owenson's book on Italy, then read it, called it 'a really *excellent* book' and subsequently wrote (on 24 August 1821) to Moore, 'By the way, when you write to Lady Morgan, will you thank her for some handsome speeches in her book about *my* books? I do not know her address. Her work is fearless and excellent on the subject of Italy – pray tell her so – and I know the country. I wish she had fallen in with *me*. I could have told her a thing or two that would have confirmed her positions' (Fitzpatrick 212).
8. For instance, Margaret Holford similarly invoked the faulty Englishness of Edward I as she wrote a Unionist poem celebrating the Scottish nationalist hero William Wallace. See Chapter 5 for more on the use of William Wallace among Romantic-era writers.
9. The full text is this: 'an asymptote is a line to which a given curve approaches without touching (*not* a hyperbola)' (264).
10. Tom Dunne, for instance, cites what he describes as the relative sophistication of Scottish historical writing compared to Irish antiquarianism to explain 'why Scott could write historical novels, while Morgan, for the most part, could only write contemporary novels suffused with history – though she could write historical novels on non-Irish themes' (139). Elmer Andrews does recognize a discontinuity between the action of the novel and the editorial voice, but rather than detecting a portrayal of different perspectives, Andrews

assumes that Owenson was unable to reconcile the contradictions of her novel, or even to understand them; to him *The Wild Irish Girl* is 'a collocation of warring impulses that are only half understood' (7). Pointing to one note's protestations that the dispossessed gentry of Ireland do not want to repossess their hereditary land (*WIG* 189), he writes,

> This assertion of the legitimacy and security of the land settlement occupies yet another footnote in a work devoted to arousing our sympathy for an intransigent Prince who takes no such view of his dispossession. Once again Lady Morgan is torn between the demands of a political programme and her imaginative sympathies. What she sees as historical necessity subverts the romance of loss. (16)

Andrews here isolates an important point of tension between the commentary of the notes and the action of the novel's plot. Indeed, the footnote he cites articulates the kind of compromise with the English, and of forgetting past injustices, that the Prince of Inishmore would not easily accept. The novel kills him off, in fact, before he has to come to terms with such a compromise.

11. In the note here cited, the editorial voice struggles to come to terms with 'a late anarchical period', shifting from hinting that English oppressors have unfairly criticized the Irish to insisting that the Irish in Wexford (site of some of the bloodiest fighting in 1798) are really British, whereas those of ancient Irish stock are less bloodthirsty; to quoting an unidentified source half-excusing Irish violence under oppression. Even in this place, the most direct address of 1798, the author/editor does not document events precisely, and she omits entirely any mention of Irish objections to England's conduct during the 1798 rebellion. That the editor chooses to invoke Wexford, of all places, calls still more attention to the novel's systematic omission of the damage England had caused to its relations with Ireland in and since 1798, as Wexford was the site of some of the most horrific English reprisals against rebels and Catholic churches in that year. See (for example) Pakenham 304–7.

12. Horatio does make 'a little offering to [the bard's] wife' (202). My point, of course, is that Horatio perceives any financial transaction with the bard as a matter requiring extreme care and propriety, given the venerable history of Irish bardic performance and patronage.

13. Only three short notes remain. One of those tells of a prohibition on the ancient Irish bards and minstrels like the Welsh prohibition in Gray's 'The Bard' (205), and another echoes the sale of the bard's harp with another moment of Irish concession to economic necessity: 'I have been informed that a descendant of the original kings of Connaught parted not many years back with the golden crown which, for so many ages, encircled the royal brows of his ancestors' (208).

14. We can gather a sense of the Maynooth institution's ongoing cultural importance from this passage of Byron's 'Additional note, on the Turks' attached to Cantos I and II of *Childe Harold's Pilgrimage*:

> In all the mosques there are schools established, which are very regularly attended; and the poor are taught without the church of Turkey

being put into peril. I believe the system is not yet printed, (though there is such a thing as a Turkish press, and books printed on the late military institution of the Nizam Gebbid); nor have I heard whether the Mufti and the Mollas have subscribed, or the Caimacam and the Tefterdar taken the alarm, for fear the ingenuous youth of the turban should be taught not to 'pray to God their way'. The Greeks also – a kind of Eastern Irish papists – have a college of their own at Maynooth – no, at Haivali; where the heterodox receive much the same kind of countenance from the Ottoman as the Catholic college from the English legislature. Who shall then affirm that the Turks are ignorant bigots, when they thus evince the exact proportion of Christian charity which is tolerated in the most prosperous and orthodox of all possible kingdoms? But, though they will allow this, they will not suffer the Greeks to participate in their privileges; no, let them fight their battles, and pay their haratach (taxes), be drubbed in this world, and damned in the next. And shall we then emancipate our Irish Helots? Mahomet forbid! We should then be bad Musselmans, and worse Christians; at present we unite the best of both – jesuitical faith, and something not much inferior to Turkish toleration. (*CPW* II.210–11)

15. Seamus Deane's brief comments on *The Wild Irish Girl* in *A Short History of Irish Literature* offer the fullest articulation of the specifically Protestant nature of the political resolution that the plot offers the reader (97–8). As my argument will make clear, I feel that Deane too quickly conflates the politics of Lord M—, Glorvina, Owenson's footnotes, and Owenson herself, but his reading usefully reminds us of the role that frustrated efforts at achieving Catholic Emancipation played in Irish Protestant Whig politics at the time Owenson wrote.

16. Much of the power of Miller's argument rests on interpreting the accusation of murder as a way to understand what is silenced by the closing marriage. Miller writes, 'Sydney Owenson gives us a heroine who is truly dangerous, one who dares, on her wedding day, to ask the question that must not be asked in a colonial marriage: "Which of you murdered my father?"' (24). While Miller does point to an element of the novel's ending that other critics have underplayed, Miller also overstates her case in saying that 'After [raising the question of murder…Glorvina] does not speak again' (27). Glorvina does speak again, largely to authorize her priest to tell her how to marry: 'I have no father but you – act for me as such!' (244). Although Glorvina is therefore not silenced in quite the way that Miller describes, one could argue that the contrast between Glorvina's delirious speech and her compliance almost immediately afterwards calls attention to the effort Glorvina must expend to forget the historical violence that lies behind her approaching marriage.

17. I am interested in the means by which Owenson's text still produces such a wide range of responses. The critics who see the final marriage as a 'genuinely as well as an overtly stabilizing resolution', in Ian Dennis's words (51), have a point: the novel presents a vision of beneficial reform, supported by a mass of detail about the evils of absentee landlords and specific remedies for the problem. It is difficult to imagine a novel interested primarily in nationalist

subversion of English colonial interests spending so much time suggesting a better system for managing those interests. Moreover, I would add that the end of the novel maintains a suggestive kind of balance: Horatio's father writes the novel's final letter solidifying the consolidating marriage, but Father John (the remaining Irish patriarch and Glorvina's explicitly adopted father) reads that letter aloud to Horatio and Glorvina. This device allows the fathers to speak with a mixed voice that Horatio and Glorvina hear simultaneously. Additionally, the planned marriage between Lord M— and Glorvina is balanced by its converse: a symbolic marriage of Horatio and her father, the Prince, when the former accepts the latter's ring (220). However unsatisfactory the resolution might be, the novel gives its readers a good deal of support for understanding the ending as a happy one and the marriage as a balanced and consensual union.

At the same time, Lew, Miller, and Ferris point to ways in which the novel's own logic calls our attention to deeper, more systemic problems that lie beyond the reach of Lord M—'s reforms. Indeed, these critics' analyses unearth a large enough body of evidence to make it difficult to imagine that the novel asks its reader to feel entirely satisfied by Lord M—'s letter. More evidence for the instability of the novel's resolution might come from the strangeness of that letter itself. Dennis points out the inadequacy of Lord M—'s protestations that his affection for Glorvina had been only 'parental' (*WIG* 246) – 'as if this somehow makes it better' (Dennis 50). I too find Lord M—'s reasoning regarding his interest in Glorvina inadequate, and I would extend Dennis's point to notice the self-serving hypocrisy of Lord M—'s advice on the maintenance of Irish estates, which he gives immediately after justifying his former marriage plans. This is the man, we recall, whose inattention caused the tyranny of his deputy Clendinning, whose cruelty remained unchecked for at least two years after Lord M— supposedly unlearned his English prejudices against the Irish.

18. See Ferris for an excellent discussion of the novel's national inflection of the sentimental conventions glorifying silent communication (*Achievement* 127–30).

19. Campbell borrows two of Stevenson's sentences, unacknowledged and somewhat out of context, and adds nothing new. Campbell writes,

> [Owenson], at least, did not seem to take these verses seriously as she insists in the Preface that they are but 'metrical trifles...bagatelles...vers de societé' put before the public only because her publisher offered her a good price, and she needed the money. They are frankly autobiographical and on the subject of love she documents at least two distinct affairs of the heart, and pleads for unimpassioned friendship, 'sentiment and sense', because love has injured her. (76)

The first sentence slightly alters this from Stevenson: 'She insists in the Preface that the verses should not be regarded as serious poetry, but as "metrical trifles...bagatelles...*vers de société*...merely and professedly amusive," put before the public only because her publisher offered her a good price and she needed the money' (90). The second summarizes Stevenson's comments on his following pages and then borrows more directly from this: 'She contrasts her childish innocent happiness with her present disillusionment, and pleads for unimpassioned friendship, "sentiment and sense," because love has injured her...' (Stevenson 91).

Campbell's alterations to Stevenson's sentences, slight as they are, change the meaning materially, at least in the first case. Stevenson charges Owenson with false modesty in the self-deprecatory Preface, while Campbell's removal of that context characterizes Owenson as dismissing her volume sincerely. It is not clear whether this is a case of sloppy copying or the intentional revision of an unacknowledged source.

20. By 'later Della Cruscan collections' I mean the verse produced by Robert Merry ('Della Crusca'), Hannah Cowley ('Anna Matilda') and others written for *The World* magazine and collected in *Poetry of the World* (London: John Bell, 1788) and *The British Album* (London: John Bell, 1790). For an introduction to this poetry, its popular success, and its rhetorical strategies, see Jerome McGann, 'The Literal World of the English Della Cruscans'.

21. In the same year Owenson published her *Lay*, Moore wrote in a footnote to 'Intolerance' (1807),

> The breach of faith which the managers of the Irish Union have been guilty of in disappointing those hopes of emancipation which they excited in the bosoms of the Catholics, is no new talent in the annals of English policy. A similar deceit was practiced to facilitate the Union with Scotland, and hopes were held out of exemption from the Corporation and Test Acts, in order to divert the Parliament of that country from encumbering the measure with any stipulation to that effect. (44)

This connection raised the question of how Scott's method of presenting Anglo-Scottish conflict as part of a romantic history to be overcome in modern unity would translate to the Irish situation, where the traumas of the recent rebellions could not rest so easily in the past.

22. Scott thus places the legislative impetus for minstrelsy's fall just before the Union of the Crowns (1603), while placing the minstrels' eventual disappearance under the House of Stuart/Stewart. In other words, his chronology does not allow for a Jacobite reading that minstrelsy died off after 1688 or 1746. The date of cultural loss moves later in Scott's subsequent works, as the novels pay close attention to eighteenth-century modernization and loss, but in the more politically delicate time of 1805, Scott puts his 'last minstrel' myth at a somewhat safer chronological distance. The 'last minstrel' motif itself had been around well before this exchange, of course, notably in Gray's 'The Bard', Percy's minstrel theories, Evan Evans's work on Welsh bards, and Owenson's own 1801 *Poems*.

23. Michael Gamer has noted this tendency in Scott regarding the framing of gothic elements. Gamer describes Scott's annotations as a manifestation of 'the anxiety [Scott] feels at invoking [gothic] devices' as well as his skill in exploiting the popularity of gothic materials while maintaining 'his authority as a historian and serious author' (535). Annotation is one of the primary means by which Scott's realism, in Fredric Jameson's formulation, 'releases a set of heterogeneous historical perspectives' (104).

24. Gamer argues for the games of this scene as a metaphor for the 'national childhood' Scott wants to create as a predecessor to the adulthood of 'British national unity' (537).

25. Owenson had written of Ossian previously: *St. Clair* includes a brief defense of the Irish claims on the ancient bard, and *The Wild Irish Girl* develops the argument further. Readers of *The Wild Irish Girl* would have remembered its extended defense of Ossian's Irishness, but *The Lay of an Irish Harp* accomplishes a similar effect in two swift strokes, by moving from the Ossianic epigraph to an Irish opening, linked by the metaphor of sleep: the command to 'awake the soul of song' in the epigraph becomes the question, 'Why sleeps the Harp of Erin's pride?' (1) in the opening poem's first line. The fact that readers after 1805 generally saw Macpherson's work as a modern, politically motivated production enforced the link between the two national 'sleeps', that of Scotland in the aftermath of the 1745 Jacobite Rebellion and that of Ireland after Wolfe Tone's uprising in 1798. The treatment of Ireland's Ossianic connections developed further in the third landmark of Ossianic studies that emerged in 1805: Scott's *Edinburgh Review* article on the Mackenzie report and the Laing edition. There, Scott takes a conciliatory stance towards Ireland (perhaps partially a result of the reduced threat of the United Irishmen). He praises Charlotte Brooke's *Reliques of Irish Poetry* and concedes the Irish claims on Ossian's birth unequivocally. Tactfully ignoring Macpherson's many attacks on Irish historians, Scott makes Macpherson's project into an example of successful Scottish assimilation into modern literature and statehood, aligning it explicitly with John Home's *Douglas*. See Chapter 1 for more on this passage.

26. Moore presumably refers to passages such as this: 'Usurpers prevail, and partial are thy courts, O! Erin; and corruption is the order of the day! That Freedom, O! Brethren of Woe, which once was yours, is driven from your isle, and now cheereth some nations abroad – but Britannia commands and oppression is joined to *your* fate!' (from the reprinted text of the poem, Clifford *Life* 33).

27. The Mackenzie report's conclusions are commonly overstated, sometimes drastically. As Fiona Stafford and others have noted, the report did not conclude that Ossian or Ossianic poems had never existed, only that Macpherson had taken more editorial liberties than he had admitted. The Committee, said the report,

> is inclined to believe that [Macpherson] was in use to supply chasms, and to give connections, by inserting passages which he did not find, and to add what he conceived to be dignity and delicacy to the original composition, by striking out passages, by softening incidents, by refining the language, in short by changing what he considered as too simple or too rude for a modern ear, and elevating what in his opinion was below the standard of good poetry. To what degree, however, he exercised those liberties, it is impossible for the Committee to determine [because of the lapse in time between Macpherson's efforts and theirs]. (152)

28. Comparison with Owenson's earlier sources helps to sharpen our sense of the choices she made here. Her 1801 *Poems* used primarily canonical English

(Shakespeare, Bacon, Pope, Otway, Thomson) and classical (Seneca, Lucan, Ovid, Anacreon, Sappho, Plutarch) sources along with a few sparse references to Continental and Irish writers. This is a source list geared to establishing a new writer's authority for an audience that does not know her. Likewise, the semi-anonymous (by 'S.O.') *A Few Reflections, Occasioned by the Perusal of a Work, Entitled, 'Familiar Epistles, To Frederick J—s Esq. on the Present State of the Irish Stage'* (1804) responded to John Wilson Croker's attack with almost exclusively Classical sources. *St. Clair* (1803), her first novel, weaves its sources into the narrative rather than citing them, but the featured writers are Goethe (*Werther* is the obvious model for the structure of the novel), Ossian, Bolingbroke, and Rousseau. The group of sources is analogous in some ways to that of *The Lay of an Irish Harp*; the cited writers form part of the characters' conversation rather than constituting a separate editorial voice. *The Novice of Saint Dominick* (1805) comes closest to the *Lay*'s model, with epigraphs from a similar gathering of writers, but it includes almost none of the documentary apparatus of the later works.

29. The very breeziness of the quotation process – 'a German poet (whose name has escaped recollection)' – reinforces Owenson's cosmopolitanism backhandedly; to forget the name of the writer is to remind the reader that she has no need to look up the line.

30. An exception to the general lack of Irish sources, the Goldsmith epigraph to Fragment XVIII, proves the internationalist rule of the Continental citations. The reason for the Irish intrusion is clear enough: the fragment is titled 'Home', and the note to the opening line ('Sad, deserted, and alone') reads,

> This trifle was scribbled on a tablet when the recollection of endeared home opposed itself to the comfortless *solitude* of an inn; for surely the term solitude is arbitrary in its application; and the heart, independent of situation, may, in the midst of the busiest haunts, shrink back upon itself *solitary* and unanswered. (79, emphasis original)

The fragment connects the alienation possible within one's country to that felt by foreigners or exiles. Where Scott strove to consolidate Britishness through animating the national ground with stories, *The Lay of an Irish Harp* uses sensibility to imply communities of feeling that subtly suggest a transnational alternative to accommodating British interests. As Trumpener writes, 'the Lowlanders' carefully sentimentalized relationship, sixty years after Culloden, toward Highland culture, has no easy parallel in Ireland' (132). Owenson takes advantage of the tension produced by recapitulating the conventions of minstrelsy in a new situation.

31. Take, for instance, a passage by Merry as Della Crusca 'To Anna Matilda', in which Merry presents his own lost happiness because he hadn't encountered Anna Matilda sooner. While Merry frequently laments the 'tyranny' of contemporary rulers, he here allows for a limited glorification of war, but only on strictly sentimental terms:

> Or had she [Anna Matilda] said, that *War's the worthiest grave*,
>   He [Della Crusca] would have felt his proud heart burn the while,

> Have dar'd, perhaps, to rush among the brave,
> Have gain'd, perhaps, the glory – of a smile.
> (*Poetry of the World* I.45)

32. Jeanne Moskal complicates the traditional equation of Owenson with Glorvina by carefully considering the editorial voice of *The Wild Irish Girl*, but Moskal nonetheless accepts the established shortcut of invoking Owenson's later nickname as a basis for sticking with that equation: 'Glorvina is the embodiment and repository of Irish culture, who can be sought but cannot herself seek. But the agency and authority of Morgan as Glorvina emerges in the footnotes, a return of the repressed. (This identification of Morgan with Glorvina lasted much of her life, as most of her friends addressed her by that name)' (177).

33. When I refer to Owenson's cosmopolitanism, I have in mind Anne K. Mellor's recent work on the idea of embodied cosmopolitanism in the work of a number of British Romantic woman writers including Owenson herself. In her discussion of the trope of marriages overcoming religious and national differences, Mellor mentions the union that closes *The Wild Irish Girl*; part of my purpose here is to add to that famous example other, sometimes more complex instances of Owenson's cosmopolitanism. Owenson's *Lay of an Irish Harp*, which I discuss below, seems to me to support Mellor's sense, following the work of April Allison, that women who legally 'lacked the constituent elements of national citizenship' created solidarity through strategies that 'exploited a cultural celebration of sympathy' (Mellor 'Embodied' 292).

3 'The Minstrels of Modern Italy'

1. When I refer to 'improvisation' in Romantic-era writing, I mean the practice of Italian *improvvisatori* and *improvvisatrici* signified by Staël's French word *improvisation*, which was generally not yet translatable into English, as I will show.

2. For example, see Stephen Greenblatt's 'Improvisation and Power', a discussion primarily of *Othello*. Greenblatt's 'improvisation' is not a Renaissance term but one that he uses retrospectively, describing 'a crucial Renaissance mode of behavior that links Lerner's "empathy" and Shakespeare's Iago: I shall call that mode *improvisation*, by which I mean the ability to both capitalize on the unforeseen and transform given materials into one's own scenario. The "spur of the moment" quality of improvisation is not as critical here as the opportunistic grasp of what seems fixed and established' (60). Greenblatt offers a persuasive reading of *Othello*, but his definition of 'improvisation' has only a vague, analogical relationship to the term's common meanings.

   In the less anachronistic 'Defoe and the "Improvisatory" Sentence', P. N. Furbank and W. R. Owens use the term differently:

   > Defoe, we feel, when he embarked upon this sentence, had only a vague idea how it would end (genuinely so; it was not merely, though it might have been, an artistic pretence that he did not know). We must not jump to conclusions from this. A little reflection will tell us that to write in this way, which we may call 'improvisatory', is quite common, and – as in

> this case – does not at all imply that the product will have less form and 'architecture' than a more premeditated style. Nevertheless, it goes against a certain hallowed tradition in prose-writing, which for a want of a better word we may call 'Ciceronian'. The Ciceronian tradition attributes special value to the *end* of sentences, and to forward planning in general. (160)

I quote this passage at length because Furbank and Owens provide an efficient and precise theory of what it means to improvise, one that strikes me as a useful way of describing the ideological potency of extemporaneous forms in general, whether in Defoe or Staël or Ellington. What I hope to accomplish here is not to contradict ahistorical theoretical definitions such as this one but to inflect them with the local specificity that Romantic writers would have understood when they developed their own theories of improvisation.

3. Throughout, I will use the Romantic-era Italian spellings of *improvvisator(e/i)* and *improvvisatric(e/i)*. English-language writers of the time used many variations of those spellings, often omitting the second 'v' (as in many of my examples here) and sometimes using 's' to form plurals.
4. The reference occurs in *Travels through France and Italy*, published in the following year. Gonda provides an excellent analysis of *OED* citations for variants of improvisation and some early British commentary on the subject.
5. The first *OED* citation of improv(v)isatrice refers to 'An honorary name given to the poetess (improvisatrice) D. Maria Maddalena Morelli Fernandez', from Matilda Betham's *Biographical Dictionary of the Celebrated Women of Every Age and Country* (*OED* 'improvisatrice'). As I note in Table 3.1, however, there was at least one eighteenth-century usage: Hester Lynch Piozzi uses the term in her 1789 *Observations and Reflections Made in the Course of a Journey through France, Italy, and Germany*.

   The *OED* also states that 'improvisation' comes from the Latin *improvisus* ('unforeseen, unexpected') via the Italian *improviso*, now spelled *improvviso* ('unprovided, extempore'). Such a confluence foreshadows later battles about the merits of improvisation, with the roots implying both an admirable ability to cope with unexpected circumstances and a less admirable lack of preparation for the unexpected.

   Our modern sense of 'improvise' as a verb developed relatively late. The *OED* gives four verb forms, all first cited between 1825 and 1835: 'improvise', 'improvisate', 'improvisatorize', and 'improviso'. ('Improviso' predated this, but only as an adjective, as in Warton's usage.) I suspect that at least some of these forms emerged before 1825, but the *OED* tells us at least that many forms were simultaneously current, and the surviving modern verb 'to improvise' is the one that shows least evidence of Italian roots, having dropped both the -o of *improviso* and the -at* or -ator* of *improvvisatore*.

   'Improvisation', the noun, came relatively early (1786), as did the adjective 'improviso'. ('Improvised' emerged much later – again the Italianate form dominates early on and then disappears. Likewise, 'Improvizer', referring to an improvisatory artist not necessarily Italian, first appears in 1829.) Shelley's use of 'improvise' as a noun (calling *Hellas* 'a mere improvise' in its preface [*CW* III.7]) was shared by Mary Shelley, but neither the *OED* nor the present writer has recorded the usage by anyone else.

6. Both the Della Cruscan poetry and *The Florence Miscellany* work to link the ruins of modern Italy with a Britain they portray as ruining itself. See, for instance, Hester Thrale Piozzi's 'Translation of Marquis Pindemonte's Hymn to Calliope' (*FM* 19–23) or Robert Merry's 'Ode on a Distant Prospect of Rome, Irregular', which for many lines describes 'visions' of war, domestic squabbling, luxury, and 'harden'd Tyranny' (*FM* 85). Without specifying whether those visions apply to 'Enlighten'd Europe', the nearest referent, or Rome, Merry allows the ambiguity to simmer for many lines until finally identifying the visions as Roman (*FM* 85). Merry's political wit often clothed politically inoffensive sentiments in phrases and syntax that suggest much riskier notions.

7. Nanora Sweet's work on Felicia Hemans points to the specifically republican resonance of Italy. Speaking of texts from about a decade later than *Corinne*, Sweet writes that Byron's and Shelley's

> evocations of classical and Italianate literature and culture ... may by read as encoding their recognition of Greece and Italy as sites of imperial struggle between Austria, Britain, Turkey, and Russia. For these two writers the particular legacy of the Greek and Italian city states is above all a *republicanism* that is superior to the unreformed constitution of the island empire; as a result, their references to Mediterranean culture generally serve to adumbrate republican values. (171)

8. Lawler's preface explains that the slightly earlier anonymous translation was produced by two men (iv). This first translation does try to work improvisation into the text in one odd usage, as the Prince 'expatiate[s] on her [Corinna's] talent for extempore effusions, a talent which resembled, in nothing, the improvisatorè, as expressed in Italy' (I.67).

9. As noted below, Letitia Elizabeth Landon translated the verse in the Hill edition.

10. In a different context, Michel Delon has also identified a 'dual' struggle in Staël's writing, a struggle

> against those who were nostalgic for the old regime, who would deny all necessity for Revolution and would look for the men and events that would have favored its avoidance; and against a fatalism which, either in invoking Providence or justifying the Terror, denies all possibility of an effect by men upon their history. (27)

11. Later in the novel comes another example of the conversational aesthetic:

> The air in Venice, the life one leads there, are calculated to lull the soul with hope: the easy swaying of the boats inclines one to reverie and idleness. Sometimes from the Ponte Rialto, a gondolier bursts into song with a stanza from Tasso, while from the other end of the canal, another gondolier responds with the following stanza. The very ancient music of these lines resembles liturgical chant, monotonous when heard up close; but in the open, at night, when the sounds stretch out over the canal like the

reflection of the setting sun, and Tasso's verses lend their beauty of feeling to the whole blend of images and harmony, the singing inevitably inspires a sweet melancholy. (302)

12. Staël's political theory in *Considérations sur les principaux événements de la Révolution française* (1818) illustrates her effort to find a theory of political moderation in more direct terms. She writes,

> the principle of heredity in a monarchy is indispensable to the tranquillity, even, I will say, to the morality and progress, of the human mind. Elective monarchy opens up a vast field to ambition . . . But the privileges accorded to birth, whether for creating a nobility or for establishing succession to the throne within a single family, need to be confirmed by the passage of time. They differ in this respect from natural rights, which do not depend on any authority or agreement.
>   . . . Legitimacy, as it has been recently set forth, is thus absolutely inseparable from constitutional limitations . . . If every change is to be condemned only because it is change, and no matter what its influence upon the general welfare and the progress of mankind, it will be easy to oppose to the older order of things that you invoke another still older order of things which it replaces. In short, what human being with common sense can pretend that a change in customs and ideas should not result in a change in political institutions? (94–6)

13. For one of many possible examples of the use of minstrelsy to express 'British fears of post-Revolutionary France', see Penny Fielding's treatment of Scott's poem 'The Bard's Incantation', written in 1804 (46).

14. Anne Janowitz has argued in *England's Ruins* that eighteenth-century ruin poetry attributed Rome's fall to its effeminate weakness: she says that in John Dyer's *The Ruins of Rome*, '[t]he source of Rome's decadence is situated in the vaginal territory that underlies the visible world of ruins on the surfaces of the landscape: it is Luxury that turned Rome's brilliance into its death-sentence' (39). *Corinne* repeats the feminizing of Rome but does so in order to focus blame on the masculine tyrannies that have suppressed Rome's greatness. Oswald, in a way the novel presents as typically English (and/or Scottish, depending on the context), repeatedly finds his Dyer-like conception of Italian history confronted by Corinne's opposing view, as in her exchanges with Oswald quoted above.

15. Many critics, including Moers and Avriel Goldberger, have explained Staël's inconsistency by attributing it to an uncharacteristic carelessness on Staël's part. Indeed, it is possible that Staël simply did not bother to distinguish the two countries consistently; throughout her writings, she mentions Scottish and even Irish works in discussions of 'English' literature, though she certainly knew enough to be more exact. Given the proximity in the text of Oswald's Scottishness and Englishness, I think of the confusion as more strategic than accidental. For my purposes here, however, the point is largely moot.

16. Such conventions had by this time been reinforced by numerous travel narratives and periodical accounts. They would return to the center of a full-length popular work in Hans Christian Andersen's *The Improvisatore* (1835; translated into a successful English edition by Mary Howitt in 1845).

17. For instance, the 'metaphor of the responsively vibrating string or chord of feeling' (326) and the play between past- and present-tense verbs (327) through which Isobel Armstrong deftly reads *The Improvisatrice* also occur in Regency metrical romances.

18. Tetrameter couplets had long been associated with easy, spontaneous verse, as in the *British Critic's* review of *The Lady of the Lake*: 'Many perhaps may read the Poem without perceiving that the whole narrative is given in the easiest, and generally the tamest measure that our language knows; the measure in which *improvisatori*, if England could produce them, would certainly speak or sing; the eight syllable couplet . . . ' (Hayden 52).

19. Angela Esterhammer has documented a contemporaneous Continental tradition of writing about the improviser 'as a misfit alienated from healthy society' ('Improviser's Disorder' 330).

20. Although Owenson and *Corinne* have separately enjoyed renewed critical attention recently, no critic, to my knowledge, has yet noticed the degree to which *The Novice* and *The Wild Irish Girl* together anticipate *Corinne*. *The Novice's* minstrel conventions, including the specific introduction of improvisation, and *The Wild Irish Girl's* plot (structured around an English visitor unlearning his prejudices by falling in love with Ireland and the antiquarian-heroine simultaneously) together provide precedents for virtually every major plot sequence of *Corinne*. I know of no reason to think Staël had read Owenson's novels; if she did, one could make a strong case that the myth of Corinne is a variant of the previous myth of Imogen. In the absence of such evidence, we can at least note the novels' similarities as a remarkable literary coincidence.

21. In the last two volumes, its morality and plot resemble strongly those of both Maria Edgeworth's *Belinda* (1801) and Jane Porter's *Thaddeus of Warsaw* (1802). Many novels had already warned of the corrupting influence of the high life, of course, but *Thaddeus of Warsaw* seems a much more specific precedent for Owenson. Like *The Novice*, it is a novel of four long volumes. Both open with a detailed account of military history and heroism, then shift suddenly to domestic life, in each case with a heavy emphasis on the suffering occasioned by aristocrats' unpaid debts. Both novels work to integrate the two plots by bringing the military characters back to play roles in the domestic plot. Staël, on the other hand, prefers macroeconomics and broad historical speculations to the details of household economy.

22. Lionel Stevenson documents the impact of *Corinne* on Owenson and her circle:

> Mme de Staël had been writing for a good many years, but it was her novel *Corinne*, published in 1807, that established her fame with the English public. Allusions to it promptly began to appear in the letters and conversations of Miss Owenson and her friends, some of whom took to calling her 'the Irish de Staël.'

Miss Owenson's own novels were already in harmony with Mme de Staël's in the prominence of their heroines. In each of her three stories the central woman character was far more distinctly drawn than the man, and in two of them she was definitely his superior in intellect and wisdom. But this had been merely the result of personal predilection; *Corinne* made Miss Owenson aware of a new cause to be championed – the defense of her own sex in a man-dominated world. In her fourth novel [*Ida of Athens*], therefore, she set herself consciously to expound the innate merits of feminine character. (111–12)

The Monthly Review noticed the influence and 'preferred *Ida* to *Corinne*' (Stevenson 119). On the other hand, *Corinne's* similarities to *The Novice of Saint Dominick* (and *The Wild Irish Girl*, for that matter) attracted the notice of some readers, at least. For instance, an 'Englishwoman of title in Rome' wrote, 'I greatly prefer Imogen [of *The Novice*] to the superhuman Corinne, whose character, though pleasing as a whole, is not always natural or consistent' (Stephenson 'Victorian Improvisatrice' 66).

23. More's work seems to have enjoyed considerable market success: first published in 1819, it had reached its 'Ninth Edition' in 1821.
24. More's change of heart about drama happened long before 1819. 'By the time that [*Percy*] was received to great acclaim in the 1785–86 season at Drury Lane, with the celebrated Mrs Sarah Siddons in the role of Elwina, Hannah More had adopted the views of the early Christian church to the theatre and would not allow herself to attend' (Evans 4–5).
25. Moers mentions Jewsbury's novel as 'an imitation of *Corinne* ... in which the heroine proclaims her admiration for fame because "it would make amends for being a woman"' (177). Julia does, of course, say those words, but the narrative systematically dismisses both her Staëlian feminism (linked here with Mary Wollstonecraft's sufferings) and her notion that fame helps anyone become truly happy. According to Jewsbury's novel (unlike *Corinne*), Julia, with proper reading and better decision-making, could have acquired worldly as well as eternal happiness.
26. I thank Michael Gamer for pointing me to the passage on Giannetti.
27. This comes from the narrator's introduction of Corinne: 'on lui répondit qu'on devait couronner le matin même, au Capitole, la femme la plus célèbre de l'Italie, Corinne, poete, écrivain, improvisatrice, et l'une des plus belles personnes de Rome' (*Corinne ou L'Italie* I.50).
28. As explained, this promised note does not seem to have materialized.
29. This comes from the narrator describing the Prince's praise of Corinne: 'Il sétendit sur son talent d'improviser, qui ne ressemblait en rien à ce qu'on est convenu d'appeler de ce nom en Italie' (*Corinne ou L'Italie* I.65).
30. This comes from the title of the famous 'Improvisation de Corinne au Capitole' (*Corinne ou L'Italie* I.73).
31. This is the same phrase as above, now used twice in succession: first to describe Corinne's own talent, then by Corinne to describe a native Italian 'talent d'improviser' (*Corinne ou L'Italie* I.123). Only the Hill translation marks a difference in the two uses: the anonymous 1807 translation translates both instances the same way, and the Lawler translation avoids the issue by referring to 'the talent for extempore poetry' (I.130, as noted in the table) and then, in Corinne's words, to 'the talent you are discussing' (I.131).

4 The Minstrel and Regency Romanticism

1. Antagonism towards Byron would hardly have been out of character for Wordsworth. In addition to the remarks quoted here, see McGann's argument in 'Byron and Wordsworth' that Byron 'did not hate Wordsworth – though he *would* have hated him had he known the whole truth' (*Byron and Romanticism* 174).

2. Other important articulations of *The Excursion*'s complexities include Frances Ferguson's chapter-length exploration of the poem in *Wordsworth: Language as Counter-Spirit*; James Chandler's comparison of the 'dialectical interchange[s]' resulting from the 'fundamental difference...that *The Excursion* is an action between characters and *The Prelude* is an action of a single character' (*Wordsworth's* 207); William Galperin's contention that the Wanderer and the Solitary have a 'peculiar kinship' and that each of them 'in the presence of the other, gradually becomes his own adversary' (47); and Alison Hickey's exploration of '*The Excursion*'s peculiar resistance to the very authority it seems to embody' (11).

3. Searching the English Short Title Catalog, the British Library catalogues, and J. R. de J. Jackson's *Annals of English Verse, 1770-1835* yields printings from the following years after 1775: 1779, 1784, 1794, 1795, 1797, 1799, 1801, 1803 (2), 1805 (2), 1806 (2), 1807 (2), 1808, 1810, 1811, 1816, 1817, 1819, 1823, 1824, and 1825.

4. This is one of a number of points at which the presumably autobiographical narrator of the poem separates himself from Edwin. '[M]y childhood', says the narrator, featured 'mighty masters of the lay' (I.xliv), as opposed to Edwin's hag. Beattie encouraged the association between his youth and Edwin's after the fact, but the first book of the poem clearly separates the two.

5. See Chapter 1 for the details of Beattie's military plans for his minstrel.

6. Everard King argues for reviving critical consciousness of Wordsworth's debts to Beattie. King has noticed Neaves's commentary on Wordsworth and Beattie, which I discuss above. King attributes the commentary to John Wilson as Christopher North, but this attribution appears to be mistaken; the letter is addressed *to* Wilson/North, and the Wellesley Index attributes the piece to Neaves on the authority of the 'Manuscript List of Early Contributors to *Blackwood's Magazine*, 1826–1870', commonly known as 'Blackwood's Contributors' Book'. King writes,

   > Since, as one suspects, many nineteenth-century readers believed [Neaves's] to be in large measure a defensible opinion, no one has ever attempted to refute Wilson's charge as a serious indictment of Wordsworth's poem; and today *The Minstrel* is an even more neglected poem than *The Excursion*. (96)

7. A side note: Merivale was sufficiently interested in Beattie to publish a continuation of *The Minstrel* (Longman, 1808). David Hill Radcliffe addresses this and other continuations in 'Completing James Beattie's *The Minstrel*'.

8. In concentrating on Wordsworth's engagement with his cultural status through the 1815 edition, I depart in emphasis from earlier treatments of the *Poems*' arrangement such as those by Frances Ferguson and William Galperin. The value of Ferguson's and Galperin's approaches lies in their skilled close

readings of the tensions and ironies of Wordsworth's prose in the volume; my approach instead emphasizes Wordsworth's interactions with his sympathetic critics, who did not customarily read in search of such ironies – or were willing to overlook them in the cause of supporting Wordsworth's poetry at the expense of Byron's.

9. Lawrence Lipking argues that Wordsworth's narrative of his own poetic life, along with Blake's, helped create a model from which later poets worked to fashion their own developmental narratives. 'The modern "epic"', writes Lipking, 'is dominated by one story and one story only: the life of the poet' (70). Lipking allows for the possibility that poets might misrepresent their own careers, '[b]ut the poet's claim to have achieved an identity, to have shaped his life into art, cannot deceive anyone for long. Either the poems themselves prove it, or they do not' (x). My interest lies in the gray area between the either/or polarities of Lipking's formulation, in the details of poets' (especially Wordsworth's) presentation of some truths rather than others at different times.

10. The complexities of the character who sings 'The Isles of Greece' have attracted a good deal of attention in modern Byron criticism. See, for example, Peter Manning, *Byron and His Fictions*, p. 219; Malcolm Kelsall, *Byron's Politics*, p. 156; McGann, *Byron and Romanticism*, pp. 44–51 and 154; and Peter Graham, Don Juan *and Regency England*, p. 190.

11. According to Radcliffe, Byron even helped to sustain Beattie's cultural prominence: '[r]ather than effacing *The Minstrel*, *Childe Harold* had an amplifying effect, swelling the number of Beattie imitations and heightening their emotional intensity' (552).

12. Maureen McLane has also noted Byron's collapse of past and present. Connecting Byron's technique to Scott rather than Beattie, she writes,

> In *Childe Harold*, Byron incorporated aspects of Scott's minstrelsy, modelling Harold's 'Goodnight Song' on 'Lord Maxwell's Good-night' from Scott's *Border Minstrelsy*. Yet Byron boldly collapsed the historical and poetic distances Scott had kept comfortably open between his narrating persona and his ventriloquized minstrel. ('Figure' 446–7)

13. Citations of the verse of *Childe Harold's Pilgrimage* and *Don Juan* come from McGann's *Complete Poetical Works* and will be given by canto and stanza.

14. McGann writes, 'The case of *The Giaour* is . . . instructive since the optional texts are distinguished by different systems of punctuation where the final intentions of the author – or even of the author working collectively with the publisher – are not definable in any clear way' (*Critique* 105). He goes on, with questions of punctuation at the heart of the example, to describe the texts available to the poem's editors and their respective claims to authority.

15. McGann makes this connection to the latter two poems in *Fiery Dust* (142).

16. See, for example, McGann's corrections of Kroeber in *Fiery Dust* (143–4).

17. In this way, Byron uses minstrelsy in *The Giaour* to purposes similar to those Peter Manning has noted in *Don Juan*: 'the condition of unfinishedness is not merely an aspect of the story, a temporary fiction exposed when the whole

is complete, but one that attaches the poet himself and his influences to the ongoing creation of the text' (*Reading Romantics* 129).

18. Byron's use of the *improvvisatore* has received the most thorough critical examination of any Romantic-era depiction of minstrels, bards, or improvisers. Among the most important analyses are those of Lindsay Waters, Jerome McGann (*Fiery Dust* 277–83), and George Ridenour (162–6). Byron's relationship with Germaine de Staël has received a full-length treatment in Joanne Wilkes's *Lord Byron and Madame de Staël: Born for Opposition* (Aldershot: Ashgate, 1999).

19. Byron's opposition to this kind of optimism does not place him simply on the side of a corresponding pessimism. Malcolm Kelsall describes the Whig progressivism of which Byron partook at this time, and the difficulties of maintaining that position in the Regency:

> The Whig tradition is one which celebrates the gradual progress of liberty, often checked by the wickedness of Tory tyranny, but which, like an incoming tide, if blocked in one place, flows on at another: from Magna Carta, to Habeas Corpus, the Bill of Rights, the American Republic, the fall of the Bastille. Leading the process for the people are the great patrician figures, men whom Byron named: Aristides and Washington, Brutus and Franklin, Fox and Windham, 'even Mirabeau'. What Byron was facing [in 1814] seemed, however, like a turn of that tide: retrogression. Abroad, the French Revolution issued in the restoration of the Bourbons; at home 'Vain is each voice whose tones could once command'. (*Byron's Politics* 55)

20. James Chandler notes Shelley's thinking along similar lines in his analysis of *Peter Bell the Third* (1819), which Chandler calls 'a tour de force and a marvelous variation on one of English writing's most-recurring themes in 1819: the question of the "future state"' (*England* 484).

21. Marilyn Butler points out that in 1816, Coleridge had criticized Byron with precisely the 'claim that Byron reached new modern heights of immorality by failing to punish his transgressive heroes' (64). Coleridge contrasted Byron's work with Thomas Shadwell's *The Libertine*; '[i]n licentiously representing the traditional Spanish story of the rake Don Juan, even Shadwell felt obliged to give it the proper ending, the hero's punishment in Hell for all eternity' (64). Byron replied, writes Butler, 'with a poem about Don Juan which shows no sign of satisfying Coleridge's requirements' (n.80).

22. For much more on Wordsworth and the political resonance of childhood, especially the complicated potential for violence that Wordsworth juxtaposes with a sense of childhood innocence, see the work of Ann Wierda Rowland, including 'Wordsworth's Children of the Revolution'.

5   The Minstrel Goes to Market

1. I cannot confirm that this Edgeworth is Richard Lovell Edgeworth, but it seems highly likely. Edgeworth wrote a letter to Sydney Owenson in 1806 where he described seeing bards at the 'Harper's Prize Ball at Granard, near this place [Edgeworth House], in 1782 or 1783' (Owenson *Memoirs* I.293).

Owenson herself mentions the Granard contests in *Patriotic Sketches of Ireland, Written in Connaught* (1807) when noting the continuing presence of 'female harpers' in Ireland: 'At the harper's prize-ball at Grannard in 1782, a woman of the name of Bridges obtained the second prize' (150, 150–1).

2. By 1800, Colley says, 'over 70 percent of all English peers received their education at just four public schools: Eton, Westminster, Winchester, and Harrow. And in the first half of the eighteenth century, sons of the peerage and the landed gentry made up 50 per cent of the pupils of all the major public schools' (167). Colley's data here come from the work of T. W. Bamford.

3. Venables, *Byzantium* [1830]. Venables was one of the Cambridge 'Apostles' and, in keeping with this advertisement, is described as a man of 'considerable humour' (Brookfield 348).

4. The dominance of heroic couplets carried over into translation as well: in 1831 Oxford published its first series of translations of its Latin Prize Poems – with a large list of eminent subscribers – all in heroic couplets (*Translations*).

5. Barbara D. Taylor has noted the tendency for prize competitors to be people excluded from university competitions. Taylor also outlines the objections to prize competitions set out by Walter Scott and, more recently, Donald Reiman (119, 121).

6. Citing the John Murray archives, Feldman reports that the first edition of 750 copies sold out, though he overestimated demand for a second; splitting the profits with Murray, Hemans received a total of more than 117 pounds for the volume by 1821 (155).

7. Though critics including this writer have referred to this as a fifty-pound prize, Nicholas Mason's research has recently clarified and corrected that assertion. The following information comes from Mason in correspondence: according to the earlier announcement of the contest ('Literary Premium' in the December 1818 *Blackwood's*), the prize money did total fifty pounds, but only half that amount went to Hemans, with fifteen going to the poet placing second and ten to the third (Mason 117).

8. I cite Hemans's poem by page number from the 1819 first edition.

9. One variant claimed to represent Harry's words faithfully, difficult as they might be for a modern, English-speaking audience; one 1790 edition, for instance, advertised itself as 'carefully transcribed' (title page). More common, however, was William Hamilton's modernized edition, with the assurance that 'the old obscure words are rendered more intelligible, and adapted to the Understanding of such as have no leisure to study the meaning and import of such Phrases, without the help of a Glossary'. The earliest edition of Hamilton's version in the British Library dates from 1722.

10. One exception to this rule is John Finlay's 1802 *Wallace; or, the Vale of Ellerslie* (published only in Glasgow, with a second edition in 1804). Finlay's poem attempts to give James Beattie's *Minstrel* the public life Beattie had intended for him, and Finlay writes in the Spenserian stanzas Beattie had helped revive, 'The design of the Poem', says Finlay,

> is to trace the effects of natural scenery, and the education of a rude age, in forming the mind of a hero – Wallace, while yet an infant, is introduced at the commencement of the poem, listening to an address

> from the Genius of his Country – its influence on his early thoughts –
> his solitary wanderings – his mother's song, imbued with the spirit of
> chivalry and romance. – The first Part concludes with the description of
> sunset, and a storm, which are supposed to rouse in his mind, feelings
> of grandeur and sublimity. – The second Part opens with a story, which
> gives an unalterable bias to his mind, thus formed – the re-appearance of
> the Genius, who prophecies his future actions – the glory of his country,
> and the terror and astonishment of his enemies. (n.p.)

Beattie's generalized nature here becomes a personification of Scotland itself;
Edwin becomes Wallace, and Edwin's unfinished future becomes the specific
national project of Wallace's resistance. Finlay uses the established nationalist
associations of the Wallace story to create new meanings for Beattie's well-
known minstrel.

Another ambivalent Wallace tale was published in Edinburgh, London,
and Glasgow: Robert Buchanan's *Wallace: a Tragedy* (1799), argues explicitly that Edward I was the enemy of rightful English liberty in opposing
the Scots:

> O strange delusion! fatal to both kingdoms! –
> Full well we know King Edward's deep-laid craft,
> First to enslave us Scots, and then to turn
> His added power against fair England's laws.
> Shortsighted, foolish Englishmen! ye forge
> Chains for yourselves, by conquering this land.
> Conquest! no, that shall never, never be.
> Our swords may for a time sleep in their scabbards:
> They'll rouse again . . . (48–9)

In this story, Wallace's death inspires revenge: six Londoners kill Edward I
out of rage at his injustice. As in other Wallace stories, criticism of England's
past government here serves as a means by which to praise England's merits
in the abstract. The warning against conquering Scotland, however, could
function either as an endorsement of the Union (because it was not a military
conquest) or as a dark hint of future violence.

11. Siddons was the son of the actress Sarah Siddons and an actor himself. He
    played the title role of John Home's *Douglas* while his mother starred as
    his character's mother. Walter Scott later wrote of his emotional reaction to
    seeing the characters played by a real-life mother and son (Staves 66–7). Henry
    Siddons's full-length tale of Wallace, while an unpolished production, does
    anticipate the development of the historical novel in some ways, preceding
    Jane Porter's *The Scottish Chiefs* (1810) by nearly two decades. Siddons also
    went on to become the manager of the New Theatre Royal in Edinburgh,
    thanks to the good wishes of Walter Scott, and Siddons produced the theatre's
    first new play, Joanna Baillie's *The Family Legend* (Parsons 208).
12. The story's intended application to contemporary circumstances becomes
    clear in a footnote about the heroic death of the Scottish (and significantly
    named) 'Stewart' in the poem. 'We may boast in our modern annals of a

similar instance of gallantry to the one exhibited in the closing scene of the illustrious Stewart', says the note, continuing,

> When the English troops stormed Monte Video, on the 3d of February, 1807, the brave Lieutenant Colonel Vassall, of the 38th regiment, was, in advancing to the breach, fatally stopped in his ardent career by a grapeshot, which broke his leg, and eventually terminated his existence. Adored by his men, numbers rushed from their ranks to support him; but as he fell, the hero exclaimed, 'Push on, my brave soldiers! It is but a leg in the service!' When the town surrendered, he cheered with his men as he lay bleeding on the ground. (247)

Lieutenant-Colonel Vassall had been the subject of Holford's only previous publication, an *Elegiac Ode, to the Memory of Lieut.-Colonel Vassall* (1808) the previous year. In her *Wallace*, the Scottish bravery of the past has become the British bravery of the present.

13. Baillie writes of Wallace in her Preface:

> His character and story are in every point of view particularly fitted either for poetry or romance; yet, till very lately, he has not been the subject, as far as I know, of any modern pen. Wallace, or the Field of Falkirk, written in nervous and harmonious verse, by a genius particularly successful in describing the warlike manners and deeds of ancient times, and in mixing the rougher qualities of the veteran leader with the supposed tenderness of a lover, is a poem that does honour to its author [Holford] and to the subject she has chosen. [Porter's] Wallace, or the Scottish Chief [sic], which through a rich variety of interesting, imaginary adventures, conducts a character of most perfect virtue and heroism to an affecting and tragical end – is a romance deservedly popular. This tribute to the name of Wallace from two distinguished English women, I mention with pleasure, notwithstanding all I have said against mixing true with fictitious history. (xviii–xix)

Baillie adds a footnote to include Hemans in her genealogy: 'Since the above observations were written, Mrs. Heman's [sic] prize-poem, on the given subject of the meeting between Wallace and Bruce on the banks of the Carron, has appeared, with its fair-won honours on its brow' (xix–xx).

14. Sarah J. Purcell's *Sealed with Blood* describes a moment that illustrates the connection to and contrast with conventional memorial rhetoric here: Purcell writes, 'One ceremonial toast in Watertown, Massachusetts, claimed that "The Bunker Hill Monument [shows] The gratitude of this generation to that which is past, and *its* claim to the gratitude of generations which are to come"' (199, emphasis original). Whereas the American toast emphasizes both present and future gratitude, Hemans's poem portrays the living generation as claiming future gratitude *rather than* expressing its own gratitude to past heroes.

15. Macpherson's note to this passage implies many later texts that give accounts of the songs of the bards on this Ossianic occasion. The note includes the following description as well as a transcription of the songs it describes:

> Those extempore compositions were in great repute among succeeding bards. The pieces extant of that kind shew more of the good ear, than of the poetical genius of their authors. The translator has only met with one poem of this sort, which he thinks worthy of being preserved. It is a thousand years later than Ossian, but the authors seem to have observed his manner, and adopted some of his expressions. The story of it is this. Five bards, passing the night in the house of a chief, who was a poet himself, went severally to make their observations on, and returned with an extempore description of, night. (253)

16. Hogg's use of multiple authorial personae in *The Queen's Wake* predates *The Private Memoirs and Confessions of a Justified Sinner* (1824) by more than a decade, illustrating the degree to which the latter work's splintered personae arise in part from the established conventions of minstrel writing.

17. For more on Charlotte's role at the time, see Peter Manning's treatment of Charlotte's political and literary importance in chapter 9 of *Reading Romantics* and Malcolm Kelsall's description in *Byron's Politics* of how Whigs, 'born for opposition', had used the Regent as a figure for the 'reversionary interest' for decades before he came to power and betrayed them, leaving the Whigs to turn to Princess Charlotte, as in Byron's 'Lines to a Lady Weeping' (11–12). Byron also penned a lament over Charlotte's death in the fourth canto of *Childe Harold's Pilgrimage* that McGann calls 'an elegy for a universe which longs to be freed of death and evil, and cannot' (*Fiery Dust* 90).

18. Hogg's editorial choices become clearer in comparison to Joseph Ritson's description of Mary in *Scotish Song* (1794). In the prefatory 'Historical Essay on Scotish Song', Ritson emphasizes Mary's own abilities as a minstrel, and speaks of her betrayal by the Scots; Hogg omits both elements. Ritson writes,

> Such was the state of Scotish song, when, in the year 1561, queen Mary returned from France to her native country. No character is to be found in history so nearly approaching excellence and perfection as this illustrious princess, before the turbulence of her unruly and fanatical subjects bewildered her senses, and plunged her into error and misfortune. At any other period, one is almost tempted to say in any other country, such a sovereign would have been the idol of her people. Not less remarkable for the accomplishments of her mind, than for the beauty of her person, she wrote the most elegant songs, and sung to her lute like an angel... Yet this princess, beautiful, elegant and accomplished as she was, and adorned with all the graces that ever centered in woman, was inhumanly persecuted by barbarous and enthusiastic ruffians, who owed her allegiance, and had sworn fidelity to her as their sovereign; and, after 19

years confinement, was deliberately murdered in cold blood by an envious, malignant, and treacherous hag, who had offered her asylum. (xlvii)

19. Given the many other playful rewritings of Scott here, the lines may well intentionally echo and undermine *Marmion*: 'Where's the coward that would not dare / To fight for such a land?' (*PW* 88).
20. In the third (Edinburgh: George Goldie, 1814) and subsequent editions, Hogg changed the lines to a milder version of a similar sentiment:

> Ocould [typo for 'O could' – corrected in later editions] the bard I
> loved so long,
> Reprove my fond aspiring song!
> Or could his tongue of candour say,
> That I should throw my harp away! (329)

21. See Chapter 4 regarding the 'Addition to the Preface' of *Childe Harold's Pilgrimage*.
22. See *Ancient Songs, from the time of King Henry the Third, to the Revolution* (dated 1790 but not published until 1792). In his 'Observations on the Ancient English Minstrels', Ritson's primary 'observation' is that the 'ancient English minstrels' as Percy defined them were in fact French troubadours imported by England's aristocracy. Ritson gives an emphatic negative answer to the question, 'Whether at any time, since the Norman Conquest, there has existed a distinct order of English men, who united the arts of poetry and music, and got their livelihood by singing to the harp verses in their native tongue of their own composing?' (iii). This argument runs contrary in some ways to Ritson's project, noted by McLane, of producing genuine English materials in *English Songs* ('Tuning' 294).
23. Sydney Owenson's *The Novice of Saint Dominick* (1805), also incorporated the golden violet theme. The troubadour-lover of Imogen, the heroine, telling her of his past, says that he determined

> to become a candidate for the golden violet instituted by the accomplished Clemence d'Isaure, countess of Thoulouse, as the reward of poetical merit. I hastened to Thoulouse in the habit of a minstrel, and sung those verses to the harp which were the first effusions of my rustic muse. My youth and rank shed an extraneous merit on my lays they intrinsically did not possess: the golden violet was adjudged me; and gratified ambition flushed her triumphs in my young aspiring heart. (II.172)

Later, Imogen's guardian de Sorville says in Provence, 'When you come to reside in this country ... I shall expect to see you a second Clemence d'Isaure, reviving the spirit of ancient poesy and song, and distributing the golden violet with your own fair hands to the triumphant minstrels' (III.91).

6   The 'Minstrel of the Western Continent'

1. In emphasizing the importance of David Gamut's character, I row against the tide of most writing on Cooper's novel (save that of Robert Lawson-Peebles,

about which more will follow), since that importance is clearest in the unusual context of transatlantic minstrelsy. Given the historical decline in the importance of minstrelsy to novel writing, it is understandable to see Gamut as a 'tiresome' fellow who leads to the conclusion 'that, like most historical novels, *The Last of the Mohicans* contains too many characters' (McWilliams 39) – or even, as W. H. Gardiner wrote in *The North American Review* in 1826, that Gamut 'is, beyond comparison, the most stupid, senseless, useless, and unmeaning monster we remember ever to have met with' (Dekker and McWilliams 110). Some attention has been paid in brief articles, however, to the roots of Gamut's character in sources other than Scott: Clay Daniel has found a source for Gamut in 'Cooper's response to the eighteenth-century Miltonic "bard" in general, and the Attendant Spirit in Milton's aristocratic entertainment in particular' (126); and Kelly Stern points to another source in the figure of the medicine man; and David Seed still another in Washington Irving's Ichabod Crane.

2. Nearly all of the literature on blackface performance in America and Britain assumes a theatrical genealogy based on the practice of blackening one's skin – for one unusually precise example, Michael Rogin refers only to theatrical face-blackening when speaking of the 'European antecedents' of 'American minstrelsy' (22).

3. To smooth out some of the roughness of these dates, I will note that some important works of my 'missing generation' appeared slightly before Moore's *Melodies* – these include Sydney Owenson's *The Wild Irish Girl* (1806) and Germaine de Staël's *Corinne, or Italy* (1807). On the other end, the starting point of blackface performance as 'minstrelsy' may have come in late 1842; this origin has been disputed from that time to this.

4. To analyze the rhetoric of minstrelsy in this way invites charges of misplaced priorities, of emphasizing semantics at the expense of recognizing the reality of the varieties of blackface performance that preceded the naming of 'Negro minstrelsy'. Those varieties have been grouped together under the name of minstrelsy by a long line of insightful critics. As W. T. Lhamon puts it in *Raising Cain: Blackface Performance from Jim Crow to Hip Hop* (1998),

> there are many reasons *not* to consider [the formation of Emmett's Virginia Minstrels] the beginning either of minstrelsy in general or the formulaic minstrel show in particular. Why should the Virginia Minstrels be said to have started things when Micah Hawkins, George Washington Dixon, T. D. Rice, and many performers imitating them had been delineating 'Ethiopians' in the western Atlantic for more than a quarter-century? Perhaps, you might say, because these forebears did not call themselves minstrels, and the bands in the early 1840s did. Naming is hardly beginning, however. It merely emphasizes one dimension of the whole. (57)

I take Lhamon's point, but I see a number of reasons for continuing to explore the implications of the transatlantic applications of the term *minstrelsy*. For example, among the 'forebears' Lhamon names, there were large differences in self-presentation. George Washington Dixon, who played the character Zip Coon, billed himself as the 'American Melodist' (Cockrell illustration 105), and a favorable review of 1834 refers to him as one of a category of 'Melodists', praising the 'Patriotism' of his 'Melodies' (quoted in Cockrell 98). Similarly, Emmett advertised himself as 'the great Southern Banjo Melodist' (Cockrell 150). In these ways, the language of Dixon's and Emmett's self-presentation and reception recalls that of Moore's *Irish Melodies* and many other similar collections, which frequently mentioned minstrels – as in Moore's 'The Minstrel Boy', even today a staple of songbooks – and established the genre of collections of 'melodies' that came to include blackface minstrel music such as Stephen Foster's *Ethiopian Melodies* (1849). On the other hand, I know of no evidence that T. D. Rice similarly used the rhetoric associated with European minstrelsy; Lhamon himself points out that only 'very late in his career . . . did Rice travel as a *minstrel* performer' (176). Lhamon's argument for an early, subversive form of blackface performance relies heavily on the biography of Rice, who seems carefully to have avoided associating himself with the term *minstrel*. In spite of Lhamon's protests, his argument itself thus points to the importance of understanding the transatlantic currency of the term *minstrel* in the first half of the nineteenth century.

5. A great deal of the existing scholarship on the origins of American blackface minstrelsy concerns this tradition of stage blackface performance. Jeffrey Cox and Julie A. Carlson have recently produced work on the history of Romantic-era British blackface performance that sheds light on the immediate prehistory of transatlantic blackface minstrelsy. Cox has argued the 'regular London theatergoer would have seen depictions of African characters or of slavery during perhaps every season of the 18th and early 19th century' (ix), and Carlson has unearthed details of those depictions in a recent *European Romantic Review* article.

6. This recent development in commentary on minstrelsy is one manifestation of a larger movement stemming from sentiments such as those of Paul Giles, who argues 'that the development of American literature appears in a different light when read against the grain of British cultural imperatives, just as British literature itself reveals strange and unfamiliar aspects that are brought into play by the reflecting mirrors of American discourse' (1).

7. Cockrell's fuller explanation is worth quoting:

> The most problematic word for me in this whole study is 'minstrels.' It is a word first applied to blackface entertainment in late 1842 for good self-conscious reasons that must have resonated broadly, for it was quickly picked up by others and became a popular convention within months of its initial employment . . . It is a word of its time, and is appropriately transforming in its impact. I try to make the case that 1842–43 was a substantially different time from 1829. What word do I then use to characterize the music, dance, and theatre treated in this book before late 1842, which does, after all, make up the bulk of my study? Would I not, by using the word 'minstrel', project anachronistically a context of understanding onto something (often) quite different? I am afraid, alas, the answer is yes; but there seems no ready alternative to the word. (xii)

8. Cockrell's contribution is to argue for the significance, not the fact, of blackface performers' belated self-naming as 'minstrels'. In pointing out the lag

between blackface performance and calling such performance minstrelsy, Cockrell builds on much earlier writers such as Hans Nathan and Robert Toll, who writes, following Nathan,

> Besides taking the name of a famous Southern state to enhance their claims of authenticity, they called themselves 'minstrels' instead of the more common 'delineators' because of the great success of the Tyrolese Minstrel Family which had recently toured America. (30)

9. A number of critics have addressed the transatlantic dimensions of later blackface performance, from the late 1830s onward. Those later Atlantic crossings have been analyzed, for example, by Reynolds (a blackface performer), Bratton, Pickering, Gilroy, and Featherstone.

10. Like so much later commentary on minstrelsy, this approach is anticipated in general terms in Eric Lott's work, which connects British and American representations of minstrelsy in passages such as this:

> cultures of the people, even 'folk' cultures, are always constructed, in this particular case by a post romantic ideology of the folk – hence the characteristic comparison in nineteenth-century discourse of minstrelsy and black secular song to the English ballad tradition. It is of course essentialist to ignore the extent to which our understanding of any culture is determined in the first place by a particular ideology of culture. Just such an ideology worked to make the elements of black culture portrayed in minstrelsy – watered down, humiliated, but unmistakably present – seem all the more naturally elements of a national 'folk.' Moreover, such ideologies of culture have most often been produced by those who do not belong to the culture that is defined, variously, as folk, traditional, popular, or oral. Which is to say that cultures of the dispossessed usually, for better or for worse, come to us mediated through dominant-cultural filters, whether it is Thomas Percy's compilation of *Reliques of Ancient English Poetry* (1765), Henry Rowe Schoolcraft's renderings of Chippewa poetry in his influential history *Indian Tribes of the United States* (1851–57) . . . (102–3)

One of my goals here is to describe the cultural developments that explain the differences between Percy and Schoolcraft (and the literature based on their respective works), differences that become visible in the context of the essential connection that Lott outlines.

11. Tim Fulford has recently written about a partial exception to this claim: Joseph Ritson's inclusion of 'The Death-Song of a Cherokee Indian' in a footnote to 'A Historical Essay on the Origin and Progress of National Song' in the front matter of his 1783 work *A Select Collection of English Songs* (Ritson ii). As Fulford observes, the song was for Ritson a present-day analog to the past songs he discusses in the 'Historical Essay', 'the epitome of the songs and ballads that Ritson wished to revive from Britain's own unlettered past' (8). Ritson's use of the song (and of many other examples of historical songs from around the world in the Essay) is typical of eighteenth-century texts that stop short of presenting international minstrelsies in parallel form in

the same volume. Ritson represents a death song in a footnote to a prefatory essay, but as he says in the preface (referring specifically to the book's fourth section), the song collection proper comprises 'the genuine effusions of the English muse, unadulterated with the sentimental refinements of Italy or France' (ix). Nonetheless, we can perceive in Ritson's practice an important early sign of minstrelsies to come.

12. Moore had showed an interest in this kind of project earlier as well, in the American poems of *Odes and Epistles* (1803) that figure in James Chandler's analysis in *England in 1819* (442).

13. Another exception is the 'Negro song' brought to Britain by Mungo Park and recently described by McLane ('Tuning' 299–302).

14. A bandore is a mandolin-like instrument 'from which we get the word "banjo"' (Greenblatt *Will* 74). In this context, it is worth noting Cockrell's observation that 'Joel Sweeney was apparently the first to play a real banjo on the stage, doing so initially in New York in 1839...In early 1843 this instrument became the heart of a *musical* ensemble – the minstrel band' (148). Combined with Cockrell's suggestion elsewhere that the terminology of 'minstrelsy' takes hold only in the early 1840s, this suggests that blackface performances became recognizable as minstrelsy when the banjo's presence created a similarity of visual iconography between the lute and the banjo. Note that the name and form of the banjo came from those of the bandore. Incidentally, a 'banjore' of this kind figures in Maria Edgeworth's *Belinda* (1801): Juba, the African servant brought from a West Indian plantation, makes a 'banjore'. After her son asks, 'What is this, mamma? – It is not a guitar, is it?' Lady Anne Percival explains, 'No, my dear, it is called a banjore; it is an African instrument, of which the negroes are particularly fond' (226).

15. The bizarreness of Chingachgook's comment clarifies the lengths to which Cooper must go to manufacture his participation in what Lora Romero has described as 'a virtual "cult of the Vanishing American" in the antebellum period' (115). Romero describes 'the historical sleight of hand crucial to the topos of the doomed aboriginal: it represents the disappearance of the native not just as natural but as having already happened' (115). Though my reading aligns more with Romero's, George Dekker offers another take on the lastness of Uncas in saying that 'Whether Cora and Uncas live or die together, he will be the last of his tribe. The choice, in effect, is between the creation of a new race to inhabit North America or the extermination or subjugation of all races save one' (72).

16. John McWilliams presents a typical view of the fair lady/dark lady genealogy presented by Cooper's critics:

> In characterizing women, male writers of nineteenth-century romantic fiction returned almost obsessively to imagining variant versions of two simplistic archetypes known as the Fair Lady and the Dark Lady. The Fair Lady – blond-haired, blue-eyed, and fully Caucasian – represents both the value of civil society and a curious innocence about it. Her responses are passive and her ideas conventional; she is physically weak, deferential to males, easily shocked, but innately decent. The Dark Lady – dark-haired, dark-eyed, and often 'tainted' by Jewish or black blood – represents the attractions of social rebellion and forbidden knowledge. (68)

By attributing this line of thinking to 'male writers', McWilliams and others omit the complications that arise from recognizing this convention's roots in *Corinne* and its many derivatives in women's writing. The continuing awareness of *Corinne*'s female characters as well as Scott's is most memorably visible in George Eliot's *The Mill on the Floss* (1860), in which Maggie Tulliver understands her own situation by analogy to the heroines of Scott and Staël.

17. The line of literary death songs may be said to culminate in Tennyson's complicated treatment of the subject in 'The Lady of Shalott', in which the Lady is represented 'singing her last song' (p. 25, l. 143) in the Sapphic style, but, partly because the poem does not represent her words, Tennyson leaves ambiguous her motives, cause of death, and other factors that are normally more straightforward in death songs. Treatments of earlier literary death songs include the work of Werner Sollors, who discusses the role of the death song in American 'Indian plays' (104–8); Julie Ellison, who attends to British representations of 'Native American melancholia' to argue that 'the Indian death song was not an exclusively North American genre but one that emerged in the North Atlantic poetry of an Anglo-American sensibility deeply preoccupied with race' (461); Nancy Moore Goslee, who pays sustained attention to Hemans's use of death songs and adds a number of works to the genealogy of British death songs; and Kathleen Lundeen, whose work is discussed below. Fulford's recent work emphasizes representations of death songs of male warriors in the eighteenth century, including one of Robert Southey's 'Songs of the American Indians' (1799). Southey's presentation of the Huron 'preparation of a funeral canoe, in which the dead man is placed for his voyage to the country of the dead' (Fulford 147–8) strikes me as an important precedent for the floating women's death songs of Hemans and Tennyson.

18. Landon's work provides a later and somewhat altered instance of what Fulford has described as a process by which

> Southey – and his readers – are 'strangers' who are drawn into sympathize with Indians' emotions because they respond to Indian oral poetry. By Englishing the Indians' songs, Southey Indianizes his readers, aligning their emotional response with those of supposedly uncultured 'savages'. The effect is to reverse assumptions about the superiority of British civilization to Indian savagery, and of writing to song. (149)

19. Lundeen has also addressed this tension in the poem, saying that 'it poses an ethical dilemma' for readers: is Hemans's 'empathy with the woman a testament to her freedom from cultural hegemony, or is it evidence of a self-serving ploy by which she can exploit another culture for her own psychological gain?' (84). Lundeen's sense that 'ethnicity exists in ["Indian Woman's Death Song"] solely in the service of gender' (88) builds on Nancy Moore Goslee's analysis of the treatment of the British self and 'Indian' other in the poem. Goslee writes of another poem, 'The Isle of Founts', that Hemans's

> treatment of tribal and cultural difference here works as a model for gender difference: that is, a fluctuating set of boundaries for 'strangers' forces us constantly to redefine what is the 'other' and what is a part of ourselves. In these poems spoken from within 'Indian' culture no strong racial difference, no 'red' against 'white' is marked, even toward the various strangers; and this sense of cultural variety with an underlying similarity extends to the collection as a whole. (246)

20. For one interesting example of the early reviewers' comments on the issue, the unsigned review in the *United States Literary Gazette* opined in May 1826 that 'Uncas would have made a good match for Cora, particularly as she had a little of the blood of a darker race in her veins, – and still more, as this sort of arrangement is coming into fashion, in real life, as well as in fiction' (Dekker and McWilliams 100). Regarding twentieth-century criticism, Baym accurately describes herself as responding to a school of '[c]ritics following the examples of D. H. Lawrence and Leslie Fiedler [who] suggest that Cora's blackness symbolizes her unacceptable sexuality, her covert affinity for Indians' (74).

21. McLane has noted the importance of masking in transatlantic minstrelsy: 'That there might be a connection between Scott's minstrelsy-as-masquerade and minstrelsy as racialized, racist US entertainment is suggested, if only metaphorically, by the very title of such as recent book as *Inside the Minstrel Mask: Readings in Nineteenth-Century Blackface Minstrelsy*' ('Figure' 447).

22. As Michael Rogin demonstrates in reference to blackface minstrelsy, the performative elements of racial imitation here are analogous to those of gender cross-dressing, and it is therefore useful to recall a split in feminist responses to men cross-dressing as women: the act of performative transgression of a binary opposition can parody and denaturalize the opposition, or the performance can reinforce the opposition as a more powerful subject speaks for a less powerful one (30–1). Rogin presents these two views as having developed in chronological sequence:

> An early feminist suspicion that cross-dressing gave men license to speak for women has been challenged by the more recent feminist, gay, and lesbian promotion of destabilized gender boundaries. In the first view, the cross-dresser acquires power over the sex whose position he speaks and reassures himself about his own identity. In the second view, however, the cross-dresser parodies and denaturalizes the binary opposition. (30–1)

23. Gamut's obsolescence as a bookish minstrel is compounded by the fact that the specific book he carries was falling out of use even in the time of the book's action. Robert Lawson-Peebles has provided, by far, the most sustained and thoughtful critical account of Gamut and his book, an account that merits quoting at length here:

Gamut has the highest praise for the text constantly by his side, the twenty-sixth edition of *The Bay Psalm Book*; published in 1744, it had therefore been in circulation for thirteen years by the time of the action of the novel. In the 1740s, however, largely as a result of the Great Awakening, *The Bay Psalm Book* was falling out of favor. There was just one further edition, in 1762. The book was supplanted by the psalms and hymns of the English dissenter Isaac Watts. Watts's publications were enormously popular, but his references to the British monarchy made his *Psalms of David* unsuitable for post-Revolutionary America and republican versions were produced by Joel Barlow and Timothy Dwight. Dwight's was the better known, and it is likely that Cooper was familiar with it, for it was published in 1802, the year before Cooper went to Yale. There were several reasons why Cooper might prefer Watts to *The Bay Psalm Book*. Watts's theology was closer to Cooper's Episcopalianism and the translations of *The Bay Psalm Book* were notoriously ungainly. The meaning of the psalms was sometimes difficult to follow, and they were occasionally hard to sing. Watts's translations were less rigid, more elegant, and there was a closer consonance between words and music...Gamut's devotion to it stacks the odds against him. (131–2)

I will revisit Lawson-Peebles's argument later in the chapter.

24. Romero addresses Gamut's attachment to books in a different way, emphasizing Cooper's association of frontier masculinity with orality in Hawkeye's dismissal of printed texts. 'Free of books', argues Romero, 'Hawk-eye liberates himself from the power that nineteenth-century domesticity gave to women' (122). She continues, 'Both the disregard for books and the association of them with the newly empowered antebellum woman are staples of the period. Although *the book* is usually associated with the reign of the father, in the antebellum period *books* seem to be associated with the reign of the mother' (122). Though this is a powerful presentation of the nature and context of Bumppo's view, the fact that it appears in Cooper's novel seems at least to complicate the equation of Bumppo's perspective with the author's, as in the claim that 'for Cooper as well as for Rousseau, words represent a whole economy of power marked as feminine' (122).

25. Hamm has documented the importance of this minstrel song by Hewitt:

American popular song seemed to come of age, suddenly, with the appearance in 1825 of 'The Minstrel's Return'd from the War' by John Hill Hewitt [103] (1801–90), son of the immigrant musician James Hewitt discussed earlier. The composer penciled the following comments on his autograph copy of the song, preserved in the Library of Congress in Washington:

The song, crude as it is, was one of my first musical efforts. It was composed in 1825 in the village of Greenville, S.C., now a city of 20,000 souls. When I returned to the North, I took this book with me to Boston. My brother James [Lang Hewitt] was a musical publisher.

> I gave him a copy to publish – he did it very reluctantly – did not think it worthy of a copyright. It was eagerly taken up by the public, and established my reputation as a ballad composer. It was sold all over the world – and my brother, not securing the right, told me that he missed making at least $10,000.
>
> . . . The composer was not exaggerating the success of his song. (102–3)

26. For more on *Childe Harold's Pilgrimage* and minstrelsy, see McLane ('Figure' 446–7) and Chapter 4 of the present work.
27. Both of these letters were written from Paris in 1826. The first is dated 9 November and addressed to Cooper's publishers Carey and Lea; the second, dated 16 November, is to Anthony Bleecker 'for the Bread and Cheese Club' (*Letters* I.180).
28. As Fulford puts it in a more general context, 'The dying Indian – a pitiable figure doomed to extinction in the face of the more advanced whites – became the stock figure that US writers developed from their British ancestors, a figure that only reinforced (albeit with expressions of liberal guilt) the self-justifying ideology that whites would inevitably supplant their more primitive neighbors' (30).
29. As Susan Manning points out, for the makers of the American union, '[i]n the absence of an independent cultural history, space stood in for time' (197). See Manning's *Fragments of Union*, especially chapter 5, for a different but related approach to the issues I address in this chapter.
30. Herder's objections to the European colonies in America are explicit at many points, perhaps most interestingly in his telling of a story of the Delawares agreeing in a treaty to be the 'woman' of a group of Indian nations, living in the middle, refusing weapons and war, and thus creating a wider peace. As Herder tells the story, this project worked until white settlers arrived:

> Unfortunately, even with the savages themselves this arrangement did not achieve its purpose for long. When the Europeans pressed closer, at the demand of the men even the *woman* was supposed to participate along with them in the defense . . . A foreign, unforeseen dominant force disturbed the beautiful project of the savages for peace among each other; and this will always be the case as long as the tree of peace does not bloom for the nations with firm, inextirpable roots *from within to outside*. (403, emphasis original)

31. Interestingly, this American genealogy of American works arguably begins with a British work, Thomas Campbell's *Gertrude of Wyoming*; as Campbell's Victorian editor writes, it 'was the first poem of any length by a British poet the scene of which was laid in America, and in it Campbell is the first European author to introduce his reader to the romance of the Virgin forests and Red Indian warriors; subjects which have since been so faithfully portrayed by Longfellow, Bryant, and Whittier in poetry and by Fenimore Cooper in prose' (Campbell 28). Campbell's poem draws unusual attention to its transatlantic subject matter by portraying the colonists of Pennsylvania as recent

exiles who make the Wyoming Valley ring with 'transatlantic story' (40, part I, stanza IV) and then rise against England in the cause of 'Transatlantic Liberty' (57, III.VI). For a perceptive treatment of *Gertrude of Wyoming* the context of 'The Death of the American Indian at the Turn of the Eighteenth Century', see Wind.

32. For an excellent and much more detailed reading of the 'Picture-Writing' section of the poem, see Virginia Jackson's recent article, 'Longfellow's Tradition; or, Picture-Writing a Nation'.

33. The contrast between the emancipatory and confining possibilities of music for blacks in the West in the nineteenth century is a recurring subject in Paul Gilroy's *The Black Atlantic*. Condemning the 'hateful antics' of blackface minstrels (89), Gilroy uses the example of the Fisk Jubilee Singers – though themselves initially received as 'Negro minstrels' (88) – as a contrary illustration of a genuinely 'unique musical culture' among nineteenth-century blacks. Gilroy's earlier formulation of the role of music in black culture resonates in interesting ways in the context of Cooper's mythmaking about the birth of the American republic. Gilroy writes,

> in the critical thought of blacks in the West, social self-creation through labour is not the centre-piece of emancipatory hopes. For the descendants of slaves, work signifies only servitude, misery, and subordination. Artistic expression, expanded beyond recognition from the grudging gifts offered by the masters as a token substitute for freedom from bondage, therefore becomes the means towards both individual self-fashioning and communal liberation. (40)

34. McGuirk writes, 'Burns dramatizes peasant speakers who assert their own authority, expressing their determination to follow Prince Charlie, or marry Tam the day they turn twenty-one, or kiss the fiddler's wife – try and stop them. In Foster's plantation ballads, by contrast, the peasants (the slave-speakers) do not rebel against their masters, having naturalized their subjugation as merely part of Father Adam's universal legacy of toil and sweat...' (16).

35. Michael Rogin develops this point at length, as in this passage: 'In the hands, disproportionately, of Irish and then of Jewish entertainers, this ethnocultural expression served a melting-pot function. Far from breaking down the distinctions between race and ethnicity, however, blackface only reinforced it. Minstrelsy accepted ethnic difference by insisting on racial division' (56). Though he does not linger to draw out the implications of a transatlantic 'minstrelsy' in detail, Rogin also connects blackface minstrelsy to Scott and Cooper in interesting ways (48–9).

36. For commentary on the suppressions of black culture upon which minstrelsy also depended, see Alexander Saxton's argument that 'the dual task of exploiting and suppressing African elements...began from the first moments of minstrelsy' (168).

37. Though the impulse to seek the founding texts of American literature in minstrelsy had faded by the early twentieth century, the impulse to mark the moment of minstrelsy's death continued. Edward LeRoy Rice's *Monarchs of*

Minstrelsy (1911) opens, 'Is Minstrelsy dying out?' (n.p.), and Harry Reynolds opens his *Minstrel Memories* (1927) claiming to write 'determined that – before the present generation passes way – at least one attempt shall be made to record one of the most remarkable and picturesque periods in the annals of British Amusements' (n.p.).

Works Cited

Abrams, M. H. *Natural Supernaturalism: Tradition and Revolution in Romantic Literature*. New York: Norton, 1971.

Addison, John William. *English Education, 1789–1902*. Cambridge: Cambridge University Press, 1930.

Allison, April. 'Transnational Sympathies, Imaginary Communities'. *The Literary Channel – The Inter-National Invention of the Novel*. Ed. Margaret Cohen and Carolyn Deever. Princeton: Princeton University Press, 2002. 133–48.

Andersen, Hans Christian. *The Improvisatore: Or, Life in Italy*. Trans. Mary Howitt. Two vols. London: Richard Bentley, 1845.

Anderson, Benedict. *Imagined Communities: Reflections on the Origin and Spread of Nationalism*. Revised edition. London: Verso, 1991.

Andrews, Elmer. 'Aesthetics, Politics, and Identity: Lady Morgan's *The Wild Irish Girl*'. *Canadian Journal of Irish Studies* 12:2 (December 1987): 7–20.

The Annual Register, or, a View of the History, Politics, and Literature for the Year 1807. London: W. Otridge, 1809.

Arac, Jonathan. *Critical Genealogies: Historical Situations for Postmodern Literary Studies*. New York: Columbia University Press, 1987.

Armstrong, Isobel. *Victorian Poetry: Poetry, Poetics, and Politics*. London: Routledge, 1993.

Arnold, Matthew. 'The Function of Criticism at the Present Time'. Vol. 3, *Lectures and Essays in Criticism. The Complete Prose Works of Matthew Arnold*. Ed. R. H. Super. 11 vols. Ann Arbor: University of Michigan Press, 1960–74. 258–85.

Augustan Review. Rev. of 'The White Doe of Rylstone . . . by William Wordsworth'. *Augustan Review* I (August 1815): 343–56.

Austin, William W. '*Susanna,' 'Jeanie,' and 'The Old Folks at Home': The Songs of Stephen C. Foster from His Time To Ours*. New York: Macmillan, 1975.

Averill, James H. *Wordsworth and the Poetry of Human Suffering*. Ithaca: Cornell University Press, 1980.

Baillie, Joanna. *Metrical Legends of Exalted Characters*. London: Longman, 1821.

Bamford, T. W. 'Public Schools and Social Class, 1801–1850'. *British Journal of Sociology* 12 (1961): 224–35.

Baym, Nina. 'How Men and Women Wrote Indian Stories'. *New Essays on* The Last of the Mohicans. Ed. H. Daniel Peck. Cambridge: Cambridge University Press, 1992. 67–86.

[Beattie, James.] *The Minstrel: Or, the Progress of Genius. A Poem. Book the First*. London: E. & C. Dilly; Edinburgh: A. Kincaid & J. Bell, 1771.

——*The Minstrel: Or, the Progress of Genius. A Poem. The Second Book*. London: Edward and Charles Dilly; Edinburgh: William Creech, 1774.

Beddoes, Thomas Lovell. *The Improvisatore, In Three Fyttes*. Oxford: J. Vincent, 1821.

Behrendt, Stephen C. *Royal Mourning and Regency Culture: Elegies and Memorials of Princess Charlotte*. New York: St Martin's Press, 1997.

Benstock, Shari. 'At the Margin of Discourse: Footnotes in the Fictional Text'. *PMLA* 98 (1983): 204–25.

Blair, Hugh. 'Critical Dissertation on the Poems of Ossian'. *The Poems of Ossian and Related Works*. Ed. Howard Gaskill. Edinburgh: Edinburgh University Press, 1996. 343–400.

Boggs, Colleen Glenney. 'Margaret Fuller's American Translation'. *American Literature: A Journal of Literary History, Criticism, and Bibliography* 76:1 (March 2004): 31–58.

Bourdieu, Pierre. *The Field of Cultural Production: Essays on Art and Literature*. Ed. Randal Johnson. New York: Columbia University Press, 1993.

—— *The State Nobility: Elite Schools in the Field of Power*. Trans. Lauretta C. Clough. Stanford: Stanford University Press, 1996.

Bratton, J. S. 'English Ethiopians: British Audiences and Back-Face Acts, 1835–65'. *The Yearbook of English Studies* 2 (1981): 127–42.

British Critic. [Rev. of] '*The Excursion*...by William Wordsworth'. *British Critic* 3 (May 1815): 449–67.

Brooke, Charlotte. *Reliques of Irish Poetry*. 1789. Rep. Gainesville: Scholar's Facsimiles and Reprints, 1970.

Brookfield, Frances M. *The Cambridge 'Apostles'*. New York: Scribner, 1906.

Buchanan, Robert. *Wallace: A Tragedy*. Edinburgh: Constable, 1799.

Burroughs, Catherine B. *Closet Stages: Joanna Baillie and the Theater Theory of British Romantic Women Writers*. Philadelphia: University of Pennsylvania Press, 1997.

Butler, Marilyn. 'Byron and the Empire in the East'. *Byron: Augustan and Romantic*. Ed. Andrew Rutherford. New York: St Martin's Press, 1990. 63–81.

Byron, George Gordon, Lord. *The Complete Poetical Works*. Ed. Jerome J. McGann. Seven vols. Oxford: Clarendon, 1980–92.

Campbell, Mary. *Lady Morgan: The Life and Times of Sydney Owenson*. London: Pandora, 1988.

Campbell, Thomas. 'Letter to the Mohawk Chief Ahyonwoeghs, commonly called John Brant, Esq., of the Grand River, Upper Canada, from Thomas Campbell. London, January 20, 1822'. *Gertrude of Wyoming: A Pennsylvanian Tale*. 1809. Ed. H. Macaulay Fitzgibbon. Oxford: Clarendon, 1889. 178–86.

Cannon, John. *Aristocratic Century: The Peerage of Eighteenth-Century England*. Cambridge: Cambridge University Press, 1984.

Carlson, Julie A. 'New Lows in Eighteenth-Century Theater: The Rise of Mungo'. *European Romantic Review* 18 (2007): 139–47.

Chandler, James. *England in 1819: The Politics of Literary Culture and the Case of Romantic Historicism*. Chicago: University of Chicago Press, 1998.

—— ' "Wordsworth" after Waterloo'. *The Age of William Wordsworth*. Ed. Kenneth R. Johnston and Gene W. Ruoff. New Brunswick: Rutgers University Press, 1987. 84–111.

—— *Wordsworth's Second Nature: A Study of the Poetry and Politics*. Chicago: University of Chicago Press, 1984.

Clifford, Brendan. *The Life and Poems of Thomas Moore*. Revised edition. Belfast: Athol, 1993.

—— Introduction to *Political and Historical Writings of Thomas Moore*. Belfast: Athol, 1993.

Cockrell, Dale. *Demons of Disorder: Early Blackface Minstrels and Their World*. Cambridge: Cambridge University Press, 1997.

Coleridge, Samuel Taylor. *Biographia Literaria: Or, Biographical Sketches of My Literary Life and Opinions*. Ed. James Engell and Walter Jackson Bate. Vol. 7 of *The Collected Works of Samuel Taylor Coleridge*. Princeton: Princeton University Press, 1970–.

——*Poetical Works*. Ed. J. C. C. Mays. Vol. 16 of *The Collected Works of Samuel Taylor Coleridge*. Gen. ed. Kathleen Coburn. 16 vols. Princeton: Princeton University Press, 1970–.

——'The Rime of the Ancyent Marinere'. 1798. *Samuel Taylor Coleridge: The Complete Poems*. Ed. William Keach. London: Penguin, 1997. 147–67.

Colley, Linda. *Britons: Forging the Nation, 1707–1837*. New Haven: Yale University Press, 1992.

Cooper, James Fenimore. *The Last of the Mohicans*. Ed. Stephen Railton. New York: Barnes & Noble, 2003.

——*The Letters and Journals of James Fenimore Cooper*. Ed. James Franklin Beard. Six vols. Cambridge, MA: Belknap, 1960.

Corbett, Mary Jean. *Allegories of Union in Irish and English Writing, 1790–1840: Politics, History, and the Family from Edgeworth to Arnold*. Cambridge: Cambridge University Press, 2000.

Cox, Jeffrey. Introduction to *Drama*, vol. 5 of *Slavery, Abolition, and Emancipation: Writings in the British Romantic Period*. Eight vols. Ed. Peter J. Kitson and Debbie Lee. London: Pickering and Chatto, 1999.

'Critical Observations'. [Introductory material in James Beattie's] *The Minstrel: Or, the Progress of Genius*. London: John Sharpe, 1819.

Daniel, Clay. 'Cooper's The Last of the Mohicans'. *Explicator* 56:3 (Spring 1998): 126–9.

Davis, Bertram H. *Thomas Percy: A Scholar-Cleric in the Age of Johnson*. Philadelphia: University of Pennsylvania Press, 1989.

Davis, Leith. *Acts of Union: Scotland and the Literary Negotiation of the British Nation 1707–1830*. Stanford: Stanford University Press, 1998.

Deane, Seamus. *A Short History of Irish Literature*. London: Hutchinson, 1986.

Dekker, George. *James Fenimore Cooper: The American Scott*. New York: Barnes & Noble, 1967.

——and John P. McWilliams, eds. *Fenimore Cooper: The Critical Heritage*. London: Routledge, 1973.

Delon, Michel. 'Germaine de Staël and Other Possible Scenarios of Revolution'. *Germaine de Staël: Crossing the Borders*. Ed. Madelyn Gutwirth, Avriel Goldberger, and Karyna Szmurlo. New Brunswick: Rutgers University Press, 1991. 22–33.

Dennis, Ian. *Nationalism and Desire in Early Historical Fiction*. Basingstoke: Macmillan, 1997.

D'Israeli, Isaac. *The Carder and the Carrier. Narrative Poems*. London: John Murray, 1803.

Duncan, Ian. *Modern Romance and Transformations of the Novel: The Gothic, Scott, Dickens*. Cambridge: Cambridge University Press, 1992.

Dunne, Tom. 'Fiction as "the best history of nations": Lady Morgan's Irish Novels'. *The Writer as Witness: Literature as Historical Evidence*. Cork: Cork University Press, 1987.

Dyer, Gary. *British Satire and the Politics of Style. 1789–1832*. Cambridge: Cambridge University Press, 1997.

Edgeworth, Maria. *Belinda*. 1801. London: Everyman, 1993.

Edinburgh Review. [Rev. of] '*An Account of the Life and Writings of James Beattie . . .* by Sir W[illiam] Forbes . . .' *Edinburgh Review* 10 (1807): 171–99.

Elfenbein, Andrew. *Byron and the Victorians*. Cambridge: Cambridge University Press, 1995.

Ellison, Julie. 'Race and Sensibility in the Early Republic: Ann Eliza Bleecker and Sarah Wentworth Morton'. *American Literature* 65 (1993): 445–74.

English, James F. *The Economy of Prestige: Prizes, Awards, and the Circulation of Cultural Value*. Cambridge, MA: Harvard University Press, 2005.

Esterhammer, Angela. 'The Cosmopolitan *Improvvisatore*: Spontaneity and Performance in Romantic Poets'. *European Romantic Review* 16:2 (2005): 153–65.

—— 'The Improviser's Disorder: Spontaneity, Sickness, and Social Deviance in Late Romanticism'. *European Romantic Review* 16:3 (2005): 329–40.

Evans, M. J. Crossley. *Hannah More*. Bristol: The Bristol Branch of the Historical Association, 1999.

Featherstone, Simon. 'The Blackface Atlantic: Interpreting English Minstrelsy'. *Journal of Victorian Culture* 3 (1998): 234–51.

Feldman, Paula R. 'The Poet and the Profits: Felicia Hemans and the Literary Marketplace'. *Keats–Shelley Journal* 46 (1997): 148–76.

Ferguson, Frances. *Wordsworth: Language as Counter-Spirit*. New Haven: Yale University Press, 1977.

Ferris, Ina. *The Achievement of Literary Authority: Gender, History, and the Waverley Novels*. Ithaca: Cornell University Press, 1991.

—— *The Romantic National Tale and the Question of Ireland*. Cambridge: Cambridge University Press, 2002.

Fielding, Penny. *Writing and Orality: Nationality, Culture, and Nineteenth-Century Scottish Fiction*. Oxford: Clarendon, 1996.

[Finlay, John.] *Wallace; or, the Vale of Ellerslie. With Other Poems*. Glasgow: Chapman and Lang, 1802.

Fitzpatrick, William John. *Lady Morgan; Her Career, Literary and Personal . . .* London: Charles J. Skeet, 1860.

The Florence Miscellany. Florence: G. Cam [1785].

Forbes, Sir William. *An Account of the Life and Writings of James Beattie . . .* Two vols. Edinburgh: Constable, 1806.

Foster, R. F. *Modern Ireland 1600–1972*. London: Penguin, 1989.

Frank, F. S. 'The Demon and the Thunderstorm: Byron and Madame de Staël'. *Revue de Littérature Comparée* 43 (1969): 320–43.

Fulford, Tim. *Romantic Indians: Native Americans, British Literature, and Transatlantic Culture 1756–1830*. Oxford: Oxford University Press, 2006.

Furbank, P. N. and W. R. Owens. 'Defoe and the "Improvisatory" Sentence'. *English Studies* 67:2 (April 1986): 157–66.

Furbo, The Abbate [Francisco]. *Andrew of Padua, the Improvisatore: A Tale from the Italian of the Abbate Furbo*. [Trans. anonymous.] London: Richard Phillips, 1820.

Galperin, William H. *Revision and Authority in Wordsworth: The Interpretation of a Career*. Philadelphia: University of Pennsylvania Press, 1989.

Gamer, Michael C. 'Marketing a Masculine Romance: Scott, Antiquarianism, and the Gothic'. *Studies in Romanticism* 32:4 (Winter 1993): 523–49.

Gellner, Ernest. *Nations and Nationalism*. Ithaca: Cornell University Press, 1983.

Giles. Paul. *Transatlantic Insurrections: British Culture and the Formation of American Literature, 1730–1860*. Philadelphia: University of Pennsylvania Press, 2001.

Gill, Stephen. *Wordsworth: A Life*. Oxford: Oxford University Press, 1990.

Gilroy, Paul. *The Black Atlantic: Modernity and Double Consciousness*. Cambridge, MA: Harvard University Press, 1993.

Gonda, Caroline. 'The Rise and Fall of the Improvisatore, 1753–1845'. *Romanticism* 6:2 (2000): 195–210.

Goslee, Nancy Moore. 'Hemans's "Red Indians": Reading Stereotypes'. *Romanticism, Race, and Imperial Culture, 1780–1834*. Ed. Alan Richardson and Sonia Hofkosh. Bloomington: Indiana University Press, 1996. 237–64.

Grafton, Anthony. *The Footnote: A Curious History*. Cambridge, MA: Harvard University Press, 1997.

Graham, Peter W. Don Juan *and Regency England*. Charlottesville: University Press of Virginia, 1990.

Gravil, Richard. *Wordsworth's Bardic Vocation, 1787–1842*. Basingstoke: Palgrave Macmillan, 2003.

Gray, Thomas. 'The Bard: A Pindaric Ode'. 1757. *Thomas Gray and William Collins: Poetical Works*. Ed. Roger Lonsdale. Reprint of 1977 paperback edition. Oxford: Oxford University Press, 1989. 52–8.

—— *The Poems of Mr. Gray*. Ed. William Mason. London: Dodsley, 1775.

Greenblatt, Stephen J. 'Improvisation and Power'. *Literature and Society: Selected Papers from the English Institute, 1978*. Ed. Edward Said. Baltimore: Johns Hopkins University Press, 1980. 57–99.

—— *Will in the World: How Shakespeare Became Shakespeare*. New York: Norton, 2004.

Hamm, Charles. *Yesterdays: Popular Song in America*. New York: Norton, 1979.

Hartman, Geoffrey H. *Wordsworth's Poetry, 1787–1814*. New Haven: Yale University Press, 1964.

Hayden, John O., comp. *Walter Scott: The Critical Heritage*. London: Routledge, 1970.

Hazlitt, William. *The Complete Works of William Hazlitt*. Ed. P. P. Howe. 21 vols. London: Dent, 1930–4.

Hemans, Felicia. 'Indian Woman's Death-Song'. *Felicia Hemans: Selected Poems, Letters, Reception Materials*. Ed. Susan J. Wolfson. Princeton: Princeton University Press, 2000. 377–9.

—— *Wallace's Invocation To Bruce. A Poem*. Edinburgh: William Blackwood and London: Cadell and Davies, 1819.

[Henry, the Minstrel, commonly called Blind Harry.] *The History of the Life and Adventures, and Heroic Actions, of the Renowned Sir William Wallace, General and Governor of Scotland ... By William Hamilton ...* Air [that is, Ayre, UK]: John and Peter Wilson, 1799.

[——] *The Life and Acts of the Most Famous and Valiant Champion, Sir William Wallace ...* Edinburgh, 1701.

Herder, Johann Gottfried von. *Philosophical Writings*. Trans. and ed. Michael N. Forster. Cambridge: Cambridge University Press, 2002.

Hickey, Alison. *Impure Conceits: Rhetoric and Ideology in Wordsworth's 'Excursion'*. Stanford: Stanford University Press, 1997.

Hogg, James. *The Queen's Wake: A Legendary Poem*. Edinburgh: Goldie, 1813.

Holford, Margaret, afterwards Mrs Hodson. *Elegiac Ode, to the Memory of Lieut.-Colonel Vassall*. Bristol: Kemp, 1808.

[——] *Wallace; or, the Fight of Falkirk: A Metrical Romance*. London: Cadell and Davies, 1809.

Jackson, J. R. de J. *Annals of English Verse, 1770–1835: A Preliminary Survey of the Volumes Published*. New York: Garland, 1985.

Jackson, Virginia. 'Longfellow's Tradition; or, Picture-Writing a Nation'. *Modern Language Quarterly* 59 (1998): 471–96.

Jameson, Fredric. *The Political Unconscious: Narrative as a Socially Symbolic Act*. Ithaca: Cornell University Press, 1991.

Janowitz, Anne. *England's Ruins: Poetic Purpose and the National Landscape*. Cambridge, MA: Blackwell, 1990.

[Jeffrey, Francis.] [Rev. of] '*Corinne, ou l'Italie*'. *Edinburgh Review* 11 (1807): 183–95.

[——] [Rev. of] '*The Excursion . . . by William Wordsworth*'. *Edinburgh Review* 24 (1814): 1–30.

Jewsbury, Maria Jane. *The History of an Enthusiast. The Three Histories*. London: Frederick Westley, 1830. 1–191.

Johnston, Kenneth R. *The Hidden Wordsworth: Poet, Lover, Rebel, Spy*. New York: Norton, 1998.

—— *Wordsworth and* The Recluse. New Haven: Yale, 1984.

Kelley, Theresa M. *Wordsworth's Revisionary Aesthetics*. Cambridge: Cambridge University Press, 1988.

Kelsall, Malcolm. *Byron's Politics*. Brighton, Sussex (UK): Harvester, 1987.

[Kennard, James J., Jr.] 'Who Are Our National Poets?' *Knickerbocker Magazine* (1845): 331–41. Rep. in *Inside the Minstrel Mask: Readings in Nineteenth-Century Blackface Minstrelsy*. Ed. Annemarie Bean, James V. Hatch, and Brooks McNamara. Hanover, NH: Wesleyan University Press, 1996. 50–63.

King, Everard H. *James Beattie's* The Minstrel *and the Origins of Romantic Autobiography*. Lewiston, NY: Edwin Mellen Press, 1992.

Landon, Letitia Elizabeth. *The Golden Violet, with Its Tales of Romance and Chivalry: and Other Poems*. London: Longman, 1827.

—— *The Improvisatrice and Other Poems*. 1825. 5th edn. London: Hurst, 1825. Rep. Poole (UK): Woodstock, 1996.

—— *The Troubadour*. London: Hurst, 1825.

Lawson-Peebles, Robert. 'The Lesson of the Massacre at Fort William Henry'. *New Essays on* The Last of the Mohicans. Ed. H. Daniel Peck. Cambridge: Cambridge University Press, 1992. 115–38.

Leighton, Angela. *Victorian Women Poets: Writing Against the Heart*. Charlottesville: University Press of Virginia, 1992.

Lew, Joseph W. 'Sidney Owenson and the Fate of Empire'. *Keats–Shelley Journal* 39 (1990): 39–65.

Lhamon, W. T. *Raising Cain: Blackface Performance from Jim Crow to Hip Hop*. Cambridge, MA: Harvard University Press, 1998.

Lipking, Lawrence. *The Life of the Poet: Beginning and Ending Poetic Careers*. Chicago: University of Chicago Press, 1981.

Longfellow, Henry Wadsworth. *The Song of Hiawatha. Poems and Other Writings*. Ed. J. D. McClatchy. New York: Library of America, 2000. 141–279.

Lott, Eric. *Love and Theft: Blackface Minstrelsy and the American Working Class*. New York: Oxford University Press, 1993.

Lundeen, Kathleen. 'Who Has the Right to Feel?: The Ethics of Literary Empathy'. *Mapping the Ethical Turn: A Reader in Ethics, Culture, and Literary Theory*. Ed. Todd F. Davis and Kenneth Womack. Charlottesville: University Press of Virginia, 2001. 83–92.

Lynch, Jack. 'Preventing Play: Annotating the Battle of the Books'. *Texas Studies in Literature & Language* 40:3 (Fall 1998): 370–88.

Mackenzie, Henry. *Report of the Committee of the Highland Society of Scotland* ... Edinburgh: Constable, 1805.

[Macpherson, James.] *Fingal, an Ancient Epic Poem, in Six Books: Together with Several Other Poems, Composed by Ossian the Son of Fingal. Translated from the Galic* [sic] *Language, by James Macpherson.* London: Becket, 1762.

Mahar, William J. *Behind the Burnt Cork Mask: Early Blackface Minstrelsy and Antebellum Popular Culture.* Urbana: University of Illinois Press, 1999.

Mahoney, John L. *Wordsworth and the Critics: The Development of a Critical Reputation.* Rochester, NY: Camden, 2001.

Manning, Peter. *Byron and His Fictions.* Detroit: Wayne State University Press, 1978.

——*Reading Romantics: Texts and Contexts.* New York: Oxford University Press, 1990.

Manning, Susan. *Fragments of Union: Making Connections in Scottish and American Writing.* Basingstoke: Palgrave Macmillan, 2002.

Marchand, Leslie A. *Byron: A Biography.* Three vols. New York: Knopf, 1957.

Martin, Philip W. 'Heroism and History: *Childe Harold I and II and the Tales*'. *The Cambridge Companion to Byron.* Ed. Drummond Bone. Cambridge: Cambridge University Press, 2004. 77–98.

Martin, Terence. 'From Atrocity to Requiem: History in *The Last of the Mohicans*'. *New Essays on* The Last of the Mohicans. Ed. H. Daniel Peck. Cambridge: Cambridge University Press, 1992. 47–65.

Mason, Nicholas. 'Felicia Hemans, "The Meeting of Wallace and the Bruce" (V, September 1819)'. *Blackwood's Magazine, 1817–25: Selections from Maga's Infancy.* Ed. Nicholas Mason. Vol. 1: *Selected Verse.* London: Pickering and Chatto, 2006. 117–28.

McGann, Jerome J. *Byron and Romanticism.* Ed. James Soderholm. Cambridge: Cambridge University Press, 2002.

——*A Critique of Modern Textual Criticism.* Chicago: University of Chicago Press, 1983.

——Don Juan *in Context.* Chicago: University of Chicago Press, 1976.

——*Fiery Dust: Byron's Poetic Development.* Chicago: University of Chicago Press, 1968.

——'The Literal World of the English Della Cruscans'. *Fins-de-siècle: English Poetry in 1590, 1690, 1790, 1890, 1990.* Ed. Elaine Scarry. Baltimore: Johns Hopkins University Press, 1995. 95–122.

McGuirk, Carol. 'Places in the Peasant Heart: Robert Burns's Scotland, Stephen Foster's American South, and Walt Disney's World'. *Scotlands* 2:2 (1995): 11–35.

McLane, Maureen N. 'Ballads and Bards: British Romantic Orality'. *Modern Philology* 98:3 (2001): 423–43.

——'The Figure Minstrelsy Makes: Poetry and Historicity'. *Critical Inquiry* 29 (2003): 429–52.

——'Tuning the Multi-Media Nation; or, Minstrelsy of the Afro-Scottish Border ca. 1800'. *European Romantic Review* 15 (2004): 289–305.

McWilliams, John. The Last of the Mohicans: *Civil Savagery and Savage Civility.* New York: Twayne, 1995.

Mellor, Anne K. 'Embodied Cosmopolitanism and the Romantic Woman Writer'. *European Romantic Review* 17 (2006): 289–300.

——*English Romantic Irony*. Cambridge, MA: Harvard University Press, 1980.

——*Mothers of the Nation: Women's Political Writing in England, 1780–1830*. Bloomington: Indiana University Press, 2000.

[Merivale, John Herman.] [Rev. of] '*Poems* by William Wordsworth'. *Monthly Review* 78 (Nov. 1815): 225–34.

[——] *The Minstrel: Or, the Progress of Genius. In Continuation of the Poem Left Unfinished by Dr. Beattie. Book the Third*. London: Longman, 1808.

Miles, Robert. *Gothic Writing 1750–1820: A Genealogy*. London: Routledge, 1993.

Mill, John Stuart. 'Thoughts on Poetry and Its Varieties'. 1833. *Autobiography and Literary Essays*. Toronto: University of Toronto Press, 1981. 341–66.

Miller, Julia Anne. 'Acts of Union: Family Violence and National Courtship in Maria Edgeworth's *The Absentee* and Sydney Owenson's *The Wild Irish Girl*'. *Border Crossings: Irish Women Writers and National Identities*. Ed. Kathryn Kirkpatrick. Tuscaloosa: University of Alabama Press, 2000. 13–37.

Moers, Ellen. *Literary Women*. 1967. Rep. New York: Oxford University Press, 1985.

[Moore, Thomas.] *Corruption and Intolerance: Two Poems. With Notes. Addressed to an Englishman by an Irishman*. London: J. Carpenter, 1808.

——*Irish Melodies*. Halifax: Milner and Sowerby, 1859.

More, Hannah. *Moral Sketches of Prevailing Opinions and Manners, Foreign and Domestic; with Reflections on Prayer*. London: Cadell and Davies, 1819.

Moskal, Jeanne. 'Gender, Nationality, and Textual Authority in Lady Morgan's Travel Books'. *Romantic Women Writers: Voices and Countervoices*. Ed. Paula R. Feldman and Theresa M. Kelley. Hanover: University of New England Press, 1995. 171–93.

Murphy, Peter T. *Poetry as an Occupation and an Art in Britain, 1760–1830*. Cambridge: Cambridge University Press, 1993.

Nathan, Hans. *Dan Emmett and the Rise of Early Negro Minstrelsy*. Norman: University of Oklahoma Press, 1962.

[Neaves, Charles.] 'Letter from Tomkins – Bagman *versus* Pedlar'. *Blackwood's Magazine* 44 (1838): 508–23.

Nisbet, Gabriel. *Caledon's Tears: Or, Wallace. A Tragedy*. Edinburgh: P. Matthie, 1733.

Owenson, Sydney [later Lady Morgan, here as 'S.O.']. *A Few Reflections, Occasioned by the Perusal of a Work, Entitled, 'Familiar Epistles, To Frederick J—s Esq. on the Present State of the Irish Stage'*. Dublin: J. Parry, 1804.

——*Italy, by Lady Morgan*. Two vols. London: Henry Colburn, 1821.

——*Lady Morgan's Memoirs: Autobiography, Diaries and Correspondence*. Two vols. London: Wm. H. Allen, 1863.

——*The Lay of an Irish Harp: Or Metrical Fragments*. London: Richard Phillips, 1807.

——*The Novice of Saint Dominick*. 1805. Four vols. London: Richard Phillips, 1806.

——*Patriotic Sketches of Ireland, Written in Connaught*. Two vols. London: Richard Phillips, 1807.

——*Poems*. Dublin: Alex. Stewart, 1801.

——*The Wild Irish Girl*. Ed. Kathryn Kirkpatrick. Oxford: Oxford University Press, 1999.

Oxford English Dictionary. Ed. J. A. Simpson and E. S. C. Weiner. Second edn. Oxford: Clarendon, 1989. *OED Online*. Oxford University Press. 4 Jan. 2007.

Oxford, University of. *Oxford Prize Poems: Being a Collection of Such English Poems As Have at Various Times Obtained Prizes in the University of Oxford*. Oxford: J. Vincent and H. Slatter, 1839.

Pakenham, Thomas. *The Year of Liberty: The Story of the Great Irish Rebellion of 1798*. 1969. St Albans: Granada, 1978.

Parsons, Mrs Clement. *The Incomparable Siddons*. London: Methuen, 1909.

Pascoe, Judith. *Romantic Theatricality: Gender, Poetry, and Spectatorship*. Ithaca: Cornell University Press, 1997.

Peacock, Thomas Love. *The Four Ages of Poetry*. 1820. *The Halliford Edition of the Works of Thomas Love Peacock*. Ed. H. F. B. Brett-Smith and C. E. Jones. Vol. 8. London: Constable, 1924. 1–25.

Percy, Thomas. *The Hermit of Warkworth: A Northumberland Ballad, in Three Fits or Cantos*. 1771. Third edition. London: Davies and Leacroft, 1772.

——*Reliques of Ancient English Poetry: Consisting of Old Heroic Ballads, Songs, and Other Pieces of Our Earlier Poets, (Chiefly of the Lyric Kind.) Together with Some Few of Later Date*. Three vols. London: J. Dodsley, 1765.

Pickering, Michael. 'John Bull in Blackface'. *Popular Music* 16 (1997): 181–201.

Piozzi, Hester Lynch. *Observations and Reflections Made in the Course of a Journey through France, Italy, and Germany*. Two vols. London: A. Strahan and T. Cadell, 1789.

Poetry of the World. Ed. Edward Topham. Two vols. London: John Bell, 1788.

Porter, Jane. *The Scottish Chiefs, a Romance*. Five vols. London: Longman, 1810.

——*Thaddeus of Warsaw*. 1802. Second edition. Four vols. London: Longman, 1804.

Purcell, Sarah. *Sealed with Blood: War, Sacrifice, and Memory in Revolutionary America*. Philadelphia: University of Pennsylvania Press, 2002.

Radcliffe, Ann. *The Italian: Or, the Confessional of the Black Penitents*. Oxford: Oxford University Press, 1992.

Radcliffe, David Hill. 'Completing James Beattie's *The Minstrel*'. *Studies in Philology* 100 (2003): 534–63.

Reiman, Donald H. 'Byron in Italy: the Return of Augustus'. *Byron: Augustan and Romantic*. Ed. Andrew Rutherford. New York: St Martin's Press, 1990. 181–98.

Reynolds, Harry. *Minstrel Memories: The Story of Burnt Cork Minstrelsy in Great Britain from 1836 to 1927*. London: Alston Rivers, n.d. [preface dated 1928].

Rice, Edward LeRoy. *Monarchs of Minstrelsy from 'Daddy' Rice to Date*. New York: Kenny, 1911.

Ridenour, George. *The Style of Don Juan*. New Haven: Yale University Press, 1960.

[Ritson, Joseph.] *Ancient Songs, from the Time of King Henry the Third, to the Revolution*. London: J. Johnson, 1792.

[——] *Scotish Song*. Two vols. London: J. Johnson, 1794.

[——] *A Select Collection of English Songs*. Three vols. London: J. Johnson, 1783.

Roberts, William. *Memoirs of the Life and Correspondence of Mrs. Hannah More*. Second edition. Four vols. London: Seely and Burnside, 1834.

Roediger, David R. *The Wages of Whiteness*. 1991. London: Verso, 1999.

Rogin, Michael. *Blackface, White Noise*. 1996. Berkeley: University of California Press, 1998.

Romero, Lora. 'Vanishing Americans: Gender, Empire, and New Historicism'. *The Culture of Sentiment: Race, Gender, and Sentimentality in Nineteenth-Century America*. Ed. Shirley Samuels. New York: Oxford University Press, 1992. 115–27.

Ross, Marlon B. 'Scott's Chivalric Pose: The Function of Metrical Romance in the Romantic Period'. *Genre* 19 (Fall 1986): 267–98.

Rowland, Ann Wierda. '"The Fause Nourice Song"': Childhood, Child Murder, and the Formalism of the Scottish Ballad Revival'. *Scotland and the Borders of Romanticism*. Ed. Leith Davis, Ian Duncan, and Janet Sorenson. Cambridge: Cambridge University Press, 2004. 225–44.

—— 'Wordsworth's Children of the Revolution'. *SEL* 4 (2001): 677–94.

Rutherford, Andrew. 'Byron, Scott, and Scotland'. *Lord Byron and His Contemporaries: Essays from the Sixth International Byron Seminar*. Ed. Charles E. Robinson. Newark: University of Delaware Press, 1982. 43–65.

Samuels, Shirley. 'Generation through Violence: Cooper and the Making of Americans'. *New Essays on* The Last of the Mohicans. Ed. H. Daniel Peck. Cambridge: Cambridge University Press, 1992. 87–114.

Saxton, Alexander. *The Rise and Fall of the White Republic: Class Politics and Mass Culture in Nineteenth-Century America*. London: Verso, 1990.

Scott, Walter. *The [Poetical] Works of Sir Walter Scott*. Ware: Wordsworth Poetry Library, 1995.

[——] [Rev. of the] *Report of the Highland Committee of the Highland Society of Scotland [. . . and] The Poems of Ossian . . .* By Malcolm Laing. *Edinburgh Review* 6 (1805): 429–62.

—— *Waverley*. 1814. Ed. Andrew Hook. London: Penguin, 1985.

Seed, David. 'Fenimore Cooper's David Gamut: A Source'. *Notes and Queries* 29:3 (June 1982): 218–20.

Shelley, Percy Bysshe. *The Complete Works of Percy Bysshe Shelley*. Ed. Roger Ingpen and Walter E. Peck. Ten vols. New York: Gordian, 1965.

Siddons, Henry. *William Wallace: Or, the Highland Hero. A Tale, Founded on Historical Facts*. London: G. and T. Wilkie, 1791.

Simpkins, Scott. 'The Remix Aesthetic'. *European Romantic Review* 3:2 (Winter 1992): 193–214.

Simpson, David. *Wordsworth's Historical Imagination: The Poetry of Displacement*. New York: Methuen, 1987.

Smart, Christopher. *On the Eternity of the Supreme Being*. Cambridge: J. Bentham, 1750.

Smith, Adam. *The Theory of Moral Sentiments*. 1759. Ed. D. D. Raphael and A. L. Macfie. The Glasgow Edition of the Works and Correspondence of Adam Smith. Rep. Indianapolis: Liberty Fund, 1994.

Soderholm, James. *Fantasy, Forgery, and the Byron Legend*. Lexington: University of Kentucky Press, 1996.

Sollors, Werner. *Beyond Ethnicity: Consent and Descent in American Culture*. New York: Oxford University Press, 1986.

Southey, Robert. *Thalaba the Destroyer*. Two vols. London: Longman, 1801.

Staël, Germaine de. *Considérations sur les principaux événements de la Révolution française*. 1818. *Madame de Staël on Politics, Literature, and National Character*. Trans. Monroe Berger. London: Sidgwick and Jackson, 1964.

—— *Corinna; or, Italy*. Trans. D. Lawler. Five vols. London: Corri, 1807.

—— *Corinna; or, Italy. By Mad. de Stael* [sic] *Holstein*. Three vols. London: Samuel Tipper, 1807.

—— *Corinne; Or, Italy*. Trans. Isabel Hill. London: Richard Bentley, 1833.

——*Corinne, or Italy.* 1807. Ed. and trans. Avriel Goldberger. New Brunswick: Rutgers University Press, 1977.

——*Corinne ou L'Italie.* Three vols. London: M. Peltier, 1807.

——*A Treatise on the Influence of the Passions, upon the Happiness of Individuals and of Nations. Illustrated by Striking References to the Principal Events and Characters That Have Distinguished the French Revolution. From the French of the Baroness Stael [sic] de Holstein.* London: George Cawthorn, 1798.

Stafford, Fiona. *The Sublime Savage: James Macpherson and the Poems of Ossian.* Edinburgh: University of Edinburgh Press, 1988.

Staves, Susan. 'Douglas's Mother'. *Brandeis Essays in Literature.* Ed. John Hazel Smith. Waltham, MA: Brandeis University, 1983. 51–68.

Stephenson, Glennis. 'Letitia Elizabeth Landon and the Victorian Improvisatrice: The Construction of LEL'. *Victorian Poetry* 30:1 (1992): 1–17.

——*Letitia Landon: The Woman behind L.E.L.* Manchester: Manchester University Press, 1995.

Stern, Kelly. 'Cooper's *The Last of the Mohicans*'. *Explicator* 56:1 (Fall 1997): 20–3.

Sterne, Laurence. *The Life and Opinions of Tristram Shandy, Gentleman.* 1759–67. London: Penguin, 1985.

Stevenson, Lionel. *The Wild Irish Girl: The Life of Sydney Owenson, Lady Morgan (1776–1859).* London: Chapman and Hall, 1936.

Sweet, Nanora. 'History, Imperialism, and the Aesthetics of the Beautiful: Hemans and the Post-Napoleonic Moment'. *At the Limits of Romanticism: Essays in Cultural, Feminist, and Materialist Criticism.* Ed. Mary A. Favret and Nicola J. Watson. Bloomington: Indiana University Press, 1994. 170–84.

Taylor, Barbara D. 'The Search for Space: A Note on Felicia Hemans and the Royal Society of Literature'. *Felicia Hemans: Reimagining Poetry in the Nineteenth Century.* Ed. Nanora Sweet and Julie Melnyk. Basingstoke: Palgrave Macmillan, 2001. 115–24.

Tennyson, Alfred, Lord. 'The Lady of Shalott'. *Alfred Tennyson* (Oxford Authors). Ed. Adam Roberts. Oxford: Oxford University Press, 2000. 21–5.

'The Tent' [including Hemans's 'Wallace's Invocation to Bruce']. *Blackwood's Edinburgh Magazine* 5 (December 1819): 627–736.

Tessier, Thérèse. *The Bard of Erin: A Study of Thomas Moore's Irish Melodies (1808–1834).* Trans. George P. Mutch. Salzburg, Austria: Institut für Anglistik und Amerikanistik, 1981.

Thomas, M. Wynn. *Transatlantic Connections: Whitman U.S., Whitman U.K.* Iowa City: University of Iowa Press, 2005.

Toll, Robert. *Blacking Up: The Minstrel Show in Nineteenth-Century America.* New York: Oxford University Press, 1974.

Tompkins, Jane. *Sensational Designs: The Cultural Work of American Fiction 1790–1860.* New York: Oxford University Press, 1985.

Tracy, Robert. 'Maria Edgeworth and Lady Morgan: Legality versus Legitimacy'. *Nineteenth-Century Fiction* 40:1 (June 1985): 1–22.

Translations of the Oxford Latin Prize Poems. First Series. London: A. J. Valpy, 1831.

Trumpener, Katie. *Bardic Nationalism: The Romantic Novel and the British Empire.* Princeton: Princeton University Press, 1997.

The United States Songster. A Choice Selection of about One Hundred and Seventy of the Most Popular Songs. Cincinnati: U. P. James, 1836.

Venables, George Stovin. *Byzantium*. Cambridge: Talbot and Ladds [1830].

Walker, Joseph Cooper. *Historical Memoirs of the Irish Bards*…London: T. Payne, 1786.

Waller, J. F. Prefatory Memoir. *[Thomas] Moore's Irish Melodies, Lalla Rookh, National Airs, Legendary Ballads, Songs &c.* London: William Mackenzie, n.d.

Warton, Joseph. *The Works of Virgil, in Latin and English*. Vol. 1. London: R. Dodsley, 1753.

Waters, Lindsay. 'The "Desultory Rhyme" of Don Juan: Byron, Pulci, and the Improvisatory Style'. *ELH* 45 (1978): 429–42.

Weisbuch, Robert. *Atlantic Double-Cross: American Literature and British Influence in the Age of Emerson*. Chicago: University of Chicago Press, 1986.

Wilkes, Joanne. *Lord Byron and Madame de Staël: Born for Opposition*. Aldershot: Ashgate, 1999.

Wilson, John [Christopher North]. [Review of] 'Wordsworth's *White Doe of Rylstone*'. *Blackwood's Edinburgh Magazine* 3 (July 1818): 369–81.

Wind, Astrid. '"Adieu to all": The Death of the American Indian at the Turn of the Eighteenth Century'. *Symbiosis* 2 (1998): 39–55.

Woodmansee, Martha. *The Author, Art, and the Market: Rereading the History of Aesthetics*. New York: Columbia University Press, 1994.

Wordsworth, William. 'Essay, Supplementary to the Preface'. *Poems by William Wordsworth: Including Lyrical Ballads, and the Miscellaneous Pieces of the Author. With Additional Poems, a New Preface, and a Supplementary Essay*. Two vols. London: Longman, 1815.

—— *The Excursion, Being a Portion of The Recluse, a Poem*. London: Longman, 1814.

—— *The Letters of William and Dorothy Wordsworth: I. The Early Years, 1787–1805*. Ed. Ernest de Selincourt, second edition rev. by Chester L. Shaver. Oxford: Clarendon, 1979.

—— *The Letters of William and Dorothy Wordsworth: II. The Middle Years, Part I: 1806–1811*. Ed. Ernest de Selincourt, second edition rev. by Mary Moorman. Oxford: Clarendon, 1969.

—— [and Samuel Taylor Coleridge]. *Lyrical Ballads*. 1798–1802. Ed. R. L. Brett and A. R. Jones. Second edition. London: Routledge, 1991.

—— *The Prose Works of William Wordsworth*. Ed. W. J. B. Owen and Jane Worthington Smyser. Three vols. Oxford: Clarendon, 1974.

—— *The White Doe of Rylstone; or The Fate of the Nortons*. 1815. Ed. Kristine Dugas. Ithaca: Cornell University Press, 1988.

The Wreath, Containing The Minstrel and Other Favorite Poems. London: Suttaby, 1815.

Yuli, the African: A Poem, in Six Cantos. London: J. Hatchard, 1810.

Zionkowski, Linda. 'Bridging the Gulf Between: The Poet and the Audience in the Work of Gray'. *ELH* 58 (1991): 331–50.

Index